Nature's Events

Nature's Events

*A Notebook of the
Unfolding Seasons*

John Serrao

Illustrations by John Wiessinger

STACKPOLE
BOOKS

Copyright © 1992 by Stackpole Books

Published by
STACKPOLE BOOKS
Cameron and Kelker Streets
P.O. Box 1831
Harrisburg, PA 17105

Cover illustrations by John Wiessinger

Cover design by Mark B. Olszewski

Printed in the United States of America

First Edition

10 9 8 7 6 5 4 3 2 1

Library of Congress Cataloging-in-Publication Data

Serrao, John, 1949–
    Nature's events : a notebook of the unfolding seasons / John Serrao ; illustrations by John Wiessinger. — 1st ed.
        p.   cm
    Includes bibliographical references and index.
    ISBN 0–8117–2560–X
    1. Nature.   2. Natural history—Outdoor books.
    3. Calendar.
    I. Title
    QH81.S463   1992   91–44937
    508—dc20   CIP

This book is dedicated to Richard B. Fischer, Professor Emeritus of Environmental Education at Cornell University. Twenty years ago his careful guidance, boundless knowledge, and contagious enthusiasm led to my pursuit of a naturalist's career. Over the years Dick Fischer has continued to instruct and direct many of our country's top naturalists and environmental educators, and his students have benefited from his advice and interest long after graduating from Cornell. It was his recommendation that led me to write this book.

Contents

Acknowledgments

I wish to extend my sincere thanks to John Wiessinger, whose excellent drawings illustrate the chapters of this book.

Most of the chapters are based on my field journals written over the past twenty years, but they include much information from original research and fieldwork done by other professional scientists and naturalists. Their publications are listed in the bibliography.

Above all I thank my wife, Felicia, for her tireless work at the word processor completing this manuscript and her many suggestions, encouragement, and support throughout this project.

Introduction

The return of the first robin to a newly greening front lawn in March . . . the blossoming of the first hepaticas and jack-in-the-pulpits through the forest leaf litter in early spring . . . the sounds of bullfrogs and the flashes of fireflies on early summer evenings and the first calls of katydids toward summer's end . . . the honking of Canada geese migrating overhead after the leaves have turned their autumn colors . . . the February songs of cardinals and chickadees, signaling that spring is on its way . . . these and many other annual events are some of nature's most cherished happenings. Year after year people look forward to seeing and recording them in their memories or notebooks as "mileposts" of the passing seasons—events that can be trusted, anticipated, and then celebrated every year.

The human world is changing at a sometimes frightening pace, and no one can keep up with every new technological advance or historical occurrence. Machines and institutions become outdated soon after they are invented, and political regimes seem to topple and fall overnight. But the natural world maintains the rhythms that have evolved over hundreds of thousands of years. It is comforting to know that countless plants and animals still carry on their seasonal activities according to ancient natural laws and cycles. And in today's complicated, changing world it is soothing to the mind to realize that these activities are dependable, reliable phenomena that occur year after year regardless of the vagaries of human ways. Perhaps it is the desire for some stabilty in their lives that draws people into anticipating and recording these natural events. Or perhaps the reason comes from the more distant past, a time when observance of the passing seasons and the activities of other living things had a much more significant role in human survival.

The study of the progression of recurring natural phenomena

over the course of a year in relation to various factors, such as weather, that affect the dates of these events is called phenology. Even though many natural events occur every year on a reliable basis, their exact timing varies from place to place according to an area's climate. One of the most important factors determining an area's climate, and thus the timing of its annual natural events, is latitude. On the average the onset of a phenological event occurs about four days later with each one-degree northward shift in latitude (about seventy miles) because of the cooler temperatures. As one moves northward, events such as the return of migrating birds and the blooming of early spring wildflowers occur at later dates. In other words, spring arrives later in the north.

Altitude produces this same climatic effect. Spring's annual events are delayed by the rise in elevation up the side of a mountain just as surely as by traveling northward. In some cases a trip to the top of a 4,000- to 6,000-foot mountain in the Northeast reveals the same phenological changes (as well as the same shifts in dominant vegetation) as driving several hundred miles north into Canada. Temperatures decrease as much as three to five degrees for every 1,000-foot increase in elevation, and this is equivalent to a two-hundred- to three-hundred-mile northward change of latitude. Such altitudinal cooling can cause the spring wildflowers to blossom more than a month later at the tops of some of the mountains than at the bases. Elevation also affects an area's precipitation since air loses its moisture as it rises up a mountain. In the Northeast the annual rainfall at the top of a high mountain may be almost double that in the lower valleys.

Other circumstances, as well, can produce surprising differences between the dates of annually occurring events in two neighboring areas: slope, exposure to the sun (north-facing versus south-facing slopes), and topographical relief (valley floors get much colder at night when the cold, dense air from hilltops sinks down). Thus, many different factors must be taken into consideration when predicting the dates of nature's events, including the very genetics of the species—some plants and animals are more responsive to their own internal biological clocks or the seasonal changes of daylengths (photoperiod) than they are to temperature and rainfall. Finally, even on the same site these dates can differ somewhat from year to year because of the weather, with unseasonably cool temperatures producing a late spring and abnormally warm weather an early one.

This book deals with forty-eight of nature's most spectacular and reliable annual events in the northeastern United States (the New England states, New York, Pennsylvania, and New Jersey). Each month is divided into four weeks, and a representative event is assigned to each week. Some events also occur in more than one month—late April and early May, for example. Most of these natural occurrences can be witnessed throughout this entire region, but a few, such as the shorebird migration, are more localized and are included because of their tremendous scope and predictability.

Assigning particular weeks to these forty-eight events was derived mostly from journal entries since 1971 from areas where I've lived in northeastern New Jersey, the Pocono Mountains of Pennsylvania, and New York's Finger Lakes and mid-Hudson Valley regions, and from many trips and vacations throughout New England, the Adirondack and Allegheny mountains, and southern New Jersey. As already explained, these events may occur at earlier or later dates from place to place depending on latitude, altitude, or other factors (and these variations are generally described in the individual chapters), but the particular dates assigned and, more importantly, the sequence in which they occur are fairly accurate representations of their annual occurrences in the northeastern United States.

It's Maple Syrup Time

MARCH I

The rising of the sap in the sugar maple trees

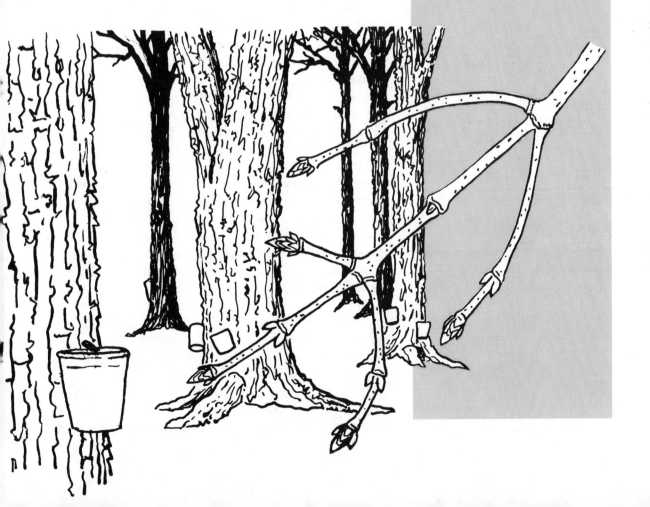

————*Observations*————

Gradually, almost imperceptibly, the days have been getting longer for the past three months. Now daylight is about to overtake the night, and the increased sunlight is beginning to warm the earth in the northeastern United States after a long, cold winter. Snow is still on the ground, ice covers the lakes and ponds, and temperatures at night still drop below freezing, but afternoons now warm up to 40 or even 50 degrees Fahrenheit, and spring is in the air. It is early March, and perhaps no other symbol characterizes this transitional time between winter and spring in the Northeast better than the hanging buckets gathering the sweet, rising sap of the sugar maples.

In his book *American Trees* Rutherford Platt calls the sugar maple a "contender for the title of the most beautiful tree in the world." "If you would see perfection," says Platt, "go look at a maple. It is like truth made into the form of a tree." Indeed, when grown in open areas, the sugar maple's form, with its almost perfectly oval outline, is a picture of harmony and balance. Like other maples, *Acer saccharum* is characterized by opposite branching: Every bud, twig, and leaf has an identical partner (unless it's been broken off) on the opposite side of the branch, a trait that is responsible for the tree's remarkable symmetry. Its winged, airplanelike fruits, which mature in the fall, are also paired together in a U shape. They develop from yellowish April flowers, which may be so numerous that the tree appears to give off a beautiful yellow haze. Nevertheless, this color pales in comparison with the flaming orange, gold, and red hues that the five-lobed leaves portray in October, making autumn landscapes within the sugar maple's range the most colorful in the world. No wonder it's been selected the state tree of New York, Vermont, Wisconsin, and West Virginia!

But now it's early March, before any of the buds have opened, and the landscape is still leafless. By a process that still is not completely understood, the alternating pattern of freezing nights and sunny, thawing days causes the maple's sap (which has been absorbing sugar from the tree) to "rise," or travel throughout the tree. As the wood enclosing the sap vessels is warmed by the sun, it expands, squeezes the vessels, and forces the sap upward, aided by the properties of cohesion and adhesion in the water molecules. This process usually starts during the last week in February and first week in March in the portions of the sugar maple's range between Virginia and southern Pennsylvania; early to mid-March in New York, northern Pennsylvania, and southern New England; and sometimes not until late March or early April in the Adirondack Mountains and the higher elevations and latitudes of northern New England. The sap stops running when the buds open later in spring.

The sap of the sugar maple is high in sugar content— generally 2 to 3 percent with some exceptional trees as high as 7 percent. (Other maple species, such as the red or silver maple, can also be tapped, but their sap is not nearly as sweet.) The sugar maple's value was long recognized by the Native Americans, and they taught the early French settlers how to slash a tomahawk into its trunk to collect this sweet liquid in hollowed-out wooden troughs.

Long before humans learned to exploit this tree, however, red squirrels knew the tree's sweet secret. They punctured the bark with their sharp incisors and left the sap to run. They returned to the tree after most of the leaking sap's water content had evaporated leaving dark, wet streaks with as high as 55 percent sugar concentration. Sugar maples often bear evidence of this squirrel activity in early spring: tiny incisions in the trunk or limbs, dripping sap, or icicles hanging from the incisions or nipped branches.

The tapping process has been greatly refined over the years by commercial collecting operations, which use evaporating tanks, hydrometers, and miles of plastic tubing connecting hundreds of trees in a forest (or "sugar bush") to draw the sap to the central sugarhouse. One of these modern operators can easily collect over one thousand gallons of sap per day and produce a couple of gallons of maple syrup every hour. By contrast, using the old-fashioned equipment of wooden or metal spiles and buckets, an individual collector can expect a reward of only one gallon of syrup after a laborious day's work of collecting and boiling down the sap.

Observations

It takes twenty-five to fifty gallons of raw sap to produce one gallon of maple syrup. Although Euell Gibbons, the famous wild-food expert, claimed to have extracted ten gallons of sap from a huge sugar maple tree in a single day (using six taps), most trees can be expected to yield no more than twelve gallons of sap per year, from which only a single quart of syrup is produced. The boiling process itself, although very time-consuming for the individual farmer or land owner, is fairly straightforward. The syrup is ready to be poured off once the temperature of the liquid reaches seven degrees above the temperature when it starts to boil. Since the sap is 98 percent water, it will begin to boil at about 212 degrees Fahrenheit at sea level, so once the thermometer reads 219 degrees, it will be syrup (these temperatures will be slightly lower at higher altitudes). One gallon of this finished syrup should weigh eleven pounds—compared to eight pounds for one gallon of water. Federal regulations stipulate that this product must be at least 66 percent sugar to be labeled maple syrup.

More than any other species of deciduous tree, the sugar maple distinctly symbolizes the northeastern United States. Although its range extends all the way down along the higher Appalachian Mountains of North Carolina, extreme northern Georgia and Alabama, and even a curious "finger" into the Big Thicket region of eastern Texas, sugar maple is most common in the North, where it is a dominant member of the northern hardwood, or "beech-birch-maple," forest. Here it thrives in the rich, deep, moist, well-drained soils of these cool, shaded forests, attaining a maximum height of 135 feet and exceptional diameters of 5 feet. Such trees might have thick, straight, rough-barked trunks free of branches for 60 feet. The canopy in these forests is often very dense, admitting hardly any sunlight in summer to the woodland floor. Since it is one of the most shade-tolerant of all eastern trees (along with beech and hemlock), it is one of the few species capable of surviving as seedlings and saplings in the shade of its larger parents. Thus, the sugar maple is considered to be a characteristic member of the "climax," or self-perpetuating, forest in the northern United States.

————*Observations*————

In addition to its importance in the maple syrup industry and its inestimable worth to the tourist industry when it produces its flaming autumn colors, the sugar maple's wood is also extremely valuable. Strong, hard, very resistant to shock (it is also called "rock maple"), and taking a beautiful polish or stain, the wood is used extensively in flooring (including dance floors and bowling alleys), furniture, and cabinets. It is also a first-rate fuel wood. However, in the past decade there has been an alarming decline in sugar maples throughout the northeastern United States and Canada, and an analysis of their annual rings has revealed very slow growth. In the late 1980s maple syrup production in Vermont (the nation's leading state in this industry, with New York and Wisconsin ranking second and third) dropped to nearly the lowest levels in this century—250,000 gallons in 1987 compared to 410,000 gallons in 1978. Many syrup producers have been forced to abandon their industry entirely.

Scientists point out that a number of causes rather than a single factor are to blame for this mysterious decline. The sugar maple is notoriously vulnerable to road salt, which is spread in winter to melt snow and ice. Over the years many roadside trees have died from this practice. Starting in the late 1970s the pear thrip, a tiny, flea-sized insect (originally a pest of West Coast fruit trees), began affecting thousands of acres of maple forests in north-central Pennsylvania. This insect was first noticed in Vermont in 1985, and three years later it was blamed for damaging a half million acres of maple forests in Vermont and a million acres in Pennsylvania, with smaller amounts in other northeastern states. Some scientists claim that the sugar maple is losing its resistance to such pests as the pear thrip, scale insects, and various caterpillars as a result of air poisoned with ozone, sulfur dioxide, and acid rain. These environmental pollutants negatively affect the sugar maple's leaves as well as the soil in which it grows. This weakens the tree's defenses and may cause it to lose the ability to withstand attacks by insects and other pests. There is a growing concern that acid rain may be a contributing factor in the decline not only of the sugar maple but of entire forests in the northeast.

———Observations———

In recent years both Canada and the United States have signed legislation to reduce the emission of chemicals responsible for acid rain and other forms of air pollution. (In 1990, after years of debate, the new Clean Air Act was finally passed by the 102nd Congress to strengthen these laws.) The era of cleaner, fresher air that hopefully will be ushered in may promise a return to health and vigor for our northern forests. One of the species that will benefit most is the dominant organism and chief symbol of these forests, the sugar maple.

March Migrants

Return of the first birds from the South: blackbirds and bluebirds, robins and red-tailed hawks, woodcocks and wood ducks, flickers and phoebes

————*Observations*————

Who hasn't been thrilled by the sight of the year's first robin on a lawn or the first bluebird perched on a fence post? Who hasn't felt a certain sense of joy and optimism upon hearing a distant honking and then looking upward to see the spectacle of hundreds of Canada geese flying northward in formation? Even the most ardent fan of winter can't help but succumb to "spring fever" when seeing these earliest winged harbingers of spring. Their annual arrival from the southern states may not be as mysterious and awe-inspiring as the later return of shorebirds and songbirds that have overwintered thousands of miles away in South America, but, coming as it does at the end of a long winter, it is certainly one of the most welcomed natural events in our calendar.

The March migrants include birds that have spent the winter months within our country's borders, usually less than one thousand (and in some cases just a few hundred) miles from their summer homes. As in all migrating birds, the urge to make these annual journeys is hormonal in origin—a physiological response to the changing daylength, or photoperiod. As days increase in length in late winter and early spring, responses by the bird's pituitary gland bring on migratory "restlessness" and increased appetite, causing the bird to eat more food to fuel the coming journey. Then, when the time arrives and the weather is right, the migrant takes off, usually in a flock, and heads for the same place where it was born or raised a family in previous springs. The actual timing of the arrival at any given location often parallels the progression of spring for many of these species. For example, Canada geese move northward roughly in step with the advance of the 36-degree (Fahrenheit) isotherm (a line drawn on the map connecting all places with the same temperature at that time), while robins follow the advance of 37-degree temperatures as they return northward. For both species this puts their date of arrival at the middle of our northeastern region during the first ten days in March. Of course, an unusually late or cool spring may delay their return by a few days, while an early spring may push it up. The many mysteries surrounding bird migration—celestial and magnetic navigation, nocturnal travel, nonstop oceanic flights, and other apparent miracles—are the subjects of continuing scientific investigation and are explored in chapter 25.

The first of the March migrants to return to the Northeast are the blackbirds, sometimes in mixed flocks of several species that have spent the winter by the millions in southern agricultural areas. Occasionally as early as the last few days in February in some locations, but most commonly in early March throughout our region, male red-winged blackbirds settle down in marshes and wet meadows and at the margins of ponds to set up nesting territories for their mates, which won't arrive until a few weeks later. Each male claims the choicest possible territory for himself by perching high on a cattail or tree branch, exposing his red-and-yellow shoulder patches for all others to see, and singing his distinctive, raucous "o-ka-ree" territorial call. If he successfully defends his territory from other males, he may gather into it a harem of several females when they arrive later in the month.

Another blackbird species that returns in early March is the common grackle, easily recognized by its shiny, purplish black, iridescent plumage. Males strut along the ground, puff themselves up on branches, and utter a call that sounds like the opening of a rusty gate. Preferred nesting sites are groves of evergreen trees in residential areas.

By mid-March a third species, the rusty blackbird, returns to New England and Adirondack bogs and marshes. About this same time a fourth blackbird, the brown-headed cowbird—famous for its parasitic habit of laying eggs in nests of other species and letting them raise its young—returns to farms and fields. One of the cowbird's favorite hosts is the eastern phoebe, a grayish brown, medium-sized flycatcher that spends the winter in the southern states and returns to nest beneath bridges, eaves, and porch roofs about the same time as the cowbird's arrival. The phoebe's annual return is one of spring's most dependable events. In my twenty years of keeping records in the New York–New Jersey–Pennsylvania region, the earliest date for seeing the first phoebe was March 16 and the latest was March 28. In the majority of those years the phoebe returned within the one-week period of March 17–23.

————*Observations*————

Two of the most colorful early March migrants have figured prominently in the lists of spring's symbols throughout the history of our area. Both members of the thrush family, the American robin and the eastern bluebird have experienced opposite fortunes this century, the former increasing in abundance with the spread of lawns and suburbs, the latter declining from loss of extensive fields and orchards and competition with starlings and house sparrows for nesting cavities. Fortunately, the past few decades have seen a great comeback for the bluebird as thousands of specially designed bluebird houses have been erected by volunteers and successfully used by these birds in raising multiple families.

Song sparrow, field sparrow, common flicker, killdeer, woodcock, and tree swallow are among the other species that return this month to nest in the northeastern United States. Meanwhile, our ponds, lakes, and wetlands are experiencing the arrival of the waterfowl. Beginning with the flights of thousands of Canada geese from our coastal bays and estuaries and mallards and wood ducks from southern swamps, one species after another passes through our region after stopping to rest and feed on our waters. The black duck, like the three aforementioned species, arrives in early March, followed in midmonth by the green-winged teal, the redhead, the wigeon, the lesser scaup, and the American merganser. Then during the latter half of March the blue-winged teal, the shoveler, the greater scaup, and the ruddy duck fly in. The majority of these ducks continue to move past our borders to nest in the flooded marshes and potholes of the Canadian provinces and our north-central states or the tundra pools of the Far North.

One of the most dramatic annual migration spectacles of all begins this month with the northward movements of the raptors. Hawks, falcons, vultures, and eagles—fifteen species of raptors in all—return to their northern breeding grounds in spring. Some lookouts that have been established to study these migrations record tens of thousands of hawks moving northward from March to June. (More details of the hawks' routes, flight patterns, numbers, and the locations of the best lookouts are described in chapter 7.) Although the majority of these hawks are broad-winged and sharp-shinned hawks, which peak in numbers later in April or May (see chapter 7), some spectacular flights of big raptors can be seen earlier in March, especially along the southern shores of the Great Lakes, which act as major detours to these migrants. Turkey vultures, with wings spanning 6 feet, begin their migrations in early March, and by the end of the month several hundred of these huge birds can be seen daily soaring masterfully overhead in dark squadrons. In the spring of 1988, 6,575 turkey vultures were recorded at Lake Ontario's Braddock Bay (north of Rochester, New York) for the season, with over 1,000 on March 30—800 in a single moving group! March is also the month of the three big buteos, named for the scientific genus *(Buteo)* to which they belong and characterized by chunky bodies, broad, rounded wings, and wide, fanned tails built for soaring.

The first to arrive, the rough-legged hawk, is also the rarest. As early as the end of February these striking black-and-white raptors with wingspreads up to $4^1/_2$ feet make their way back to their open-country breeding grounds in northern Canada after spending the winter in the northern United States. About 500 are counted at Braddock Bay each spring, with daily numbers reaching 50 or more by the end of March. The red-shouldered hawk, a handsome *Buteo* with dark reddish brown underparts, a dark, white-banded tail, and a 40-inch wingspread, also begins to appear in early March. The earliest raptor to complete its migration, it gradually builds up to numbers as high as 200 a day by the middle of March and peaks by month's end with as many as 1,000 per day. On one exceptional day at Braddock Bay in the spring of 1988 over 3,200 were counted. By the first week of April, however, this hawk is rarely seen flying past the lookouts.

The most common March raptor is the red-tailed hawk, perhaps the best-known hawk in the northeastern United States. Commonly seen soaring over farms and fields on wings spanning 4 feet or more, these robust birds are recognized by the dark band across their white bellies and the reddish tail of the adults. Sometime during the first half of March Canadian red-tails, which have overwintered in our northern states, begin to return, and from now until

———*Observations*———

————Observations————

the beginning of April over 1,000 birds may be counted on exceptional days with southerly winds at Lake Ontario's main lookouts (ten to twenty times the daily numbers seen during this same time period at hawk lookouts along the Appalachian ridge of Pennsylvania and northern New Jersey). During some springs as many as 10,000 red-tails are counted at Braddock Bay.

Besides the incredible numbers of migrating hawks soaring overhead, part of the thrill of participating in a raptor count in March is the possibility of seeing one or more of the really rare and powerful birds of prey in migration. During this month the goshawk, our largest *Accipiter* hawk, returns to Canada, as does the very rare peregrine falcon. And the two largest raptors of all—the bald eagle and the golden eagle—may also make an exciting appearance when a cold front approaches and winds are from the south. On March 22, 1984, eleven golden eagles and four bald eagles passed over Derby Hill, a lookout near Lake Ontario's eastern end. To see just one of these magnificent birds gliding on dark wings spanning 7 or 8 feet certainly makes braving the cold air of the Great Lakes and the strong winds of March worthwhile.

The Flight of the Woodcock

A most unusual bird and its strange courtship ritual

While flocks of honking Canada geese speed overhead, silent hawks soar along lakeshores and ridges, and colorful robins and bluebirds return to our lawns and fields, another March migrant has been secretly making its way back northward without much fanfare. In both appearance and behavior the woodcock is certainly one of our strangest birds, yet few people are aware of its presence as it lies perfectly camouflaged by day among the brown leaves and dried grass. Emerging under the cover of darkness, it performs a spring courtship ritual that makes it one of the most unusual and entertaining of all the birds in our region.

Although closely related to the sandpipers, the American woodcock (also known as timberdoodle and mud snipe) is not an inhabitant of the open beaches and sand dunes. It prefers, instead, wet, overgrown fields, alder thickets, and young, brushy woods near streams throughout the eastern United States. Short, chunky, and from 10 to 12 inches long, the woodcock's shape superficially resembles that of a bobwhite quail, but with shorter legs. Its colors are those of the forest floor: a mottled mixture of russets, browns, grays, and blacks intricately woven into an extremely well camouflaged pattern that renders the bird invisible as it sits motionless among the dead leaves.

Except for its close relative the common snipe, the woodcock's head is unlike that of any other bird in our region. It is essentially neckless, and its large, dark eyes are set so high on its head and so far back that its ears are actually in front of them. Its long, thin beak ($2^{1}/_{2}$ to $2^{3}/_{4}$ inches long) functions like forceps, probing the soft ground for earthworms. The tip of its upper mandible is hooked and equipped with a flexible hinge, so that when the beak is stuck into the ground, its tip can curve up or down and can open and clamp onto worms. Both the tongue and the beak tip have raspy surfaces that prevent slippery worms from escaping, and the beak has a series of sensory pits beneath its thin, soft skin casing, enabling the woodcock to feel for and identify its unseen prey beneath the soil. (It was once believed that a woodcock fed by sucking up nourishment from the mud through its tubelike bill.)

About 75 to 85 percent of its diet is earthworms, with the remainder soft insects and seeds, and the woodcock may eat more than its own weight in worms each night. Extremely long intestines help it digest such heavy meals. The unusual placement of its large eyes enables the woodcock to scan its surroundings for owls, hawks, foxes, and cats (apparently its chief predator) with its beak submerged and its head touching the ground.

Its amusing, awkward appearance is in marked contrast to the woodcock's graceful courtship performance, exhibited shortly after its return to our region in early March. Upon its arrival a male woodcock establishes a territory (or reclaims a former one) in a clearing, usually near a wet area bordered by alders, aspens, gray birches, and various shrubs. Sometime between sunset and darkness it struts around this site in an erect posture, uttering strange, nasal "peent" sounds, much like the tones of a raspy beeper and somewhat suggestive of the flight call of the nighthawk. After repeating this sound several times at five- or six-second intervals, the woodcock suddenly takes off without warning and flutters upward, producing musical twittering sounds as it ascends in wide spirals as high as 300 feet into the air. Then the twittering stops and the woodcock begins its dive, sweeping rapidly across the sky and making soft, liquid gurgling and chirping sounds, which grow louder and louder until it seems as if the bird will actually crash into the ground or the tree tops. But, instead, about 20 feet above the ground it pulls out of the dive and silently flutters down on almost the same patch of ground from which it took off. Then it resumes its strutting and "peenting" once again for a few minutes before launching into another exhibition flight.

Woodcock-watchers often wait until the bird takes off at the start of its nuptial flight, and then they move closer to that point. They are sometimes rewarded with a very close look at a woodcock by flashlight or twilight when it returns to earth. On some large and particularly desirable territories it is possible to see two or three male woodcocks displaying simultaneously in the air against the setting sun, with the sounds of spring peepers whistling from nearby swamps.

This performance continues evening after evening with remarkable consistency, beginning about a minute later on each successive night as the month progresses. If

—————Observations—————

the male succeeds in attracting a female with his court-ship flights and mates with her, she will lay four eggs on the ground and incubate them for three weeks. Toward the end of this period the incredibly well camouflaged female will sit tight on her eggs even when touched by a human. The eggs split lengthwise when hatching—another unique feature of the woodcock—and the young are precocial (able to leave the nest and follow their mother within hours).

A very few woodcocks may linger in the warmer parts of our region near springs and swamps if the winter is mild and earthworms are still available near the surface. The great majority, however, leave in autumn and spend the winter in the Gulf states, especially Louisiana, where up to 50 percent of the country's woodcocks overwinter in the swamps along the Atchafalaya River. Here they hunt earth-worms until February, when the northward migration to their breeding grounds in the northern states and Canada begins. By the end of that month the southern swamps may be almost empty of woodcocks. They reach southern New Jersey by the last days in February, Pennsylvania by early March, and the New England states during the second and third weeks of this month.

Around the turn of the century the woodcock was al-most hunted to extinction in some northern states (much of it by illegal poaching and market hunting), where it is still considered a classic gamebird and its dark meat a delicacy. But new regulations, stricter enforcement, and wildlife management policies have helped it to make a comeback.

Although very hardy (often returning north when snow still covers the ground), a woodcock can't survive long without food. If a hard freeze prevents it from getting earthworms, starvation comes quickly. In the 1940s thou-sands of birds died from unusually cold weather in their primary wintering state, Louisiana. Then in the 1960s DDT and other pesticides started showing up in the tissues of woodcocks, a result of these chemicals seeping into the ground and being picked up by earthworms. (The same predicament befell robins on college campuses sprayed with DDT, often with fatal results.)

DDT was banned in 1972—another lucky break for the woodcock. Today its main problem is one it shares with many of our other wild creatures: loss of habitat. When overgrown fields, young-growth woods, and wetlands are converted into shopping malls and residential developments or naturally grow into mature forests, fewer open areas remain for the woodcock to find cover, earthworms, and the space it needs for its courtship flights. Since about 1970 woodcock numbers have declined by 36 percent in the East because of such changes in land-use patterns. Hopefully, today's emphasis on preserving wetlands, both for their value as wildlife habitat and their functions in water purification and flood control, as well as efforts in some states to stem the loss of farmlands, will benefit the woodcock and ensure that it will continue to launch itself into the twilight every March.

4

Awakening Amphibians

MARCH IV

Wood frogs, spring peepers, and spotted salamanders emerge to breed in ponds

Another ancient spring ritual is performed under the cover of darkness each March in our region. The players in these acts possess smooth, moist skin rather than feathers, and instead of winging their way back north from warmer southern areas, these creatures emerge on cue from the cold, thawing soil where they spent the winter months. They are the amphibians, five species of which reawaken during the first warm, rainy weather in March in the northeastern United States. Ice remains on the northern lakes and snow lingers in the ravines, but now it begins to disappear as daytime temperatures approach 50 degrees Fahrenheit. Once the ground thaws out, the renewed growth of vegetation and the damp soil give the balmy air that unmistakable earthy aroma of early spring.

The stage is now set for the arrival of the earliest amphibians to the swamps, small woodland pools, and shallow, marshy borders of ponds and wetlands. Their biological clocks tell them that the time to emerge into the outside world is near. These same clocks have prevented them from being fooled into premature reawakenings and emergences during midwinter thaws when the breeding season was still weeks away. But now the winter portion of their clocks has run out, and the newly warmed earth tells them that winter is indeed ending. Only one more environmental signal is required to bring these creatures out of hiding: the first March rains, which soak through the thawed forest soil where they have spent the winter months in suspended animation. Then they emerge en masse—thousands of frogs and salamanders hopping and crawling across the moist earth, usually at night, bound for the same waters where they were spawned in previous years.

Studies in New York, Pennsylvania, and Connecticut have concluded that once the air temperature reaches a certain critical level, the emergence of the spotted salamander—one of the earliest amphibians to breed throughout most of the Northeast—always coincides with either the first rainfall of early spring or the rapid melting of the snow cover. The critical temperature required to precede this event is from 45 to 55 degrees Fahrenheit, depending on the location. According to a ten-year study in Missouri these amphibians apparently need to feel that the ground temperature at the surface has become warmer than that of their burrows, which lie about 12 inches below the ground. Similar studies in southern Michigan also have found that these salamanders migrate to their breeding areas during the first rain following the disappearance of snow and the thawing of the ground.

During their journey from forest to wetland pools the spotted salamanders are often accompanied by other early amphibians that have been awakened by the same spring rains and that have the same instinctive urge to enter the water. The closely related, but more localized and uncommon, Jefferson's salamander, the wood frog, and the spring peeper all emerge at this time, while the red-spotted newt is already in the water, having spent the winter months beneath the ice of ponds. The environmental cues that guide these amphibians as they migrate as much as a half mile back to their watery birth places include odors emanating from the muck and algae of the wetlands, the open horizon above the ponds, and—probably in the case of the spotted salamanders—an imprinted memory of their own birth place and route home.

I have found that the average date for the first emergence of spotted salamanders and wood frogs in the New York–New Jersey–Pennsylvania region is March 16. The earliest date was March 5, after an extremely mild February (1976), while the latest date was March 28, during a late, cold spring. Similar dates have been recorded by others in Connecticut, while farther north in the Albany, New York, region near the Vermont border the dates range from about the middle of March to the first week of April.

Why do these cold-blooded animals emerge to breed at such early dates, while the waters are still ice cold? The answer is related to the breeding habitat: small, shallow, generally temporary woodland ponds and swamps that fill up with rain and melting snow in winter and spring. By breeding in these small, isolated habitats rather than in the larger permanent ponds and lakes, their tadpoles are spared predation by turtles and fish. But the amphibians are forced to reproduce at the earliest possible dates to ensure that their aquatic descendants have enough time to metamorphose into air-breathing, terrestrial frogs and salamanders before the ponds and swamps dry out in late summer.

Returning to the water to reproduce has apparently been a condition of their lives for over 300 million years, ever since amphibians evolved from fish to become the earth's first air-breathing, land-dwelling vertebrates. Despite all those millennia and their divergence from those first primitive forms into today's twenty-five hundred worldwide species of frogs, toads, and salamanders, amphibians as a group still depend on the earth's wet places. Because of their thin, permeable skins and varying degrees of cutaneous respiration they are relegated to ponds, streams, swamps, damp soil, and rotting wood. Although many tropical species have developed interesting exceptions to the rule, the great majority of this country's amphibians must return to the water each year to lay eggs. From these eggs develop tiny gill-breathing larvae or tadpoles. After an underwater existence that varies from a few weeks to a couple of years, depending on the species, the amphibians lose their gills and emerge into the air as adult frogs, toads, or salamanders with lungs (except for the lungless family of salamanders, which breathe entirely through their skins and mouth linings).

At 8 or 9 inches in length and resembling a thick, black rubber toy decorated with bright yellow spots, the spotted salamander is our region's largest salamander. Slow moving on land, it performs unusual underwater "nuptial dances" once it enters the breeding pond. In groups of up to forty or fifty individuals the males gyrate their bodies, fan their tails, and nudge and rub against the females in an attempt to arouse their interest, possibly with the aid of some stimulatory chemicals secreted into the water. If sufficiently excited by this foreplay, a receptive female then follows a male as he swims away from the group and deposits spermatophores (small, gelatinous packets of sperm) onto the underwater debris. Taking one of these into her genital opening, the female becomes fertilized. Within a few days she deposits on underwater sticks one to three jellylike clumps, each containing fifty to one hundred black eggs and swollen almost to the size of a tennis ball. Within two or three weeks these adult salamanders (as well as their close cousins the Jefferson's salamanders, which have been breeding in a similar fashion in the same ponds) leave the water and return to the woods for an underground, molelike existence until next year's March rains bring them out again. In the water their eggs hatch in five to six weeks into tiny, gilled larvae that feed on aquatic life and metamorphose into miniature spotted salamanders, which leave the water by fall.

In their breeding activities frogs rely on sound rather than dance. The males of each species possess a unique mating call that attracts only the females of their own kind. The two earliest frogs in our region have entirely different calls. That of the 3-inch wood frog sounds remarkably like a quacking duck, and a pond full of these brown, black-masked frogs in March has probably fooled many people into believing that a flock of mallards was present in the water. The only frog found as far north as Alaska and Labrador, the wood frog is truly a species of the northern woods. Remaining in the icy waters for only about two weeks, the wood frogs return to the forest after leaving large, tapiocalike clumps of eggs attached to sticks just beneath the surface of the water. Unlike salamanders, frogs fertilize their eggs externally (like fish). The male clasps the female's waist from the back (the amplexus position) and spreads his sperm onto the eggs as she voids them into the water. As many as one thousand tiny black eggs are contained in a single wood-frog clump, and they hatch in two or three weeks into tadpoles, which transform into frogs by late summer.

The spring peeper, our smallest frog at only 1 inch in length, is also one of our loudest. Used to attract the female, its high-pitched, birdlike whistle can be heard a half mile away. The peeper's loudness results from its ability to distend its throat into a huge bubble almost as big as the frog itself, essentially creating its own sound amplifier. (The vocal pouches of a male wood frog are smaller and expand from its sides rather than from beneath its throat.) Spotting by the light of a flashlight one of these shy, diminutive treefrogs blowing its bubble while thousands of

———*Observations*———

————*Observations*————

its invisible companions produce an ear-ringing, almost deafening, chorus from the marsh vegetation is certainly one of the thrills of visiting a northeastern wetland on an early spring night.

Unlike the wood frog and spotted salamander, the peeper continues its breeding activities until the end of spring when it finally returns to the woods to climb among the shrubs. As a result it shares its aquatic habitat with other amphibians that follow in an orderly, predictable sequence as water temperatures warm up and become more conducive to each species' specific temperature preferences. In mid-April the spotted pickerel frogs and northern leopard frogs begin breeding. By the end of April, after a few 70-degree days, the American toads enter the waters for just a few days, filling the air with musical, sustained, birdlike trills created in their huge throat bubbles. The toads leave their eggs in long, ribbonlike strings rather than big clumps. In May the shorter, melodious trills of the gray treefrogs burst through the air, especially on humid or rainy nights. The last two frogs to breed—the green frog (which makes a sound like the plunking of a banjo string) and the big bullfrog (named for its deep, loud, bellowing calls)—don't reproduce until the water temperature is in the seventies, bringing the progression of the amphibians to a close in June (see chapter 12).

Because of their thin, permeable skins, amphibians are greatly affected by pollutants. Several species have experienced definite decreases in numbers in recent years, and scientists have blamed pollutants in the air and chemicals entering the waters where amphibians live and breed, as well as the stocking of predatory gamefish into these ponds, for this decrease. In New England and the Adirondack Mountains acid rain is said to be a factor contributing to decreasing wood-frog and spotted-salamander populations. These two species are especially vulnerable to this problem since they breed in vernal woodland ponds—a habitat that often becomes highly acidified in early spring when it is filled by melting snow concentrated with acids. Many of these habitats in the Northeast no longer support amphibians (just as some of the larger lakes and ponds in New England are now devoid of fish because of acid precipitation), and others have been found to contain frog and salamander larvae that are deformed from extremely high acid levels.

The destruction of wetlands (swamps, bogs, marshes) by development has historically been the most serious threat to these amphibians' survival. Since this country was first settled, over half of its original 200 million acres of wetlands has been lost to dredging, filling, channelization, and other operations designed to render them "useful" to developers. Despite attempts by the Bush Administration in 1991 to remove wetlands from protection by "redefining" them, stringent regulations to protect remaining wetlands now remain in effect in several northeastern states as well as at the federal level (the Clean Water Act of 1977), and resolutions to reduce the emissions responsible for acid rain and other forms of pollution also have been signed recently by both Canada and the United States (the new Clean Air Act of 1990).

Only by preserving our remaining wetlands and keeping their waters clean can we continue to take pleasure in venturing into the swamps on spring evenings to witness the ancient rites of the amphibians.

5

Resurfacing Reptiles

APRIL I

Garter snakes, painted turtles, and others greet the warmth of spring

Observations

The snow has melted away, the ponds have thawed, and the April sun shines longer and more intensely with each passing day. Daytime temperatures reach the fifties and sixties, and this renewed warmth signals another group of cold-blooded creatures to awaken from their long winter's sleep and greet the spring. Not as cold-hardy as the amphibians, reptiles shun the icy waters and cold rains that attract the frogs and salamanders in March. Our northern snakes and turtles require the sun's warmth to raise their body temperatures to certain levels before they can pursue their breeding and feeding activities for another season. Once they emerge from hibernation in April, they bask in the open sunlight on rocky ledges, logs, or the banks of ponds, soaking up the rays like sun worshippers.

The earliest reptile to emerge from hibernation in the Northeast is also the most widespread and familiar species—the eastern garter snake. Like the spotted salamanders, garter snakes emerge from their underground dens after several days of warm weather have raised the temperature of the ground surface above that of their sub-surface dens (the reversal of the winter months, when the frost-free dens are warmer than the frozen surface). Usually this occurs a week or two after the early amphibians begin breeding in our area, thus the first garter snakes are seen toward the end of March in northern New Jersey and southern New York and the first or second week of April farther north in New England or in the cooler mountainous areas.

A few days after the garter snake emerges, the northern water snake makes its appearance. This brown, thick-bodied reptile is often mistaken for the poisonous water moccasin of the southern states; however, there are no poisonous water snakes north of Virginia. Water snakes (and sometimes garter snakes) hibernate near or beneath the shores of lakes and ponds—they've even been known to spend the winter covered with water—so that's where they are first seen basking in early spring, sometimes by the dozens.

Later in April the next snake to emerge is the black racer, a shiny black, 5- to 6-foot snake, which often hibernates in dens with the even larger, unrelated black rat snake and the two poisonous snakes of our region—the copperhead and the timber rattlesnake. (Actually, a third poisonous species, the massasauga, or swamp rattlesnake, is found in extreme western Pennsylvania and near Lake Ontario in west-central New York.) These black racer dens are holes or crevices in rocky areas, deep enough to escape penetration by frost throughout the winter months. They may contain hundreds of snakes, all four species sometimes hibernating together and going their own separate ways upon emergence. The copperhead and timber rattler are among the last snakes to come out in the spring, usually not until May, when warm spring weather has become more firmly established.

Upon emerging from hibernation the first priority for a snake—even before eating its first meal in months—is mating. The gestation period for many of these species is three months, so if their babies are to be born before autumn's cool weather returns, they must mate as soon as possible. Before becoming fully active, copperheads and rattlers intermittently bask in the sun on ledges at the den sites, then retreat underground again at night when the temperatures drop. Once the weather remains warm enough, they mate and then disperse from the dens. (In Manitoba the red-sided garter snake—the species found farthest north of any North American snake—emerges by the thousands in late April from hibernation in limestone pits and immediately mates before leaving the den site, sometimes as many as seventy-five males converging on a single female in a frenzy.)

Another "early riser" among the reptiles is the painted turtle, our region's most common turtle. In 1976 I saw one of these attractive reptiles sunning itself on a log in a northern New Jersey pond as early as February 26, the mildest February on record throughout most of our region. This preceded by a week the emergence of the wood frogs and spotted salamanders that year. In most years, however, painted turtles don't awaken from their hibernation sites in the mud at the bottom of ponds until about the same time as the appearance of the garter snakes. At that time it is not unusual to see twenty or thirty of these

———*Observations*———

6-inch, colorful turtles sunning themselves on a log in a northeastern pond.

Like the snakes, turtles begin breeding soon after emerging from their winter sleep. In our aquatic species mating is an underwater affair and, in the case of painted turtles, seldom observed by humans. When the much larger snapping turtles awaken from the pond bottoms two or three weeks later, however, their breeding activities are more noticeable. The pond appears to boil when two of these twenty- to forty-pound behemoths wrestle and tumble as they mate just beneath the surface. These acts are preludes to a more significant, and generally more noticeable, natural event that occurs two months later: the turtles lumber ashore to lay eggs, then return to their watery domain (see chapter 13).

6

"Shadfish" and Shadbush

When the buds open on the serviceberry, the shad are in the rivers

————Observations————

In terms of both the consistency of its timing each year and the number of individuals that participate, the migration and spawning of the American shad in our rivers every April certainly deserves to be on the list of nature's events. Granted, not many outdoor enthusiasts—or even professional naturalists—record this event in their journals every year, but if they were able to see beneath the murky river waters, they would witness a spectacle as amazing as any bird migration.

Millions of $1^{1}/_{2}$- to $2^{1}/_{2}$-foot shad—bluish green with silvery sides—leave the Atlantic Ocean and enter the larger eastern rivers, returning to their places of birth of four or five years ago. In our northeastern states they begin to arrive in the rivers at the end of the first week in April, when water temperatures exceed 40 degrees Fahrenheit, and for the next five or six weeks the fish keep coming, the males arriving first and the largest egg-laden females last. Averaging 4 pounds but reaching 13 in exceptional cases, the big females are filled with 115,000 to 450,000 eggs. Like the salmon in the western United States, the shad (along with the alewife, its smaller cousin in the herring family) is an anadromous fish—it lives in salt water but spawns in fresh water.

After swimming up the Hudson, Delaware, Susquehanna, and Connecticut rivers for some distance from their saltwater homes, the shad begin to spawn. Sometime between sunset and midnight, with much vigorous splashing near the surface, the male shad fertilize the females' eggs as they void them into the water, where they slowly sink to the bottom. After reproducing, the emaciated adults swim downriver once again. Many of them, especially those that have traveled the farthest upstream, die after spawning, and only about 5 percent survive to spawn again the next year. The eggs hatch in about a week, and the tiny fish are nurtured through the spring and summer months in marshes and coves where they feed on aquatic crustaceans and insects. By September they are 3- to 5-inch-long fingerlings, and, like their parents, they begin to migrate down the rivers to the Atlantic Ocean, reaching it by October or November. Once in the ocean the young shad mingle with others from different rivers and from the

Chesapeake Bay. The Gulf of Maine appears to be a favorite mingling area. Males mature in the ocean after four years, females in five, and, guided by familiar chemical odors, they miraculously return to the river of their origin to produce the next generation of shad.

The American shad, *Alosa sapidissima* ("shad most delicious"), is native to the Atlantic coast from the Gulf of St. Lawrence south to Florida. Long prized as a table delicacy (along with its eggs), this "aristocrat of the herrings" was introduced by New York's Seth Green in 1871 to California, where it has become the source of a successful fishery industry. Historically, the Hudson River has been one of the most important rivers in North America for shad, but since colonial times this fishery has been characterized by wide fluctuations in productivity. The record catch was over 4,300,000 pounds in 1889 (almost matched in 1942), and the record low, 40,000 pounds, was in 1916. From the mid-1930s through the 1950s over a million pounds of shad were netted and removed from the Hudson River every year, but soon afterwards sharp declines in the fishery occurred. Similar trends were experienced in the Delaware River of New York, New Jersey, and Pennsylvania, where annual counts of migrating shad at Lambertville, New Jersey, revealed very low numbers (100,000 to 200,000 per season) in the 1970s compared to a few million in the earlier years of this century.

Many fishermen attribute the much-reduced numbers to overfishing, but the pollution of our northeastern rivers by raw sewage and chemicals may have been an even greater contributing factor to the decline of the shad. Artificial propagation, scientific management, and serious efforts to clean up the rivers during the past two decades have resulted in an encouraging growth once again in the number of shad returning to our rivers each April. Indeed, counts at Lambertville exceeded 830,000 shad in 1989, an increase attributed to dramatically higher levels of dissolved oxygen in the Delaware River following improved sewage-treatment methods. The construction of elaborate fish lifts and passageways at various dams along the Susquehanna in New York and Pennsylvania has allowed that river to once again support an annual shad run.

———*Observations*———

Along the banks of these eastern rivers, and spreading up to the tops of the ridges and hillsides that drain into them, a flower is beginning to bloom at this time from the buds of smooth, gray-barked trees. Named after the fish swimming up the rivers as it blossoms, the shadbush is overlooked all year long except for this season, when it produces the first colors amidst the bare, gray-brown woods of mid-April. A small, shrubby tree that usually grows in clumps of multiple trunks less than 30 feet tall, it is dwarfed by the oaks, maples, and birches that surround it. But when the masses of white flowers with five ribbon-like petals burst from their pointed buds, suddenly the trees become very noticeable throughout the forest. This usually occurs from early to mid-April in New Jersey and New York, late April to May in the Poconos of Pennsylvania and at lower elevations in New England, and not until June on Mount Washington.

Actually, several species of *Amelanchier* live in our region, and they are all extremely similar in appearance. It takes an expert to separate them into species based on habitat, flower morphology, and whether the blossoms appear before or after the leaves. Throughout their range they are known by many different names: shadblow, because the flowers appear like puffs of white steam or smoke in the leafless woods; Juneberry, after the fruits that ripen in early summer; and serviceberry, or "sarvis," named either after the coincidence of its blooming with the appearance of the preachers who resumed their traveling services in the Appalachian Mountains each spring or from a corruption of *Sorbus*, the genus name of the mountain ash tree, which is a very close relative.

The shadbush resembles other members of the apple or rose family in both its fruits and its flowers. The fruits look very much like small red or purplish crab apples, but they're delicious, both to humans and a great variety of wildlife. Over forty species of birds, skunks, raccoons, foxes, squirrels, and especially black bears (which often break down the branches) relish the Juneberries. After the fruits are gone in early summer, the shadbush once again seems to disappear into the lush, green forest until the following April when the shad return to the rivers.

7

Return of the Raptors

The great spectacle of the spring hawk migration

————Observations————

Above coastal beaches, atop rocky mountain vistas, and along the southern shorelines of the Great Lakes, the skies of April are the stage for one of nature's most spectacular annual events. Unlike the movement of the shad, this migration is witnessed by hundreds of people. Returning from their southern wintering grounds, thousands of raptors—hawks, falcons, vultures, and eagles—pass through our region from March through May, reaching a peak in the second half of April. When weather conditions are just right during this season, the air may be crammed with soaring, gliding hawks making their way back to the northern forests where they were born.

Birds of prey take advantage of various weather conditions and topographical features to save energy during their long migrations. Many species use tail winds, thermals, updrafts, and other aids to give them free lift. Thus, certain sites in our region figure as very productive lookouts in spring or fall (or, rarely, both seasons) because their topographical features, combined with the direction of the prevailing winds, are ideal for the production of these energy-saving factors. Great numbers of raptors tend to concentrate at the sites that lie along their intended migration route. People also concentrate at these lookouts, recording the numbers of hawks, the weather conditions, and other data each year. This information, gathered over the years from many lookouts across our region, has been invaluable in shedding light on the population trends of each raptor species and the different aspects of its migratory behavior (see chapter 26).

In the spring the raptors look for winds from the south to push them back north. These favorable tail winds often follow the passage of a low-pressure weather system and its associated front through our region. Raptors not only use these tail winds, they also take advantage of strong thermals, rising bubbles of warm air generated by the increasing temperatures in these weather systems (see chapter 26). Hawks also seek out free rides on updrafts— winds deflected upward by blowing against the sides of mountains and ridges. In autumn, when northwest winds prevail in our region, ideal updrafts are created against the northeast-to-southwest-oriented Appalachian Mountains. In spring, however, the migration is much more dispersed in the Appalachian region because the southerly winds generally strike the ridges obliquely and create weaker updrafts.

Nevertheless, some fairly impressive numbers can still be seen at some of these mountain lookouts at this season. For example, at Raccoon Ridge in northwestern New Jersey about 4,000 raptors can be counted in spring (20 percent of the ridge's autumn totals). More than half the total number of hawks seen each spring at Raccoon Ridge and other lookouts atop Kittatinny Ridge (the eastern section of the Appalachians extending from northwestern New Jersey into eastern Pennsylvania) are *Buteos*. The broad-winged hawk predominates, with smaller numbers of red-tailed and red-shouldered hawks. These three species are characterized by broad, rounded wings and fan-shaped tails designed for soaring on the thermals and updrafts rising from the ridge country.

The best coastal lookout in spring is at Sandy Hook, a long, narrow peninsula jutting northward toward New York Bay from the north end of New Jersey's Atlantic coast. As hawks following the coast northward reach Sandy Hook, they become concentrated there since they are reluctant to cross the open water. (The same phenomenon accounts for the tremendous numbers of southbound raptors—ten times the totals seen at Sandy Hook—that are counted each fall at Cape May, New Jersey.) More than 6,500 birds of prey are counted migrating past Sandy Hook during an average spring (the record is over 8,000). Almost 2,000 of these are American kestrels, a colorful, robin-sized falcon and the smallest of our fifteen raptor species. The merlin, its slightly larger and much rarer northern cousin, generally accounts for 150 to 250 sightings, which is by far the largest total seen at any of our region's spring hawk lookouts, inland or coastal. Only 2 or 3 of the much larger and endangered peregrine falcons—the world's fastest flying bird—are seen there each spring.

With their streamlined bodies, long, pointed wings, and extremely swift, powerful flight, falcons are built for the open country rather than the woodlands. During

————Observations————

migration they are much more abundant along the coast, where the wide-open terrain suits their style and there are plenty of migrating shorebirds and songbirds to pursue. They comprise from 30 to 50 percent of the total number of raptors seen at Sandy Hook in the spring, compared to only 5 to 10 percent at the Appalachian lookouts. The coastal dominance of the falcons is even more pronounced at Plum Island, Massachusetts, where kestrels amounted to almost 300 of the 420 raptors counted in the spring of 1989. On the other hand, the situation is reversed with hawks, which depend on updrafts and thermals during migration. Of Sandy Hook's average spring total of over 6,500 birds of prey, only about 150 are broad-winged hawks, which account for half the numbers seen at the Appalachian lookouts.

Sooner or later many of these migrating raptors—perhaps the majority—meet up with the southern shores, or "plains," of the Great Lakes as they continue northward into Canada's vast forests. Here they face a dilemma. They hesitate to fly over a large expanse of cold, open water because of the absence of thermals and updrafts to keep them aloft, so they turn east or west and follow the shoreline until a break or bend allows them to continue northward. As they approach the end of one of these detours, or "diversion lines," their numbers may have grown considerably since other hawks are continually joining them from the south in a broad migration front, especially on southerly winds. Certain lookouts along these shores witness tremendous concentrations of raptors—by far the greatest numbers seen anywhere in our region in spring.

Some of the hawks turn west upon reaching Lake Erie and travel around its western end, but most turn northeast and eventually reach Erie's neighbor, Lake Ontario. Here, again, some turn west and follow Lake Ontario's southern shoreline to its western end, where they can resume their trip to Canada. A lookout at Grimsby, Ontario, near the lake's western end, is the best place to see this contingent of migrating hawks. Most of the raptors, however, turn east upon reaching Lake Ontario's southern shore and ultimately attain its eastern end, where they veer north into Canada. All along the lake's southern plains other hawks have been joining this main contingent from the south.

Three lookouts—one at Braddock Bay, just north of Rochester between the lake's eastern and western ends; the second at Sodus Bay, forty-seven miles east of Rochester; and the third at Derby Hill, New York, at the lake's southeastern corner—are the best places in the northeastern United States to enjoy the spectacle of the spring hawk migration. Well over 60,000 migrating raptors are sometimes counted flying past Braddock Bay and Derby Hill in a single spring!

Fifteen different species of raptors are regularly included in the numbers seen at all these lookouts. Each species has its own timetable as it migrates back to its breeding grounds. Throughout the month of April those species that made up the vanguard of the hawk migration in March and early April (see chapter 2) are slowly being replaced by later species. Red-shouldered hawks have almost completely finished their migration by the end of March. Turkey vultures peak at the Great Lakes at the end of March and first week of April, when some spectacular displays of more than 1,000 of these big raptors pass by in a single day. After mid-April they slow down considerably. The red-tailed hawk experiences a similar decline at this time, although it is not unusual for several hundred of these *Buteos* to be seen on mid-April days at Derby Hill and Braddock Bay. The big rough-legged hawk has a much more protracted migratory season than the other *Buteos,* and all through March and April it is possible to see 30 to 50 of these big northern hawks on certain days. As temperatures get milder and those warm southerly winds of April increasingly dominate the weather of our region, hawkwatchers become anxiously impatient for the arrival of the next big wave.

Several species of raptors are included in this "changing of the guard," and each begins to reach its peak through the month of April. From the end of March to mid-April 100 to 300 kestrels per day may migrate over both Sandy Hook and the Great Lakes (more than 1,000 of these tiny falcons were counted at Braddock Bay on April 14, 1983).

The sharp-shinned hawk and its larger, much rarer cousin the Cooper's hawk also peak in April. Both are

———Observations———

Accipiter hawks (as is the huge and even rarer goshawk), which are characterized by short, rounded wings and long, rudderlike tails that enable them to swiftly pursue smaller birds through forests. In migration their flight is characterized by alternately flapping several times and then gliding. "Sharpies" may number more than 100 per day at the inland mountain lookouts in middle to late April and more than 500 at Sandy Hook, where they outnumber even the kestrel as the most abundant spring raptor (averaging over 3,500 per year out of 6,700 total hawks). It is usually near the end of April or even the first week in May that sharp-shinned hawks peak at the Great Lakes. At this time more than 1,000 sharpies a day are commonly seen at the Lake Ontario lookouts, especially when winds come from the south. As many as 14,000 have been counted in a single spring at Braddock Bay.

Only about 200 Cooper's hawks are seen at Sandy Hook each year, with peak days of 30 in late April. Although annual totals for this *Accipiter* are much higher at the Great Lakes (up to 1,300 at Braddock Bay with peaks at 100 to 200 per day in early April), it is still much less common than its smaller cousin.

The harrier, or marsh hawk, has the longest migration period of any of the raptors, starting in early March and continuing into late May. Its buoyant, sailing flight, white rump, and narrow 42-inch wingspread identify this bird. It is most numerous along the coast and in the Appalachians during the second and third weeks of April, when 15 to 30 birds can be seen on peak days. At Braddock Bay, where more than 2,000 harriers were counted in the spring of 1988, the peak occurs earlier in the month or even at the end of March, when 150 to 275 of these graceful raptors may sail by in a day.

When the osprey, or fish hawk, suddenly returns north at the beginning of April, it is easily recognized by its black-and-white coloration and crooked, 6-foot wingspread. The numbers seen at each of our region's lookouts are between 100 and 500 per year (the higher figures coming from Lake Ontario), with peak flights of about 50 to 100 ospreys per day occurring at the end of April and beginning of May.

The first broad-winged hawk usually appears in our region just about the middle of April, returning north after spending the winter as far away as Bolivia or Peru. It is always the last of the fifteen species of raptors to return in spring. Slightly larger than a crow but chunkier, with broad, rounded wings, it is a handsome raptor with reddish brown underparts and prominent black-and-white bands across its wide tail. Yet, soaring alone high in the sky, it is easily overlooked as it flies way above the tree tops. Soon more broad-wings arrive, 10 and 20 at a time in soaring "kettles" circling upward or in gliding squadrons rapidly moving toward the horizon. Finally the day comes when the April sky is dark with broad-winged hawks—hundreds of moving birds covering the entire field of view. Groups of several hundred pass together overhead, only to be instantly replaced by hundreds more. Hour after hour they circle overhead and then glide away until by late afternoon the sky appears empty and calm again. If good weather conditions continue the next day, hundreds or even thousands more may move through our region. Hawkwatchers stare upward in awe, necks stiff and forearms weary from lifting binoculars as they keep track of one of nature's greatest displays.

It is not uncommon for the bulk of the broad-winged hawk migration to take place in just a three- or four-day period if the weather conditions are ideal (winds from a southerly direction). At Raccoon Ridge in New Jersey, Hook Mountain in southern New York, and Hawk Mountain, the famous autumn lookout near Drehersville, Pennsylvania, as many as 500 broad-wings may be seen on these peak days in middle to late April. At Montclair Quarry, a lookout in the Piedmont region of northeastern New Jersey, more than 1,000 have been recorded on some of these rare days. This hawk-watch station, situated neither along the coast nor in the Appalachian ridges, is nevertheless emerging as one of our region's best lookouts south of the Great Lakes. Almost 9,000 raptors were counted there in the spring of 1989, including 5,000 broad-wings, 1,000 sharp-shins, 500 turkey vultures, 475 kestrels, and 300 red-tails.

In late April the broad-wings reach their peak at the Great Lakes lookouts. As a cold front begins to approach

————*Observations*————

this region and warm winds blow from the south, more than 10,000 broad-wings can be seen at Derby Hill, Sodus Bay, or Braddock Bay in a single day. Almost 20,000 were counted at Braddock Bay on April 27, 1984, and in the three-day period of April 27–29 that year over 35,000 broad-wings appeared over both Braddock Bay and Derby Hill! On the other hand, during the spring of 1989, which was characterized by an abnormally cold, wet April, the total count of broad-wings at Braddock Bay for the entire season was 18,000. When the weather isn't right, broad-winged hawks don't appear at the lookouts in great concentrations; but when nature cooperates, their numbers may be unbelievable.

With the cold lake water acting as a barrier, the broad-wings hitchhike on the southerly winds and move in a narrow, concentrated band past the lookouts along the shore. After this peak period good flights of thousands of broad-wings may continue into May, and some days in early June may even produce more than 100, the great majority of these being immature birds, which migrate later in the season. But the really magical time to be at these lookouts is during the last two weeks in April, when it is possible to enjoy not only hundreds (or thousands) of broad-winged hawks overhead but also good numbers of kestrels, sharp-shinned hawks, harriers, ospreys, and maybe even a few bald eagles and peregrine falcons. During this time there also exists the exciting possibility of seeing the largest and rarest of all the raptors in the northeast. On April 21, 1979, 5 golden eagles were seen migrating past Braddock Bay, and two years earlier, on the exact day, the unbelievable total of 10 golden eagles (half of the spring total) passed over Derby Hill in just a ninety-minute period from 3:15 to 4:45 P.M.!

8

Woodland Wildflowers

APRIL IV

The forest floor is carpeted with color

——*Observations*——

For many of those who mark the progression of the year by tracking nature's annual events, nothing is more symbolic of spring than the appearance of the first wildflowers. The early spring breeding rituals of wood frogs and woodcock are secretive, mostly nocturnal performances that are witnessed by few people. Even the appearance of the first robins and bluebirds can be false alarms—they may very well be Canadian visitors that have spent the entire winter in our northeastern states rather than our "own" birds returning to greet the spring. But when the forest floor suddenly transforms from brown leaves and bare earth to patches of white, yellow, and green, then spring has definitely arrived. The magical appearance of the first wildflowers probably does more to break the doldrums of a long winter than any other natural event. As the world becomes colorful once again, dispositions are also transformed in profound ways. "Spring fever" takes hold and prompts many people who had held themselves "prisoners" indoors for months to become restless and anxious to spend their hours outdoors again. There is much to look forward to in the coming months at this most active and stimulating time of the year.

Many of our earliest woodland wildflowers sprout from underground tubers, bulbs, rhizomes, or rootstocks—structures that store the plant's food and enable it to produce early leaves and flowers after a long winter's dormancy. Since they are under the earth, these plants cannot sense the increasing length of the day in spring, so it is probably the increasing warmth that is the stimulus initiating their spring emergence. However, an internal "clock" also may be involved, as well as the necessity to experience the cold months of winter before popping up. These factors ensure that the plant won't emerge prematurely during an abnormally warm spell in midwinter. Once its winter dormancy is broken, then the warm weather of April activates the underground plant to send up its leaves and flowers. This is why, unlike the many birds that reappear each spring within precisely the same week, flowers often vary by as much as two or three weeks in their flowering dates from year to year, depending upon the weather. And the same species may bloom a week or two later in a sheltered ravine, north-facing slope, or elevated summit than in an exposed, sea-level site.

Many of the earliest spring wildflowers are cup or dish shaped, with deep centers and shiny, reflective petals (commonly white or yellow). These traits enable the plants to reflect sunlight off their petals and focus it onto their central reproductive parts, where the warmth is retained by the flower's shape. The heat that accumulates from the spring sunlight in this way may actually raise the temperature inside a hepatica, anemone, trillium, or marsh marigold several degrees above that of the air. A few species, like hepatica, also have very downy or fuzzy interiors, which help to retain heat. Not only is heat retention beneficial to the flower in accelerating the development of its pollen and seeds in the chilly April weather, it also may provide warmth for the pollinating insects that the flowers depend on. The glossy white or yellow flower parts also help to attract the attention of bees, flies, and butterflies. (Red trillium, or wake-robin, employs a different strategy: Its flowers smell like rotten meat to attract carrion flies, giving rise to another one of this beautiful but odoriferous flower's names, "stinking Benjamin.")

Even though the vagaries of the spring weather change the dates from year to year, there is still a certain order in which the wildflowers appear each spring. Following skunk cabbage (which emerges in the wetlands in late winter), the first flower of spring in our region is coltsfoot. It is related to and is sometimes mistaken for the dandelion, but it differs by sending up its bright yellow flowers on scaly stalks long before its first hoof-shaped leaves appear. Late March or early April is when this alien flower appears in disturbed areas like roadsides and railroad embankments.

The first true woodland flowers appear soon afterwards, usually beginning in very early April with hepatica, an exquisite gem in the buttercup family with a varying number of petallike sepals (usually five or six but sometimes up to twelve) ranging from white to pale lavender to deep blue. Hepatica's leaves have three liver-shaped lobes

————*Observations*————

——Observations——

(*hepar* is Greek for liver) and, like many plants, were once used as medicinal cures for ailments of the body part that they resembled (the so-called doctrine of signatures).

Following hepatica's appearance is trailing arbutus (known as mayflower in Massachusetts), a wonderfully fragrant, evergreen, ground-trailing relative of azalea and blueberry. By mid-April bloodroot, spring beauty, trout lily, Dutchman's breeches, and red trillium arrive. Later in the month there are marsh marigolds, over a dozen species of violets (white and yellow as well as various shades of blue and purple), white trillium, dwarf ginseng, fringed polygala, rue anemone, wood anemone, blue cohosh, wild ginger, and the toothworts.

By the end of April the woodland wildflower display is at a peak, and the leaves of the species that will flower in early May have also begun to emerge by the thousands in the rich woodland soil and leaf litter: Canada mayflower, jack-in-the-pulpit, Solomon's seal, white baneberry, wild geranium, and many others. The thick shoots of mayapple emerge now, resembling colonies of tightly wrapped, folded umbrellas, which gradually open wide in early May and reveal waxy, greenish white flowers. Along dry rock ledges and cliffs more-specialized species are also in bloom in late April—rock cress, early saxifrage, moss phlox—and the leaves of the beautiful columbine have also begun to appear from the cracks and crevices. In a few short weeks the forest floor has been transformed from a drab, gray-and-brown covering of dead leaves to a changing multihued carpet of delicate flowers and leaves. Daily walks in the woods are almost a necessity to keep up with the accelerating pace of nature's parade of flowers.

By mid-May, however, the parade ceases almost as abruptly as it began. Once the trees above these plants sprout their leaves and the forest canopy closes, the sunlight necessary for the growth and reproduction of these smaller plants is cut off. During the weeks in which the woodland wildflowers have been emerging, the buds of the trees and shrubs also have been bursting open, primed by the increasingly longer days of April. Like the underground parts of the wildflowers, the buds of woody plants must first experience a period of frigid winter weather in order for their dormancy to be broken. Then, as days lengthen in spring and reach a certain critical duration, hormones are released by light-sensitive pigments in the buds that apparently keep accurate track of the increasing daylight in order to prevent the premature formation of leaves. These hormones make the buds ready to open on the warm days of late April and early May.

The emerging leaves of some trees can be just as beautiful and magical a transformation as the appearance of wildflowers. When the outer bud scales of shagbark or mockernut hickory drop off, for example, delicate inner scales are revealed, which gradually expand until they resemble tulip petals, and the entire tree appears to be in bloom. Then the scales roll back to reveal a cluster of new, pale green leaves joined at their tips like the fingers of a hand. As beautiful as this process is, however, it spells the end of another season for the wildflowers, many of which soon turn yellow in the shade of the forest and disappear for another year.

———*Observations*———

9

The Big Hatch

MAY I

Mayflies and stoneflies, swallowtails and saturniids, inchworms and other insects

——————*Observations*——————

The regreening of the landscape seems to occur with an alarming suddenness each spring. Within the brief span of just a few warm days in early May the buds completely open to release millions of tiny, embryonic leaves expanding into the sunlight, beginning with the maples and birches and ending with the oaks and ashes. The forest now becomes a darker, cooler, more humid environment as countless green leaves from the canopy down to the lower shrubs and herbs intercept most of the incoming sunlight and add their own moisture by constantly transpiring water vapor from their pores. Even more important, the green leaves provide an almost unlimited source of food for our region's primary herbivores, the insects.

As soon as the green leaves appear, an army of leaf-eating insects emerges to dine on them. Many of these are the caterpillars that hatch from eggs that were deposited on bark or branch by adult moths last summer. Millions of tiny inchworms, loopers, underwing larvae, and tussock moth caterpillars emerge and begin to munch on the leaves or hang from silken strands to the ground and disperse to other parts of the forest. At times in early May these suspended caterpillars are so numerous that walking through the forest becomes very uncomfortable as sticky webs and tiny larvae cling to faces and arms. A steady rain of droppings falls from the canopy above as the caterpillars devour the greenery.

Another caterpillar that emerges from its egg in early spring is the tent caterpillar, two different species of which occur in our region. One, the forest tent caterpillar, lives in colonies on a variety of deciduous trees but does not actually build a tent. The other, the more familiar eastern tent caterpillar, hatches from a shiny, compact egg mass wrapped around the twig of a wild cherry or apple tree. As soon as the first leaf buds open on these trees, the tiny caterpillars all emerge from their egg case and spin a small silken tent in the crotch of a limb. This serves as a shelter from predators when these fuzzy, colorful caterpillars aren't feeding on the foliage. As they grow bigger through the spring, they enlarge the tent until it becomes a foot or more in diameter and resembles a thick, messy mixture of webbing, droppings, and caterpillars. When fully grown, the caterpillars leave the tent to spin a cocoon in some sheltered location. Small cherry trees may be completely defoliated by these colonies, but new leaves grow and the trees usually recover.

An even more destructive caterpillar, which hatches from soft, tan egg sacs on the bark of trees in early May, is the gypsy moth larva. Introduced into this country from Europe over a century ago, this insect has become one of the nation's most successful pests and is now found virtually anywhere oak trees grow. Upon emerging from the egg mass the tiny black caterpillars cluster together in a tight group around the mass. Then they crawl up to the branches or disperse on silken strands like parachutes in the breeze. During some years when the gypsy moth population is particularly high, the forests may be almost completely defoliated by July (see chapter 18).

Not all of the spring caterpillars hatch from eggs at this time. Some species, like the woolly bear and other tiger moth caterpillars, overwinter in this larval stage and awaken in spring to spin cocoons and metamorphose into adult moths. Other species spend the winter in the pupal stage and then become winged adults in early spring. One familiar butterfly that does this is the spring azure, a small blue butterfly that appears about mid-April and is easily noticed as it flutters over the mostly bare ground.

During the last days of April and first week in May each year the first swallowtail butterflies emerge from the well-camouflaged chrysalises (the pupae of butterflies) that were suspended from bark or branches. Two very large and beautiful species commonly appear in our region at this season: the yellow, black-striped tiger swallowtail and the black, greenish marked spicebush swallowtail. After mating the female swallowtails seek out the particular species of trees and shrubs that their caterpillars prefer (cherry, ash, or tulip tree for the tiger; sassafras or spicebush for the other), lay their eggs there, and die soon afterwards.

Our region's largest, most spectacular moths have also spent the winter in the pupal stage, waiting until the warm May weather to emerge, usually under the cover

—————*Observations*—————

of darkness. Their pupae, however, unlike the naked chrysalises of the butterflies, are contained within thick, silken cocoons that have spent the winter either attached to or suspended from twigs or down in the forest leaf litter, depending on the species. These moths are all members of the family Saturniidae, commonly called giant silk moths, and since they fly at night, they are rarely able to be appreciated for their beauty and size. With a wingspread exceeding 6 inches, the cecropia moth is our country's largest moth and also one of the most attractive with its huge wings and thick, furry body colored in various shades of brown, tan, and red. Almost as large is its close relative the polyphemus moth (named after Polyphemus, the Cyclops blinded by Odysseus), easily recognized by the large blue-and-yellow eyespots on each of its tan hindwings. But the most beautiful giant silk moth of all—and considered by many to be our country's most attractive insect—is the luna moth. With lavender-bordered, pale green wings spreading over 4 inches and long "tails" sweeping out from the bottom wings, this exquisite insect rivals the most beautiful of the woodland wildflowers. None of these giant silk moths possesses functional mouth parts, so no food is taken during the brief one- or two-week lifespan. The energy required for flying, mating, and reproducing was stored by the gluttonous caterpillar a summer ago.

Meanwhile, beneath the waters of our streams, rivers, lakes, and ponds another hatch is occurring with the arrival of May's increasing temperatures. The warming of the waters is followed by the emergence of millions of winged insects that have spent their immature stages clinging to underwater rocks or crawling in the gravel. So important are these insects as food for trout and other fish that many have been given common names by fishermen, who create ingenious artificial imitations in an attempt to lure their quarry. Most famous are the delicate mayflies, which may live only a day or two as adults but create quite a scene with their mating swarms comprised of thousands or millions of winged insects "dancing" in the air. Although mayfly species continue to emerge from the water into the summer, the most productive month in the northeastern United States is May.

May also brings on the metamorphosis of other aquatic insects into winged adults able to leave the water and fly into the warm spring air. Stonefly nymphs—squat, crawling, flattened insects with two long tails—emerge onto rocks and tree trunks, shed their skins, and flutter (or run) away as winged adults. Caddisflies resemble small moths with their wings folded rooflike over their bodies. They begin to emerge from streams and ponds in May after spending their immature lives as caterpillarlike larvae that encase themselves for protection in bits of debris, plant stems, or even tiny pebbles.

Then, as every outdoor person well knows, early May also brings on the emergence of the one insect that probably does more to ruin the enjoyment of this season than any other—the blackfly. Metamorphosing from maggotlike larvae attached to underwater stones, the tiny, biting flies swarm around our faces and arms in their quest for blood. Soon, like the caterpillars dropping on silken lines from the trees, these nuisance insects will in turn serve as important meals for countless hungry songbirds returning to our forests from the tropics.

10

Waves of Warblers

Birders prepare for the "big days" of mid-May

——————Observations——————

Before the first light of dawn the forest music begins. As the sun rises above the horizon and illuminates May's fresh, pale green foliage, the melodies increase in intensity and variety, with one songbird after another adding its voice to the early morning chorus. It all started very simply way back in February, when the nonmigratory resident birds like the cardinals and chickadees began to sing in response to the lengthening days of late winter. They were joined in March by robins, bluebirds, and song sparrows coming back to our area after spending the winter in more southern states. Additional species contributed to the chorus through April, and now, as the pace of the spring bird migration greatly accelerates in May, the musical score of morning's bird chorus is much more elaborate. Dozens of different species—thrushes, warblers, vireos, orioles, tanagers, finches—sing their specific melodies from perches in the trees and shrubs. The woods are alive with music, and birders awaken without the aid of alarm clocks, anxious to catch glimpses of these colorful songsters flitting among the branches. Some of the species will remain to raise families this summer, but others will move on, not to be seen again until their southward migration through our region in the fall.

The timing and the sequence of nature's annual events are truly remarkable. No sooner do the new leaves emerge on the trees and shrubs than an army of caterpillars hatches from winter eggs to consume them. And returning north just in time for this springtime feast are the insect-eating birds that spent the winter months in the Tropics. Most of the birds that come back to the Northeast in May have overwintered in Mexico, Central America, the Caribbean Islands, and even South America. (Some of the mysteries of these tremendous annual trips will be explored in chapter 25.) Traveling over one thousand miles back to their breeding grounds each spring requires lots of energy, so when these birds are not flying, they are picking insects off leaves, twigs, and the ground or snatching them right out of the air. Their constant activity, melodious voices, brilliant colors, and sheer variety make May the best month of the entire year to go out and enjoy nature's most splendid creatures.

During the first three weeks of April arrivals from the

Deep South and the tropics begin to trickle into our region while the trees are still leafless. These include the first species of warblers—our most popular, colorful, and diversified group of woodland birds, with thirty to thirty-five different species passing through our region per year. Each of these small, 5- to 6-inch birds has its own particular song, color pattern, habitat, and behavioral repertoire that set it apart from its relatives, as well as its own dependable migration schedule. The first to return are usually the palm, yellow-rumped, and pine warblers, three species that may have spent the winter in our southern states (a few yellow-rumped, or myrtle, warblers occasionally spend the winter in our northeastern region, especially along the coast where they feed on the fruits of bayberry, or myrtle).

Also during this time the first of the truly tropical migrants returns to our area: the Louisiana waterthrush. Actually a species of warbler, with its spotted breast and ground-dwelling habits it more closely resembles a thrush or even a tiny sandpiper with its bobbing movements. The waterthrush's song is one of the most joyful sounds of this season. Three loud, clear whistling notes followed by a jumble of twittering sounds echo from the sides of deep ravines and stream valleys where the bird hops from stone to stone in the flowing water. It is the essence of a wild, undisturbed, reawakening forest in spring.

By late April the prairie, yellow, and black-and-white warblers begin to arrive as the pace of the spring migration quickens. During the first few days of May these and other warblers are joined by some of the most colorful, larger songbirds, which have also spent the winter over one thousand miles away: the scarlet tanager, the rose-breasted grosbeak, and the northern (Baltimore) oriole. The brilliant reds and oranges of these three species symbolize the tropical forests from which they came. Also returning in the first week of May are the less colorful but incomparably melodious wood thrush and veery, whose haunting, flutelike songs lend an ethereal quality to the woods at dawn and dusk. Several species of flycatchers come back during the first ten days of May—kingbird, least flycatcher, and great crested flycatcher—as well as our tiniest bird, the ruby-throated hummingbird.

————Observations————

By the middle of May the woods are filled with activity and song. In the trees are dozens of additional species of warblers and three or four kinds of vireos, while thrushes and ovenbirds search the leaf litter for insects and flycatchers and cedar waxwings snatch them in midair. Permanent residents, like woodpeckers and nuthatches, and earlier migrants, like sparrows, towhees, and kinglets, also become increasingly active as the nesting season approaches. This is the peak of spring in the northeastern United States, and since the 1970s this has become the traditional season when groups of birders take to the woods, fields, and shores for their annual "Big Day," "Spring Count," or "Birdathon."

Usually occurring right smack in the middle of May when the warbler migration is at its peak (perhaps a week later in northern New York and the higher elevations of New England), birdathons are friendly—but serious and well-prepared—competitions among birding clubs or unattached groups of individuals to record the most species of birds in a single day. It is common for a group to exceed one hundred species of birds during one of these forays, including twenty to twenty-five different warblers. A few of the very experienced, "semiprofessional" New Jersey birding groups (including one that enlisted the help of master birder–author–artist Roger Tory Peterson) have even exceeded the magical two hundred number by covering one end of the state to the other in twenty-four hours. This extraordinary total says as much for the experience and preparation of these birders as for the wonderful diversity of New Jersey's habitats, including farms, fields, both northern hardwood and mixed oak forests, and the Atlantic shore. (Has the number of birds returning to our region each spring really decreased in the past few decades? Chapter 15 will deal with this very serious and alarming possibility.)

During the last week of May the spring migration decreases in intensity. The arrival of the two latest warblers—the blackpoll and the mourning warbler—usually occurs at this time, and birders generally see this as a sign that their favorite season is drawing to a close. The migration of a few other late species—yellow-billed and black-billed cuckoos, nighthawk, gray-cheeked thrush, wood pewee, and several of the other flycatchers—continues into very early June. Then the season of passage gives way to the season of nesting and raising another family of birds that will experience their own southward journeys in a few short months.

————Observations————

11

Beachcombers on the Bay

*The arrival of
horseshoe crabs
and shorebirds*

———Observations———

Away from the hemlock ravines and northern hardwood forests, far from the songs of the Louisiana waterthrush and scarlet tanager, other events are taking place this month that surpass even the warbler migration in both magnitude and international significance. Like the early May arrival of the woodland songbirds just when hordes of caterpillars are feeding on newly formed leaves, these events are outstanding examples of nature's precise timing. On the beaches and mudflats along the Delaware and New Jersey sides of the Delaware Bay, two apparently unrelated natural happenings are simultaneously taking place among creatures as different in appearance, habitat, and behavior as any in our region. Yet one group depends completely upon the other for its survival, and together they result in one of the most overwhelming natural history spectacles in this country.

Emerging in spring from the depths of the Delaware Bay and nearby Atlantic Ocean where it has spent the winter, one of our most primitive creatures begins to make its way to the shore. Virtually unchanged in appearance for 300 million years (based on fossil evidence), the horseshoe crab is not a crab at all but a distant relative of the arachnids, a group that includes spiders and scorpions. Its shield-shaped body, including its sharp, stiff tail, is 20 inches or more in length and is covered with a carapace, or armored shell. By May the first of these horseshoe crabs are reaching the shoreline.

Just about in the middle of the month, coinciding with the time of either the new moon or full moon, the invasion of the beaches begins. Thousands of crabs are pushed toward the shore by the high tides, then, shortly after the waves begin to recede, the first males begin to slowly and clumsily make their way onto the sand. For miles along the water's edge the beaches may be lined with a solid mass of horseshoe crabs several rows deep, waiting for the females to arrive. This occurs as the tides continue to ebb, and the males scramble for mates when the females crawl onto the beach. Groups of ten or more males may surround a female until one finally succeeds in attaching himself to the rear of her shell with his pedipalps (a pair of specialized, leglike appendages near the head).

Riding her up the beach, the male waits for the female to dig a nest in the wet sand 2 to 8 inches deep, into which she deposits her eggs—from fifty thousand to eighty thousand in number. Each egg is round, olive green to brown in color, and the size of a pinhead. They come out in clumps about $1/2$ inch to 4 inches across, which become clustered together in the nest. The male fertilizes them as they leave the female's body, then they both cover the nest with sand and return to the water.

This scene is repeated day after day throughout the month, with each new invasion of horseshoe crabs coinciding with an incoming tide. The peak occurs between May 18 and 28, when the beaches around Delaware Bay may be crammed with ten thousand crabs per square mile, and there may be fifty nests in every square yard of sand. Over a million horseshoe crabs may participate in this reproductive orgy, a number unmatched anywhere else along the entire Atlantic coast of the United States. Then, suddenly, during the first few days of June it is all over, and the beaches are littered with the upside-down carcasses of horseshoe crabs unable to right themselves and stranded by the outgoing tides.

If this event occurred all by itself, it would still be called unparalleled as a natural history spectacle. But it is ultimately responsible for another happening, the success of which is completely dependent on the horseshoe crab's reliability from year to year. Returning from wintering areas thousands of miles away in Peru, Chile, Brazil, Suriname, Patagonia, and all the way down to Tierra del Fuego, the shorebirds arrive at Delaware Bay just when the horseshoe crabs are reaching the beaches.

Unbelievable as it may seem, most of these birds have made a nonstop flight of over two thousand miles lasting several days between takeoff from South America and landing at the bay. One species, the red knot, for example, completes its four-thousand-mile trip from southern Argentina to Delaware Bay in a single, nonstop flight of sixty hours. Depleted of fuel and famished after this incredible odyssey, the shorebirds begin to feast on the eggs of the horseshoe crabs, pecking at those that have been washed out of the nests and digging for those still buried.

————Observations————

The number of shorebirds that arrive at Delaware Bay during these last two weeks in May can be as high as 1$\frac{1}{2}$ million—the largest concentration anywhere in the eastern United States. Over 400,000 may be present simultaneously on peak days. A single fifteen-mile stretch of beach may contain 250,000 shorebirds at one time, a moving carpet of birds gorging on crab eggs. As many as a dozen different species may be included, the most numerous being the semipalmated sandpiper, sanderling, red knot, ruddy turnstone, and dunlin, followed by the short-billed dowitcher, semipalmated plover, black-bellied plover, least sandpiper, and willet. Thousands of laughing gulls also join the feast, flying in from their nesting areas in nearby marshes to take advantage of this excessive but temporary bounty.

For several of these shorebird species the numbers present at Delaware Bay during this brief time may represent a majority of their populations in the entire continent. A tremendous flock of shorebirds on Moore's Beach, northwest of Cape May, New Jersey, was estimated to contain over 200,000 semipalmated sandpipers one day in May 1985. It is thought that perhaps 80 percent of all the red knots in the entire Western Hemisphere pass through Delaware Bay in three weeks. Comparable percentages are estimated for New World Atlantic populations of sanderlings and ruddy turnstones.

In their two or three weeks spent at the bay the shorebirds consume unimaginable quantities of horseshoe crab eggs. Some estimates exceed one hundred tons, and scientists have calculated that a single sanderling eats as many as ten thousand eggs every day for two weeks! The result is a doubling of its weight, from about 50 grams when it first landed, lean and hungry after its long flight, to 100 grams before the next leg of its long and continuing journey to the breeding grounds.

Staying only long enough to regain their weight, the shorebirds soon take off to resume their northward migration. Most are gone by the end of May, and after the first week of June the beaches are almost empty. They still have another two thousand miles to go before reaching their breeding grounds in the Arctic tundra, where the very brief summer is the ultimate reason for their extraordinarily hurried ways. In fact, after nesting in June many species begin their return journey to South America in July. It is the abundant supply of insects and other small creatures as food for themselves and their young during the short Arctic summer that makes such a long trip worthwhile.

Delaware Bay represents eastern North America's main and final gathering place for all these shorebirds before continuing their migration to their Arctic breeding grounds. Neither a nesting area nor wintering area, it functions as an extremely important stopover, or "staging area"—a critical link in the chain connecting these other two seasonal homes for the shorebirds. Staging areas may be thousands of miles from both breeding and wintering homes, and many, like Delaware Bay, may be impossible to replace due to their strategic location along the migration route and the coincidental appearance of an abundant food source. In this case the shorebirds must congregate at precisely the right place (Delaware Bay) at precisely the right time (the latter part of May) to be able to replenish their food stores. After this spectacular but short-lived episode the role of the staging area for these species discontinues until the next May.

For these millions of shorebirds the protection of Delaware Bay is just as important as the preservation of their Arctic breeding grounds and South American wintering areas. Perhaps it is the loss of similar but unrecognized staging areas in the past that has been partly responsible for the decline in the numbers of many shorebird species over the years (in addition to the effects of wetland development and wanton slaughter in the past century by market and sport hunters). Even though they are now protected by law and number in the tens of thousands, these shorebird species are still very vulnerable because they all gather in one limited area at the same time. A single major springtime oil spill in Delaware Bay—one of the world's largest petrochemical ports and the scene of intense oil-tanker traffic—could be disastrous to a large proportion of this continent's shorebirds.

Since many of the beaches surrounding the bay are privately owned and threatened with development, this

————*Observations*————

also poses a potential problem to the survival of these birds. A landmark step toward ensuring this survival came in 1989 when Governors Kean of New Jersey and Castle of Delaware signed a resolution proclaiming the lower estuary of Delaware Bay a reserve in the Western Hemisphere Shorebird Reserve Network. This network's purpose is to highlight key staging areas for shorebirds throughout the world and to work to protect them. It was founded by a coalition including the National Audubon Society, World Wildlife Fund, International Association of Fish and Wildlife Agencies, and Cape Cod's Manomet Bird Observatory.

In the case of Delaware Bay, New Jersey's Department of Environmental Protection joined with Public Service Electric and Gas Company to generate a land-acquisition fund to purchase key beach areas. Other private conservation groups like the New Jersey Conservation Foundation, The Nature Conservancy, and the National Audubon Society are likewise buying important parcels around this bay, where for a few brief weeks each May one of nature's truly sensational events continues to follow the timeless movements of the tides.

12

Bellowing Bullfrogs, Trilling Treefrogs

The breeding of late-spring amphibians

————Observations————

A lone veery sounds its haunting, flutelike call as the sun sets behind the pond's tree-lined horizon. Darkness falls, the thrush's melody fades away with the light, and all is quiet. But not for long. It is now the end of May, and a new chorus of frogs is beginning to emerge from the ponds and wetlands. The early spring calls of the wood frogs have been a memory for almost two months, and the spring peepers and American toads have completed their noisy breeding rituals, too. But now the frogs of summer are taking their turns at adding the dimension of sound to the swamps on warm evenings in late May.

The ranges of a few of these amphibians barely extend into our region. The Pine Barrens of southern New Jersey, for example, is the northern limit of the range for the carpenter frog, a small, 2½-inch brown frog with four yellowish stripes down its back. When these frogs issue their plunking calls from the sphagnum bogs, it sounds just like a group of carpenters hammering nails. Interspersed with these calls is another sound very characteristic of late spring and early summer nights in New Jersey's pinelands. In fact, the fast-repeated, nasal "quonk-quonk" calls of the Pine Barrens treefrogs are heard very few other places in the world. Outside of the cedar swamps and sphagnum bogs of these pinelands, this gorgeous green treefrog with light-bordered lavender stripes along its sides is found in only a few small, isolated colonies along the southeastern coastal plain.

At the other extreme in our region is the mink frog, a 3-inch, tan species with lots of dark blotches on its back and the habit of giving off a strong, garliclike odor resembling a mink's when captured. This species inhabits ponds and streams in the Far North of Canada, northern New England, and the Adirondack Mountains, where its rapid succession of metallic clucking sounds can be heard starting at the end of spring.

About a month after the American toads breed at the end of April (see chapter 4), another toad briefly takes its place in shallow ponds and roadside ditches to lay eggs. Known as Fowler's toad, this species differs in appearance from the American toad by its smaller size, white, unspotted belly, and three or more warts contained in each large, dark spot on its back (the American toad has only one or two). But its chief difference is its habitat, which is generally restricted to the coastal plain and the sandy borders of lakes and large river valleys. Its voice is also unmistakably unique—a loud bleating call somewhat like that of a sheep or a baby crying "waah." After breeding these toads hide during the day in ground burrows or under logs and emerge at night to catch moving insects with flicks of their sticky tongues.

In addition to these four localized amphibians there are three other frogs whose calls should be familiar to anyone who has ventured near a pond in the northeastern United States in late spring and summer. One of the most common and widespread of all American frogs, the 4-inch green frog is found wherever there is fresh water—ponds, lakes, wetlands, and rivers and small streams. Its familiar call can best be compared to the plucking of a loose banjo string, and, as with all frogs, only the male produces the call to attract a mate. The male green frog also has a bright yellow throat and large eardrums (tympani) that distinguish it from the female.

Many people are surprised to learn that the unseen bird trilling from way up in a tree is really a well-camou-flaged frog sitting on a branch. The gray treefrog usually only comes down to breed in ponds (or swimming pools) in early summer and then returns to its lofty perch in the woods to wait for unsuspecting tree crickets, beetles, moths, and other insects. Its amazing camouflage stems from its ability to change the concentration and distribution of pigments flowing from cells just beneath its skin. Usually the same color as tree bark—gray with some darker blotches—the treefrog also can become brown, black, greenish, or almost white, and its granular skin can change in texture from dry and shiny to moist and slippery. As it sits motionless on a limb or in a knothole with its legs tucked neatly under its 2-inch body, it resembles a small bump of wood. Like all treefrogs, adhesive discs on its toes enable it to cling to both horizontal and vertical surfaces. Starting around the end of May and continuing into the summer, the gray treefrog's short, loud, melodious trill bursts forth from the woods on humid and rainy evenings and on days when the skies darken with rain clouds and distant thunder signals them to begin their chorus.

———*Observations*———

————Observations————

Just as surely as the arrival of spring is announced by our smallest frog, the spring peeper, its departure and the first warm days of summer are heralded by the deep, booming calls of our largest frog, the bullfrog. From late May through July the bass, throaty "jug-o-rum" bellows are as characteristic of warm summer nights as the flashing of fireflies over a lush, dew-covered meadow. Capable of carrying over a half mile on a still evening, it is the loudest sound to come from any cold-blooded animal in our region.

Female bullfrogs are drawn to the loudest calls, which are produced by the biggest males. Seizing her around the waist from the back in the amplexus position for as long as forty-five minutes, the male deposits sperm over the female's ten to twenty thousand eggs as she deposits them in the water in a thin, frothy mass around the stems of aquatic plants. In only about four days these eggs hatch into algae-eating tadpoles that may not metamorphose into frogs for two years, becoming up to 5 inches long before they do. It takes another year or two for the frogs to reach sexual maturity and then perhaps an additional two to four years to become full grown, 1-pound, 8-inch giants with an additional 7 inches of back legs.

Besides attracting a female, a bullfrog's voice serves a territorial function. A big male will float on the surface of the pond like a bright tennis ball with his yellow throat expanded, intimidating the other males in the pond with his loud bellows. If another male enters his territory, which ranges from 6 to 20 feet in diameter, the male begins shoving and jostling the intruder, gouging it with his thumbs, locking forelegs, and finally holding it underwater until it escapes and leaves his domain.

A big male may also attract several smaller "satellite males" that lurk around the edges of his territory and try to intercept females drawn to his loud calls. Some of these small males may succeed in fertilizing a female's eggs, but the big males rule the pond. The largest ones may mate with six different females, all irresistibly drawn to the voice that best symbolizes the end of spring and the start of a new season in the northeastern United States.

13

Turtles Ashore

JUNE I

Aquatic turtles leave the water and lumber ashore to excavate nests

————Observations————

Two months have passed since the first painted turtles swam to the surface to bask in the sun after spending several months hibernating in the bottom mud. A strong urge now grips these reptiles, an urge so powerful that it causes them to leave their aquatic habitats and crawl ashore, where unfamiliar terrain and a host of predators endanger them. These dangers are minimized by timing their emergence from the waters to coincide with the very early morning or late afternoon hours, especially during rainy weather, and by remaining ashore only as long as it takes to lay the eggs that will become the next generation of turtles.

Usually during the first week of June throughout our region (and as early as the last week of May in New Jersey) the first painted turtles climb ashore. One of our most attractive turtles, it is marked with red-and-yellow stripes on the legs, neck, and head, and red bars and crescents on the edges of its 6- to 9-inch carapace, which is smooth, flat, and dark olive to black in color (the bottom shell, or plastron, is yellow). The painted turtle is most often seen basking on logs or rocks in ponds and lakes, sometimes in the company of many others. But now the females leave the water to fulfill their reproductive duties.

A female turtle may wander some distance from the water to find just the right place to lay her eggs, but generally the nests are excavated somewhere near the open shores, such as on dams, causeways, or nearby roadsides. An open, well-drained site with loose, sandy or loamy soil is selected. After firmly planting her front legs in the ground, the turtle starts scraping away the soil behind her with her back legs. Each leg works alternately, reaching downward to scoop up a small mound of soil, hauling it up, and dumping it to the side while the other leg replaces it in the hole. About 1 inch below the surface the hole is widened into an underground chamber. When finished, the entire nest resembles a flask in shape. When her legs can reach no deeper (about 4 inches), the female painted turtle urinates to moisten the nest. Then she is ready to lay eggs.

Each white egg is about 1 inch long and elliptical in shape. From two to twenty may be dropped into the nest, although most commonly a clutch contains five to ten eggs. After the eggs are laid, the nest is refilled with soil by the hind legs, the front legs are finally relaxed from their grip, and the turtle drags her shell over the nest to cover up any signs of her presence. Then she returns to the safety of the water. A female painted turtle may lay a second clutch of eggs later in June, or even as late as the first week in July, but the peak of their nesting activity in our region is early June.

The first week of June also brings a second species of turtle out of the water, one that is rarely seen basking in the sun and prefers to hunt for food in the murky depths of its habitat. Because of its large size (its shell reaches 18 inches in length), prehistoric-looking appearance, and nasty disposition, the common snapping turtle creates quite a stir when discovered on land. Dragging its long, spiked tail, with its massive head and wrinkled neck hanging down and its body raised off the ground, the snapping turtle is an awesome sight, especially when it lunges forward and strikes like lightning with its powerful jaws. However, it wants nothing more than to be left alone to lay eggs and return safely to the water, where it scrupulously avoids people and poses no danger to swimmers.

Weighing as much as 25 pounds (males may be almost twice as heavy), a female snapping turtle may appear clumsy on land, but she excavates her nest as gracefully and deftly, and in very similar fashion, as the much smaller painted turtle. The nest is dug 4 to 7 inches deep, and then up to fifty eggs (usually fifteen to thirty) are dropped into it. Each egg is 1 inch in diameter, spherical rather than elliptical, and bears a remarkable resemblance to a Ping-Pong ball. A female produces only a single clutch of eggs (and she never sees her offspring) before returning to the pond, shallow lake, swamp, marsh, or river. Here she will hunt frogs, fish, insects, aquatic plants, carrion, and perhaps even an occasional duckling or gosling in much the same manner that these relicts of the dinosaur age have been doing for 200 million years.

One of the more fascinating aspects of turtle reproduction is the influence of temperature on the incubating eggs. With both freshwater and ocean turtles cool nest temperatures (75 to 80 degrees Fahrenheit) will result in most, if

———*Observations*———

not all, of the eggs hatching into males, while warm temperatures (over 88 degrees Fahrenheit) yield all females. Intermediate temperatures produce a mixture of both sexes.

Although these two aquatic turtles do their best to cover up their nests before returning to the water, many of the eggs are dug out and eaten by skunks, raccoons, foxes, and opossums. Crinkled, white shells scattered around empty holes are evidence of the work of these predators. About three months after the eggs were laid, those nests that somehow escape this fate will produce hatchling turtles, some of which will dig to the surface and find their way to the pond. But others will remain underground for their entire first winter, waiting until next spring to come out and join the others in the water.

14

The Laurel Spectacle

JUNE 11

Our showiest shrub blooms

―――Observations―――

In Pennsylvania, where back in 1933 it was chosen to be the state flower, mountain laurel blooms right at the beginning of the tourist season. School is out, summer is about to officially begin, and people flock to the Poconos, the Alleghenies, and other mountainous parts of the state to enjoy one of the Northeast's most spectacular annual events. There are laurel festivals and other events in honor of this beautiful shrub, and pamphlets published by tourist agencies, vacation bureaus, and state parks describe the best roads and vistas for viewing the large, showy blossoms.

Mountain laurel grows from New England west to Indiana and all the way down to northern Florida. A large, evergreen shrub up to 35 feet tall with multiple, twisting trunks, it grows best across our region in rocky, well-drained woodlands with light shade and acid soil, although it also does very well in the flat, sandy New Jersey Pine Barrens. Sometimes mistaken for its close relative the rhododendron, it usually grows in drier, more exposed locations (rhododendron thrives in cool, wet, shaded ravines, along waterfalls, and in dense swamps), and its leaves are only about a third the size of rhododendron's. Furthermore, the laurel's mid-June peak blooming period is three or four weeks earlier than that of the rhododendron.

Both mountain laurel and rhododendron are members of a large, widespread family of plants called the Ericaceae, or heaths. There are over thirteen hundred species in the world, growing especially well in such harsh habitats as the Arctic tundra, mountain summits, acid bogs, and the English moors, which are carpeted with heaths. Many heath plants are evergreen, and the fact that they don't have to invest energy each year into producing a completely new crop of leaves enables them to outcompete deciduous shrubs in these harsh, sterile, nutrient-deficient environments.

In the northeastern United States other close relatives of mountain laurel are wild azaleas (including the pinkster, the early mountain, the swamp white, and the incomparable, pinkish purple rhodora of bogs and scrub barrens), blueberries, huckleberries, and cranberries, the small wintergreen and trailing arbutus, and specialized denizens of acid bogs like leatherleaf, bog rosemary, and Labrador tea. Its closest relative is sheep laurel, a smaller shrub found in bogs and dry pine-oak woodlands, which produces its deep pink blossoms below the upper leaves rather than in terminal clusters. Another name for sheep laurel is "lambkill"—like many of the other evergreen heaths, including mountain laurel, its leaves contain a toxin that can cause illness or even death in cattle and sheep.

Although a hillside covered with flowering mountain laurel shrubs can be a breathtaking sight, a closer look at the individual blossoms reveals an even more wonderful structure of nature. Each flower is saucer shaped, five lobed, and pinkish white, the intensity of the pink often being greater in bright, open exposures like the edges of cliffs and tops of mountains. Shrubs growing in shadier forests usually produce mostly white blossoms. Growing in dense clusters at the tips of the branches, the flowers create a vivid contrast with laurel's dark, shiny, leathery leaves.

The blossoms are not only gorgeous, they are functional as well, since they are highly specialized for being pollinated by insects, especially bees. The inside of each flower resembles a ten-ribbed parasol or umbrella. Near the outside edge of each rib is a tiny pit into which is inserted a thin, straplike stamen (one of the male flower parts). The stamens all arise from the center of the flower and then bend separately like arched bows, each one sticking into its own pit. They are set to go off like triggers as soon as they are touched by insects visiting the flower to get nectar. A touch by a busy bee releases the pressure, and one or more stamens spring from their pits to slap pollen all over the insect's back and head. Showered with pollen, the insect leaves the flower and visits another, thus cross-pollinating the species and ensuring the continued success of this showy and fascinating plant.

15

The Nesting Season

Songbirds raise their families, but in lesser numbers for many species

---Observations---

The season of the spring passage is now over for our birds. Even the latest migrants have arrived on their breeding grounds to raise their families. The non-migratory species that remain in our region all year are already feeding hungry mouths. Ruffed grouse lead precocial chicks through the forest by late May; cardinals, chickadees, crows, tufted titmice, and downy woodpeckers bring insects to their babies before the end of that month; and during the first few days of June the Louisiana waterthrush, one of the first tropical migrants to return in April, flies to its secret nest beneath the stream banks with its beak crammed full of insects. As the summer solstice approaches, one bird after another that returned to the Northeast during the mid-May peak of the spring migration begins to settle down to the task of nesting.

Usually returning to the same area as in the previous year, the male songbird begins to establish a territory and attract a mate. Both of these important tasks are implemented by singing. Under hormonal control and stimulated by the intensity of daylight, the song of the male bird is indispensable to his success in raising a family. Most species are born with the innate ability to recognize the correct song of their species, and they must hear this song at an early age in order to learn it and copy it correctly. (A few exceptions, like the mourning dove, are born with the ability to sing their correct songs without having to hear them first.) Once a bird has learned its specific song from a model (usually its parent), it can then develop its own repertoire of variations on the main theme. A male wood thrush, for example, may create as many as twenty-five different song patterns, each one slightly different but recognizable as the song of a wood thrush and together distinguishing him as an individual among all the other male wood thrushes in the forest.

With warblers there are both primary and secondary songs, each used by the male for different purposes and at different times. As soon as he arrives on the breeding grounds, a male warbler will begin singing his primary song—the one that most birders recognize as the unmistakable, familiar voice of that species throughout its range. This song's purpose is to attract a female to his territory early in the season (she usually arrives north a few days after the male). The male also produces a secondary song (or songs), which may sound somewhat different from the primary song and usually varies from region to region in the species' range but is shared by all the males in a given area. This song is directed toward other males in the area and is meant to defend a territory and a mate. At first the primary song is performed much more frequently—sometimes hundreds of times an hour after sunrise—than the secondary song. But once the male has secured a mate, he switches to his secondary song in order to drive away other competing males. Then, when his mate has settled to the task of incubating their eggs and is no longer pursued by other males, and his investment in the next generation is thus assured, the male switches back to his primary song again, perhaps in the hope of attracting a second mate.

In many of our songbirds the females apparently choose their mates on the basis of his voice. Males with the loudest songs or the most diversified repertoire (in mockingbirds, for example) are chosen over others. It is no coincidence that such males also happen to be the older, more experienced ones, capable of choosing and defending the choicest, largest territories and providing the best parental care. These males have managed to survive longer, too, which is an indication of superior genes. Of course, other traits, such as brilliant colors, flashy plumes or tail feathers, and even "body language," may also play roles in attracting mates (as well as in defending territories), but the songs of male birds—as melodious and soothing as they are to hear on early summer mornings—unquestionably fulfill a vital role in the perpetuation of the species.

Bird songs serve another unintended purpose, one that is of invaluable assistance to naturalists and ornithologists studying the populations and distributions of these vocal, but often secretive, animals. In studies designed to determine the kinds and numbers of birds breeding in certain areas, the songs of the male birds are often the most useful criteria. A male bird singing in the same location for much of the breeding season (June and July) usually indicates the presence of a nesting pair. Breeding-bird surveys and censuses use these clues to draw up maps showing the numbers and locations of each species of bird nesting in a given area.

Such censuses were carried out by the National Audubon Society from 1946 to 1984. In 1965 the United States Fish and Wildlife Service started a series of breeding-bird surveys, consisting of a large number of predetermined car routes across the continent. Each route begins a half hour before sunrise and contains fifty stops, each a half mile apart. At each site volunteers listen for three minutes to record all singing birds, then they move on to the next stop. More recently, individual states, like New York and Pennsylvania, have completed their own breeding-bird atlases, massive efforts several years in the making that enlisted the services of hundreds of birders to map the state's bird distributions. Coordinated and tabulated by scientists from state wildlife agencies and from universities, these atlases provide invaluable information about each state's roster of breeding birds, their regional distributions, nesting dates, general abundance or rarity in the state, habitat preferences, and the occurrences of new nesting locations for rare or unusual species. The atlases will serve as baseline studies to chart future changes in the abundances and distributions of these birds.

Veteran birders who have been involved in many of these surveys over the years have echoed some very grave concerns about the decline of several species of birds in our region. These concerns, unfortunately, have now been verified as fact by many scientific studies of breeding birds in the northeastern United States. Some of our most colorful and beloved birds are disappearing from their former homes in New York, New Jersey, Connecticut, and many other states. Study after study by the Smithsonian Institute, World Wildlife Fund, United States Fish and Wildlife Service, and other organizations has revealed remarkably similar downward trends in the same groups of birds. Many of these studies have been carried out in sanctuaries and parks, essentially protected from outside disturbance, and yet the birds are still disappearing.

In New Jersey's 165-acre Greenbrook Sanctuary, where I served as director from 1975 to 1986, breeding-bird censuses have been carried out biennially since 1946. Many of the species that were the sanctuary's most abundant breeders through the 1950s experienced unbelievable declines by the 1970s. Some, like the ovenbird, black-throated green warbler, chestnut-sided warbler, hooded warbler, American redstart, blue-winged warbler, and yellow-throated vireo, have disappeared completely from the sanctuary after being present in numbers as high as ten to twenty-five breeding pairs per year in the 1950s. Others, like the veery, red-eyed vireo, black-and-white warbler, Louisiana waterthrush, and wood pewee, fell to 20 to 30 percent of their former numbers. Meanwhile, species like the chickadee, downy woodpecker, blue jay, tufted titmouse, robin, and white-breasted nuthatch were holding steady or even increasing in numbers. Remarkably similar trends with the same species of birds and during the same time period have been found during censuses across the entire northeastern United States.

Many scientists blame the increasing fragmentation of our forests for these declines. Over the past three decades large expanses of formerly undisturbed forests across the northern United States have been broken apart into smaller, disconnected parcels by housing developments, shopping malls, and roads. This fragmentation and shrinkage into smaller woodlands increases the amount of "edge" into which nest predators like cats, dogs, raccoons, blue jays, grackles, and crows can penetrate. It also allows easier access by humans. Another culprit that finds these fragmented parcels more to its liking is the brown-headed cowbird, which lays its eggs in the nests of other birds for them to incubate and raise to fledglings. There has been a tremendous increase in both nest predation and cowbird parasitism in birds that inhabit smaller forest fragments surrounded by developments compared to those that nest deep in the interior of large parks or wilderness areas where these predators are either absent altogether or have great difficulty finding the nests. Also, the possibility of "reinforcements" replacing losses due to predators or parasites is not as likely in a smaller, isolated parcel of woods as

―――*Observations*―――

in a large tract of forest containing many other birds.

Why are some birds decreasing while others seem to be thriving? The species most at risk are those that migrate back to our region from tropical America—the warblers, vireos, flycatchers, and thrushes, for example. Arriving here late in the spring, they have time to raise only one clutch of babies, so a single predatory or parasitic event could wipe out the entire season's productivity. Permanent residents like chickadees and blue jays and short-distance migrants like robins, which arrive in early spring, can produce two or three clutches of eggs per season (and their clutches are generally larger), so there's more chance of success. In addition, the tropical migrants tend to be much more vulnerable to discovery because of their open, cup-shaped nests, often built on or near the ground where they are more visible (as opposed to the chickadees, woodpeckers, nuthatches, and titmice, which nest in the safety of tree cavities). The tropical migrants are also, by their very nature, more attracted to the quiet, undisturbed interiors of vast forests than to smaller parcels surrounded by humans and their pets and vehicles.

More and more scientists are looking beyond our country's borders for an additional explanation of the decline of our birds. Almost without exception the species that are disappearing from the northeastern United States are those that spend the winter months in Mexico, Central America, the Caribbean Islands, and South America. Those that don't migrate to the Tropics have not experienced these devastating declines in numbers. The deforestation of the world's tropical countries has been well documented, and it has been estimated to amount to the staggering loss of over 40 million acres a year worldwide, an area almost the size of the state of Washington. In our own hemisphere the chopping and burning of tropical forests to convert them to settlements, farms, commercial timber lands, and cattle ranges (from which cheap beef is exported to the United States) have been found to coincide very closely in timing with the declines of the birds that spend the winter there.

Sixty different species of "our" birds spend the winter in mature tropical forests, living in our region for only the four or five months from May to September. These include twenty-nine species of warblers, five vireos, five flycatchers, four thrushes, and various tanagers, orioles, grosbeaks, and cuckoos—exactly those species that are declining in the forests of New York, New Jersey, New England, Pennsylvania, Michigan, and the Maryland–Washington, D.C., region. Most of these species overwinter in Mexico, northern Central America, and the Caribbean, where the rate of deforestation has been the highest, with smaller percentages overwintering in southern Central America and South America. The areas where these birds overwinter are smaller than their nesting grounds so many more are concentrated together. Thus, the destruction of a given amount of tropical forest will have a much more devastating effect than the loss of the same amount of North American woodland, where the birds are much more dispersed. For example, the Bachman's warbler, which once nested in many southeastern states, overwintered exclusively in Cuba, which has converted most of its forests to sugarcane fields. Today it is feared that the Bachman's warbler is close to extinction.

Three decades ago Rachel Carson spoke of a "silent spring" resulting from the poisoning of songbirds by pesticides sprayed throughout our country. Today, as fewer and fewer of the warblers, vireos, thrushes, and other tropical migrants return to our northeastern states each spring, the forests are becoming increasingly silent for other reasons. The analogy of our world as "spaceship earth" takes on greater meaning when we realize that these small feathered creatures, which travel thousands of miles each year between hemispheres, are as profoundly affected by matters in their tropical wintering homes as in their northern homes in our northeastern United States.

16

Ten Thousand Points of Light

JUNE IV

The flashing of fireflies

Observations

Being outdoors on an early summer evening can be a very sensual experience, one that evokes pleasant memories of carefree, youthful feelings, which, sadly, are all too often lost upon reaching adulthood. The sweet fragrance of grass in a dew-covered meadow, the sounds of bullfrogs calling from a nearby pond, the soothing caress of the warm summer breezes, and the sight of countless stars twinkling overhead at the end of the longest days of the year—all these sensations that characterize an evening in late June are felt by too few people once the chores of everyday life take hold of their daily rhythms.

Another symbol of early summer evenings that surely belongs with these other memories is the firefly. What child hasn't experienced the thrill of chasing fireflies on warm June nights, capturing them in a jar, and bringing them indoors to watch them work their magic in a darkened room? As adults this same experience can be even more exciting once the secrets of the firefly's magic are known.

Fireflies, or lightning bugs, are neither flies nor bugs; they are members of the beetle family, Lampyridae. Like all beetles, a firefly's outer wings (the elytra) cover its body like a two-parted shield, with the two halves meeting in a straight line right down the middle of the insect's back. The two membranous inner wings are folded beneath this protective sheath and can be expanded for flight once the outer wings are flipped open. Unlike most beetles, however, a firefly's elytra are soft and loose, offering less in the way of protection. Fireflies share with other beetles (and with butterflies, moths, bees, wasps, and flies) the process of complete metamorphosis, developing into reproductively mature insects in a series of very dissimilar stages: egg, larva, pupa, and adult beetle.

The soft, flattened, segmented larvae of fireflies are often called glowworms and are equipped with long, hollow mouthparts (mandibles) for preying on other small creatures. Emerging from burrows or from beneath logs at night, glowworms capture snails, worms, and caterpillars in their jaws, inject them with digestive enzymes, and then feed on the liquefied prey. After about a year a full-grown glowworm transforms underground into a pupa that resembles a stiff, enlarged, motionless larva. The miracle of metamorphosis changes this pupa into an adult firefly, which, in many species, eats nothing during its brief one-week life span.

The one trait that immediately sets fireflies apart from almost all other beetles (except a few click beetles) is bioluminescence—the production of light. On the bottom of the abdomen, near the tail end, the firefly's external skeleton becomes transparent, plainly revealing the pale yellow light-producing organs within its body. In each light organ thousands of cells called photocytes are arranged in cylinders, through which nerves and tracheae, or breathing tubes, pass. The tracheae open to the outside via breathing pores called spiracles. Inside the photocytes are packed tiny granules containing the chemicals responsible for one of nature's most coveted secrets, a mystery to humans for many centuries but now finally understood as a result of chemical analyses in the laboratory.

Fireflies create their light by oxidizing a chemical called luciferin. The oxygen for this reaction enters through the insect's spiracles and through the tracheae into the light cells where the luciferin is concentrated. An enzyme-catalyst named luciferase (also present in the light cells) must be present, as well as some magnesium. The energy that powers this chemical reaction is adenosine triphosphate (ATP), the same molecule that is responsible for most muscle movements and bodily functions in animals, and it is all triggered by a nerve impulse.

The flash that results from this chemical reaction inside the firefly's body is nearly 100 percent light, with hardly any heat produced as a side effect. (By contrast, less than 10 percent of the energy in a light bulb is light, with over 90 percent wasted as heat.) This efficient "cold light" may appear yellow, green, blue, or even orange, depending on the species of firefly. But the function is always the same: communication between male and female for the purpose of mating. (Glowworms also produce light, the function of which is unknown, but it possibly advertises their unpalatability to predators.)

There are over 130 species of fireflies in North Amer-

—————*Observations*—————

ica, at least 30 of which occur in our northeastern states (they are curiously absent from the western United States). Some of these are active in late spring, others in July and early August, and a few black species in the genus Ellychnia (which lack light-producing organs) are commonly seen basking on tree trunks in late winter and early spring. But the peak of firefly activity in the Northeast is late June, when several species may be courting and mating simultaneously during the first hours after sunset. I have seen roadsides, horse pastures, wet meadows, and river banks alive with thousands of blinking lights during the last week of June in northeastern New Jersey, upstate New York, and the Pocono Mountains of Pennsylvania, and these evenings remain some of my most unforgettable experiences in the outdoors.

Each kind of firefly has its own specific flash pattern, ensuring that it attracts only a mate of the same species. For example, in *Photinus pyralis*, a common and well-studied species found from southern New York to northern Florida, the male emerges from hiding in the vegetation around sunset and takes flight. (Scientists have found that fireflies possess an inherent twenty-four-hour rhythm that functions like a clock in initiating their nightly activities.) Every six seconds he emits a yellow flash of light lasting about a half second, during which he dips down and then rises up again in a short, flying "hop," so that the flash sometimes appears like a J-shaped arc (especially in time-lapse photography). It is thought that this maneuver increases the chances of the two sexes seeing each other.

Two to three seconds after seeing the male's flash, the female (which, as in most other species, does not fly) flashes with a one-second burst of light from her perch in the tops of the grass or other low vegetation, usually aiming her abdomen in the male's direction. Upon seeing this response—with the aid of a pair of large compound eyes— the male turns accurately toward the female's position and flies over to her, repeating his signal and hovering for a few seconds after each flash. Landing in the grass a few feet away, the male walks toward the female as they both continue to exchange these specific signals with each other at the exact intervals until they meet and mate. About a half hour after sunset almost all activity is over for that evening. Sometimes a chain reaction is set off when several males flash in unison in response to a female, and their lights stimulate another nearby female to flash, which is seen by males close to her, and so forth. (This synchronous flashing is much more prevalent in Southeast Asia, where many trees along river banks may be covered with thousands of fireflies all flashing in unison and producing an unbelievable spectacle.)

So ingrained is its behavioral repertoire that a firefly, either male or female, can easily be fooled into producing its correct flash response to a penlight or small flashlight that imitates the flash pattern of the opposite sex, and males will even land on the artificial light in the grass. In fact, several species of *Photuris* fireflies (including *Photuris pennsylvanica*, one of the most common fireflies in the Northeast) have evolved an ingenious trick to capitalize on this behavior. The predatory females actually mimic the responses of other species and fool the males into landing near them, after which they seize and eat the males. One species, *Photuris versicolor*, can even adjust her "aggressive mimicry" to imitate and lure four different species. She recognizes the male of her own species by his flash pattern and allows him a safe landing.

Other northeastern firefly species produce flash patterns that differ in one or more characteristics—the duration of the signal, the interval between flashes, the number of light pulses, or the flight pattern of the male. For example, *Photinus consimilis* males fly in a slow, horizontal path about 3 to 6 feet above the ground, emitting as many as nine quick pulses of light in succession, pausing ten seconds, then repeating the flash pattern. A common New Jersey species, *Photinus scintillans*, emits a single sharp flash lasting only a quarter second, with a time interval of two and a half seconds between flashes. In *Photinus ardens*, a species present in northern sphagnum bogs and wet pastures, the male flashes two or three fast pulses, each a half second apart, then pauses six seconds before repeating; the female's response is a double pulse of light. And in *Photinus marginellus*, a northeastern species found near lawns and roadside shrubs, the female waits less than a

————Observations————

half second before responding to the male's flash pattern.

Fireflies inhabiting the same region during the same season may also stay reproductively isolated by flying at different times of the evening (anytime from a half hour before to an hour after sunset), flying at different heights above the ground (from tree top to grass level), or by utilizing different habitats—stream banks, meadows, marshes, open lawns, or woodlands. But the most reliable means of ensuring that all the different species of fireflies living in the same area (and often very closely resembling one another) are attracted to only their own kind for mating is their different flash patterns. This is also a very economical and efficient way to find a mate in a world full of potential predators. By a simple, species-specific "flash answer" signal and by severely restricting the time spent actively seeking mates to no more than ninety minutes every evening, each kind of firefly minimizes its exposure to enemies, yet still manages to create one of nature's most dazzling displays in the dark.

17

Basking Beauties

JULY I

Butterflies seek the summer sun

————Observations————

Many people receive their first introduction to nature as children by chasing butterflies on sunny summer days. Butterflies are easy to see yet elusive, beautifully delicate yet strong, swift fliers, and ubiquitous in both country meadows and suburban backyards. These ingredients, plus their completely harmless, gentle natures, make butterflies one of nature's most appealing and popular groups of creatures.

During the first days of July the sunny roadsides, fields, and borders of ponds become increasingly lush with fragrant, colorful summer wildflowers. Many of these plants are important sources of sweet nectar for the butterflies that have been emerging from their chrysalises at this season. Common milkweed, swamp milkweed, and orange milkweed (also called butterfly weed) rank as three popular hosts for butterflies. Other July favorites include the dogbanes, butter-and-eggs, purple loosestrife, spotted knapweed, teasel, and members of the mint family like heal-all, wild bergamot, bee balm (or Oswego tea), and the mountain mints. Later in the month the butterflies flock to the thistles, joe-pye weeds, sunflowers, and, around the edges of ponds and wetlands, one of the best of the "butterfly bushes," the buttonbush. In return for the flowers' nectar, which it tastes with its feet and then sips through its long, strawlike proboscis, a butterfly brushes against the plant's sticky pollen with its furry body and carries it to another flower of the same species to effect cross-pollination.

Swallowtails, sulphurs, and a few other butterflies are also commonly found "puddling" in large groups around the edges of moist sand or roadside puddles in summer. Some, like the red-spotted purples and the banded purples, also congregate on and around bird droppings, mammal dung, campfire ashes, and even decomposing animals. Almost without exception these butterflies are all males, and it is believed that they are sipping sodium present in solution in these wet areas rather than drinking water. Apparently, male butterflies have a greater need than females to replace the sodium lost during their mating activities.

A third place to look for butterflies is on tree trunks

coated with oozing sap. Sometimes dozens of mourning cloaks, red admirals, pearly eyes, red-spotted purples, commas, and wood satyrs visit these trees to partake of the sweet liquid. The butterflies often become so engrossed in drinking (or else intoxicated by the fermenting sap) that they can easily be photographed or even picked up with fingers.

Butterflies need to attain a certain body temperature (at least 80 degrees Fahrenheit) in order to fly, and they use their broad wings to soak up the sun's warmth and raise their temperatures after cool summer evenings. Basking in the sun is a habit common to many species, each with its own characteristic pose. Yellow sulphurs, orange sulphurs, painted ladies, American coppers, and several of the small blues often bask laterally, folding their wings closed and tilting them sideways to expose them to the sun while perched on a leaf. Monarchs, swallowtails, wood satyrs, fritillaries, buckeyes, and question marks usually bask dorsally with their wings spread fully out in the sunshine. Many of the small hairstreaks, whites, and wood nymphs are called "body baskers"—they narrowly angle their wings so that only their bodies receive the solar radiation.

Painted ladies, red admirals, question marks, commas, and mourning cloaks can also raise their body temperatures by rapidly contracting their thoracic flight muscles to produce internal heat, almost like a bird or mammal shivering. If temperatures get too hot, butterflies will either close their wings and orient them parallel to the sun's rays or take shelter in the shade.

With their bright, gaudy colors, diurnal nature, and habits of basking in the bright sun and fluttering among the flowers, butterflies are among the most highly visible of all summer creatures. Their presence or absence in an area, as well as their increase or decrease over time, is easily noticed. In 1971 the Xerces Society was formed to monitor populations of North American butterflies, preserve their habitats, and help educate the public about the plight of certain species. Named after the Xerces blue, one of the first North American butterflies to become extinct in 1943

————*Observations*————

when its last habitat was destroyed in San Francisco, the society sponsors an annual butterfly count throughout North America around the Fourth of July.

Several species of butterflies have been declining in numbers over the years, mainly due to the loss of their habitat. For example, in the northeastern United States, the Karner blue has disappeared from Pennsylvania and most of New England because of the destruction of its pine barrens habitat, where its food plant the wild lupine grows. The only areas where it still survives are a locality near Concord, New Hampshire, and the Albany Pine Bush in New York State, a unique pine barrens community that has been greatly reduced in size over the years by shopping malls, office complexes, and the New York Thruway.

Today The Nature Conservancy and the New York State Department of Environmental Conservation are trying to preserve much of what's left of the Albany Pine Bush to prevent the endangered Karner blue from going the way of its close relative the Xerces blue. Its disappearance might not create as much of an uproar as the extinction of a larger, more glamorous animal, but it would be just as irreversible and just as effective in reducing this planet's rich diversity.

18

Alien Invasion

The gypsy moths emerge in the woods

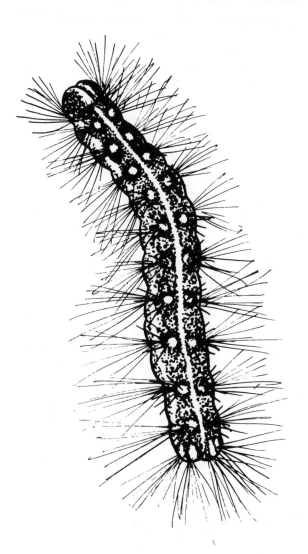

—Observations—

Fluttering through the oak forests in July is a close relative and look-alike of the butterfly, but this insect is not searching for wildflowers or tree sap. Male gypsy moths, unlike most moths, fly during the day like butterflies, and the objects of their searching flights are female moths. Peaking throughout our region by mid-July, the moths emerge from brown pupae attached by flimsy strands of silk to tree trunks, branches, and shrubs. The brownish tan males can easily be mistaken for butterflies with their $1^1/_2$-inch wingspreads and fast, fluttering flight through the woods. The much plumper females have creamy white wings with dark, wavy markings, but they can't fly because they are so heavy with eggs. So they simply wait for the males to discover them after they emerge from their pupae.

In order to ensure its discovery, a female secretes a scent, or pheromone, which the males detect via their feathery antennae. After mating she deposits on tree trunks and buildings four hundred to five hundred eggs in a soft, buff-colored, $1^1/_2$-inch mass covered with the hairs from her own body. Death then follows very quickly for the adult moths, but the eggs will remain dormant at their attachment sites for the next ten months, hatching into tiny, fuzzy black caterpillars in early May just when the leaves are emerging on oaks, beeches, and other trees. It is at that time that the gypsy moth's presence becomes noticeable once again—not from the flying adult moths but from the voracious caterpillars that defoliate the hardwood forests.

It was back in 1868 that gypsy moths were first imported into this country to Bedford, Massachusetts, by Leopold Trouvelot, a French scientist who hoped to crossbreed them with silk moths and improve the silk industry. They escaped, however, and by 1889 severe defoliation of oaks and other trees was noticed around the Boston area. By the turn of the century the gypsy moth was widespread in New England, New York, and New Jersey, and in 1932 it reached Pennsylvania. Today, as a result of its ability to spread to different regions of the country as egg masses attached to cars and recreational vehicles, the gypsy moth is found as far west as Oregon and south to Virginia.

Like many other accidentally introduced exotic organisms, without the natural predators, parasites, and diseases that controlled its numbers in its native Europe, Asia, and North Africa, the gypsy moth was able to expand and proliferate unchecked until it became one of our country's most destructive—and controversial—pests. By 1980 the gypsy moth was responsible for the defoliation of 5 million acres of forest each year in the Northeast alone. In 1981 a new record was established—12 million defoliated acres nationwide. In 1990 almost 4$\frac{1}{2}$ million acres of trees were defoliated just in Pennsylvania, which has earned the dubious distinction of experiencing the greatest gypsy moth damage.

Most of this defoliation occurs from mid-June (in New Jersey) to early July, when the caterpillars reach their full size and each consumes several leaves a day. Their favorite trees are oaks (especially chestnut oak and white oak), followed by aspen, witch hazel, beech, hickory, sassafras, basswood, and white birch. Not as preferred but eaten nevertheless when the caterpillars run out of the above species are maple, cherry, black gum, dogwood, white pine, ash, yellow birch, and black locust. Their least preferred foods are the leaves of the hemlock, pitch pine, and tulip tree. (During some very heavy gypsy moth infestations the tulip trees distinctively stand out in the forests as being the only trees with leaves.) After eight weeks as caterpillars the insects metamorphose into brown pupae wrapped in very flimsy cocoons; they then transform into the adult moths about two weeks later.

In summers with very high gypsy moth populations an oak forest may appear to be in its winter condition—not a leaf remains on any tree or shrub. Droppings fall from the canopy like rain, and caterpillars are crawling everywhere—on tree trunks, along the ground, across roads, and even into lakes and ponds. When the adult moths emerge in July, the males seem to be equally ubiquitous in the forest as they search for the females. And then the tree trunks, branches, and even the buildings become covered with egg masses, several thousand masses per acre in some years, foretelling another bad year to follow. Most trees can survive two successive years of defoliation if they're healthy, and even three if there is sufficient rainfall,

————Observations————

but a prolonged drought may cause many of the trees that are defoliated for three successive years to die.

One of the first weapons employed in the battle to fight this alien destroyer was the deadly poisonous lead arsenate. Then from the 1940s to the early 1960s DDT was sprayed by airplane over thousands of acres of forest. This practice was gradually abandoned when the devastating side effects of DDT and other persistent pesticides on fish, robins, eagles, falcons, and other nontarget wildlife were detailed by scientists like Rachel Carson, whose book *Silent Spring* became a landmark in the environmental movement. DDT was finally banned in this country in 1972. The next poison touted as the answer to the gypsy moth problem was carbaryl (marketed as Sevin), an ingredient in flea powder, but it became implicated as a killer of aquatic insects, bees, and other beneficial insects, and some studies showed that it caused headaches, nausea, respiratory problems, and possible birth defects in mammals. The aerial spraying of Sevin was gradually phased out in many municipalities in the early 1980s.

One popular replacement has been Dimilin, a chemical that kills the caterpillars by preventing them from molting (shedding their skins). But even this "safe" substitute kills other insects like bees, mayflies, and butterflies, and labels warn against spraying it near streams and lakes. And, like all insect sprays, it may indirectly have a very negative effect on bird populations by destroying the caterpillars and other insects they eat and feed to their young.

Many people have been fighting for alternatives to chemical controls of the gypsy moth for decades. Ironically, after more than fifty years of spraying increasingly greater amounts of stronger and stronger poisons on thousands of square miles of forests, the gypsy moth problem grows worse each year. In fact, the insect experienced some of its biggest population explosions during the heyday of DDT spraying in the 1950s. Poisons not only kill any natural predators and parasites that might exert control over the gypsy moth, they also result in the survival of vigorous, resistant "super caterpillars" that pass on their resistance to hundreds of offspring. Thus, more quantities of stronger chemicals must be used in successive years on a never-ending treadmill.

Scientists are quick to point out that almost every serious insect pest in our country has become more numerous and more destructive after the initiation of a poisonous spray campaign to control its numbers. They are all still with us, and our lands continue to get drenched with poisons that seep into the soil and groundwater and may produce dangerous, unknown side effects. In the 1950s almost every government agency and many scientific groups assured us that DDT was completely safe to humans, birds, fish, and mammals. Then, less than a decade later this poison began to reveal its true, deadly colors.

Since 1905 natural controls on the gypsy moth have been brought into this country from Europe, Russia, and Japan where this insect does not experience such periodic outbreaks of destruction. During the 1960s about two dozen different species of parasites, predators, and disease-causing organisms were released in the northeastern United States after rigorous testing in the lab to eliminate the possibilities of any negative side effects. Tiny wasps and flies lay their eggs in various stages of the gypsy moth (egg, larva, or pupa) and may kill over 70 percent of the pests in some years, but during extremely bad outbreaks their overall effect may not be enough to decrease the defoliation.

Other natural controls have successfully produced dramatic reductions in gypsy moth populations. *Bacillus thuringensis* is a bacterium that infects and kills leaf-eating caterpillars and may reduce heavy defoliation by gypsy moth larvae by over 60 percent. It has been mixed with water and used as a spray (marketed as Bt) by various municipalities, but it is comparatively expensive since it must sometimes be sprayed twice during particularly heavy moth years. Also, it kills all leaf-eating caterpillars, including those of the beautiful butterflies and moths and those eaten by birds.

A naturally occurring nucleopolyhedrosis virus has played an even greater role in causing gypsy moth populations to crash by infecting caterpillars during very high outbreaks and killing them by the millions. This virus (specific to the gypsy moth) is always present, attached to the foliage, and when consumed by the caterpillars it causes "wilt disease": The caterpillars appear to just wither away

—————Observations—————

and die as they stick to tree trunks. In 1990 another disease, this one caused by the Japanese fungus *Entomophaga maimaiga*, killed off up to 90 percent of the gypsy moth caterpillars in an unprecedented, massive population collapse in several northeastern states in late June after a peak outbreak of the insect. This fungus was intentionally introduced to control the gypsy moth in Massachusetts in the early 1900s, but it wasn't really noticed again until 1989 and 1990—perhaps these two very wet summers, plus unusually high numbers of caterpillars, caused it to flourish. Millions of caterpillars suddenly died, hanging upside down on tree trunks with their bodies turned to mush.

Recently, scientists have discovered yet another natural control of the gypsy moth—their own food sources. As trees become defoliated by the caterpillars, natural defensive chemicals called phenols are released into their leaves, resulting in a stunting of the caterpillars' growth, a consequent reduction in the numbers of eggs laid by the adult moths, and thus fewer caterpillars the next year. But these phenols also reduce the effectiveness of the virus disease on the caterpillars, and so there is now hope that perhaps a new phenol-resistant virus will evolve to work along with the trees' own defensive chemicals.

There is great hope that these parasites, predators, and diseases will exert enough control over the gypsy moth that spraying can be minimized or eliminated. Since the 1970s many parks, wildlife sanctuaries, and nature preserves have initiated a "let nature take its course" policy. On the National Park Service lands in the Northeast (for example, the seventy-thousand-acre Delaware Water Gap National Recreation Area in New Jersey and Pennsylvania) a "no spray" policy is also now being followed. The results: These natural areas remain completely green, vital, and full of life even after some severe gypsy moth defoliations. The frequency of these peak outbreaks occurs every eight or nine years as compared to four or five years in areas where sprays have destroyed the moth's natural biological controls. Most trees grow new leaves after defoliation, and those that don't are replaced by other trees that fill the gaps in the forest over the years. These replacement trees may be species less palatable to the gypsy moth, so the forest and the insect may be gradually accommodating each other.

Some sanctuaries are even finding some beneficial effects of the gypsy moth on the forest ecosystem, as defoliated trees permit more sunlight to reach the lower shrubs. This results in lusher growth and greater fruit production, benefiting insects, birds, and mammals. Studies of several northeastern forests that have not been sprayed by chemicals have shown that 75 percent of the trees survive heavy gypsy moth infestations, and the forest quickly recovers. In the 1970s and 1980s in unsprayed forests of northeastern and central Pennsylvania, 90 percent of the forest stands that were heavily infested suffered timber losses less than thirty dollars per acre, and only 5 percent lost more than half their timber volume.

Far from being an ecological disaster or a health hazard, the gypsy moth is more of an aesthetic nuisance that will never be eradicated. Instead of futilely fighting it with more dangerous chemicals sprayed over an environment already overburdened with poisons, humans must learn to live with it. The forests and the gypsy moths are gradually adjusting and accommodating each other, and the environment will be healthier for it.

————Observations————

19

The Fruits of the Season

Blueberries, huckleberries, blackberries, and raspberries

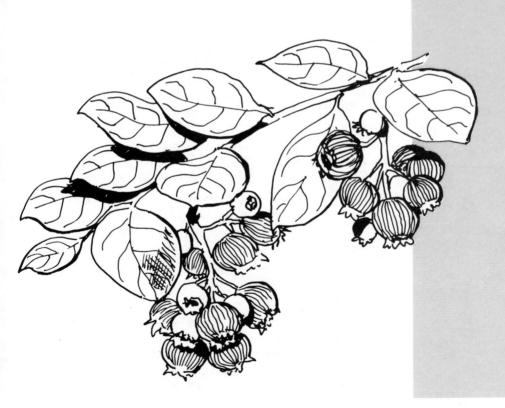

———*Observations*———

Starting with the first tiny, succulent strawberries that grow wild in the fields in June, a succession of delicious fruits ripens throughout the summer. Blueberries, huckleberries, raspberries, blackberries, and dewberries are the tastiest and most popular wild fruits in our northeastern states, and July is the month when species from each of these groups begin to ripen. Their abundance in the forests, thickets, barrens, and wetlands add immeasurably to the enjoyment of an outing on a hot day in July.

These fruits of the summer season, like those of most trees and shrubs, have evolved to attract fruit-eating animals as aids in the dispersal of their seeds. Most of these "berries" have many tiny seeds that, instead of being valued as an important source of food in themselves, are merely consumed whole by the fruit-eaters as incidental parts of the meal. Thus, the seeds pass through the animals' digestive systems unharmed and are deposited some distance away in the droppings, effectively spreading them to new habitats.

Unlike the autumn fruits, which are rich in fats and are valuable sources of energy for birds during their long migrations, the summer fruits have very low fat contents but are high in concentrations of sugars and other carbohydrates. This causes them to spoil and rot quickly after ripening. So to make them easily accessible to wildlife, these fruits are either low-growing (within easy reach of skunks, bears, raccoons, foxes, and other sweet-toothed mammals) or they quickly fall to the ground upon ripening so mice and chipmunks can find them and disperse their seeds.

One further interesting adaptation possessed by many of these fruits is the succession of different colors during their ripening stages—from green to red or pink and finally to black or blue. One theory is that wildlife (especially birds, which are highly attuned to nature's colors) are alerted by these color changes that the fruit is ready to be harvested. This prevents the berries from rotting and going to waste if they fall unnoticed to the ground below the bush, where the chances of germinating and growing successfully are very slim.

The blueberry bushes are a widespread group of

plants, with over thirty different *Vaccinium* species in our northeastern states. Brightly colored, reddish or greenish stems (both colors are often present on the same bush) covered with tiny bumps, or "warts," characterize most of our species. In spring the bushes produce fragrant, creamy white, tubular, bell-shaped flowers that are sometimes tinged with pink and are very attractive to bumblebees, honeybees, and small butterflies. Each fruit that ripens from these flowers contains approximately sixty-five seeds that are so tiny they aren't noticed when the fruits are being eaten. Four different species—two highbush and two lowbush—are much more common than the others and dominate the shrub layers in many of the woodlands of our region, especially where the soils are acidic and deficient of nutrients.

The first to produce ripened fruits is the early low-bush blueberry, *V. angustifolium*, which grows from 1 to 3 feet high in dry, shallow, rocky or sandy soils of sunny habitats like exposed mountain ridges or open pine-oak barrens. At the very end of June in New Jersey and southern New York, perhaps one to three weeks later throughout the rest of our northeastern region, the sweet, light blue fruits (covered with a whitish, frosty coating, or "bloom") begin to ripen. A second species, the late lowbush blueberry *(V. vaccillans)*, ripens in similar dry habitats a few weeks later and may be quite abundant in our northern areas and higher elevations even into September. This species differs from the earlier one by its slightly darker fruit (it has a fainter, duller bloom) and its broader, egg-shaped leaf with a whitened underside and generally smooth margins (the leaf of the early species is narrow with fine-toothed edges and lustrous green on both sides). Both lowbush blueberries are sweet and delicious.

In the wetter areas of bogs, swamps, and the shores of lakes and ponds, two species of highbush blueberry attain heights of up to 15 feet, with multiple trunks covered with loose bark. The common species, *V. corymbosum*, has large, dark blue fruits covered with a whitish bloom and leaves that are generally smooth except for a few hairs on the underside veins. This is the species that most people visit during their summer blueberry-picking expeditions

———*Observations*———

—————*Observations*—————

(and the one that has been hybridized into the commercial blueberry). A similar species, the black highbush blueberry *(V. atrococcum)*, has leaves with densely hairy or woolly undersides and sour, black berries without a whitish bloom. Both species ripen throughout our region starting in late July and continuing through the month of August. (Another close relative of the blueberry, known as deerberry—*V. stamineum*—also bears ripe fruit at this season, but its berries are large, hard, greenish, and inedible to humans.)

Between the ripening times of the lowbush and highbush blueberries, a close relative is beginning to bear sweet, delicious fruits that are often mistaken for those of the *Vacciniums*. The huckleberry *(Gaylussacia baccata)* sometimes forms dense, low (up to 3 feet high), impenetrable thickets in acid soils of dry pine-oak barrens as well as in moist woods and bogs. Like the blueberry bushes, its twigs may be reddish or greenish, but they are not covered with "warts." Also, the undersides of the elliptical leaves have distinctive, golden resin dots that sparkle when turned toward the sunlight. But the biggest difference between the blueberry and the huckleberry is the fruit. The latter's is black and contains ten large, nutlike seeds that are easily noticed when chewing the huckleberry. A second species, the tall huckleberry *(G. frondosa)*, also known as dangleberry, grows up to 6 feet high and has dark blue fruits covered with whitish powder. Both of these huckleberries ripen from mid-July to early August in the Northeast.

Blueberry and huckleberry seeds do not germinate very well, and all these plants do most of their propagation via a creeping, spreading root system, or rhizome, which sends up new shoots as it runs underground. The result is a clone that expands from year to year and covers an increasingly larger area. Some clones are estimated to be over one thousand years old, based on their annual rate of growth and the acreage they cover. A southern species, the box huckleberry, is said to be represented by some huge clones over ten thousand years old!

Dangling from stems armed with sharp prickles and bristles, the tasty, juicy berries of the *Rubus* bushes pose a challenge to those who attempt to sample them and to botanists who try to identify them. Blackberries, raspberries, thimbleberries, wineberries, and dewberries—the common names for this confusing group of plants—begin to produce their fruits in July. Technically these fruits are aggregate fruits, not berries. Every blackberry, for example, is composed of many miniature fruits, or drupelets, each one with a soft outside and a single hard seed within. All the drupelets are attached to a core, or receptacle, and the entire cluster is what is recognized as the fleshy blackberry fruit.

Raspberries as a group are generally characterized by round stems and leaves that are green above but white beneath. When picked, the ripe berries easily separate from their dried receptacles, which remain like knobs on the bushes. Thus, a raspberry fruit has a hollow core, giving rise to another common name: thimbleberry. The first of the raspberries to ripen, sometime in middle to late July, is the black raspberry *(R. occidentalis)*, easily recognized by its black fruits and its purple stems covered with a white bloom. Like many of the other *Rubus* bushes, its stems, or canes, arch down to the ground and root at their tips—a very effective method for a bush to spread out and cover a large area. This creates dense, thorny thickets, or "brambles"—great places for small animals to hide and birds to nest.

The red raspberry, *R. strigosus*, ripens a bit later than its black-fruited relative and has green, erect stems with slender prickles. A close relative known as wineberry *(R. phoenicolasius)* has been introduced into the Northeast from its native Japan and is now common in some areas of New York, New Jersey, and Pennsylvania. Its arching, rooting canes are densely covered with reddish, sticky, gland-tipped hairs, and its juicy, bright red fruits are delicious.

The last of the raspberry bushes to produce ripe fruit (late in August) is also the most uncharacteristic member of the group. Purple-flowering raspberry *(R. odoratus)*, named after its large, roselike, purplish pink flowers, lacks prickles and bristles and has leaves (green on both sides) that closely resemble large maple leaves, unlike the three-

————Observations————

to five-parted leaves of the other raspberries. Its fruit is a dull red, very shallow thimble, somewhat mealy in texture but very tasty.

Blackberry bushes have angled, green or reddish ridged stems (not round), lack a white bloom, and are armed with very stout, painful prickles. Like those of black raspberry and wineberry, the canes arch over and root into the ground to form spreading thickets. The leaves have green (not white) undersides and, like those of the raspberry bushes, are divided into three or five leaflets. However, unlike the leaves of the raspberries, which are spaced out in pairs along the stem, these leaflets are palmate, spreading out from a central point. The big difference between the two groups is the fruit. A blackberry (which develops from a showy, white, five-petaled flower) separates from the stem with its core intact and is thus a solid fruit, unlike the hollow, thimblelike raspberry. The most common and widespread species in our region is the mountain, or Allegheny blackberry, *R. allegheniensis*, which ripens from late July to early August and may continue to bear big, juicy fruits into September.

The closely related dewberries also ripen at this time. Two of these low, trailing vines are found in our region. Swamp dewberry, *R. hispidus*, is common in the wetter places, covering the ground with its vinelike, bristly stems. Its leaves are shiny and semi-evergreen (they turn reddish in winter), and the sour fruits may be red or black. The common dewberry, *R. flagellaris*, which spreads over the ground in dry, open fields with its long, prickly stems, plays havoc with the feet and ankles of those picking its large, sweet blackberries. But, like the pricked fingers, blue-stained teeth, and purple-stained clothing, these minor inconveniences are all part of the splendid summer ritual of sampling some of nature's sweetest delicacies.

20

Sounds of Summer

JULY IV

Cicadas, katydids, grasshoppers, and crickets

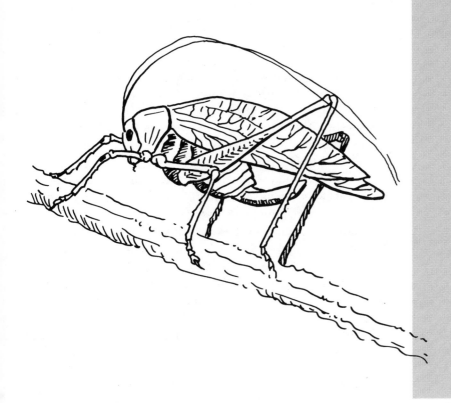

———Observations———

Dawn breaks much more softly and quietly now. Gone are the spring melodies of thrushes, warblers, and other songbirds that combined to produce the varied, early morning choruses of May and June. By late July most of these birds have finished raising their broods and no longer use their voices to attract mates or defend territories. Only the red-eyed vireo continues to sing its monotonous phrases through the hot summer days in northeastern forests.

But the late summer days and nights are by no means empty of sound. A new chorus has been gradually replacing that of the birds, growing louder and more persistent as the season progresses. Chirps, buzzes, clicks, and trills emanate from the rubbing and vibrating of various body parts against one another. It is the summer chorus of cicadas, grasshoppers, crickets, and katydids—each species producing its own distinctive sound. The purpose of these sounds is the same as the songs of birds, the flashes of lightning bugs, the scents of moths, and the calls of frogs: to attract members of the same species for mating and perhaps to compete for choice mating partners and territories among males. The insect chorus may not seem as musical to our ears as the songs of birds, but to naturalists and others who take pleasure in recording the signs of the seasons, these sounds are as symbolic of the approach of the "dog days" of August as the bird melodies are representative of the rebirth of spring.

A shrilling sound begins to echo from the trees as soon as the late July sun has risen high enough to heat the earth toward the 80-degree mark. Starting like a rattle, then accelerating in frequency and growing louder and louder until it becomes a strong buzzing, it is the familiar pulsating call of the male annual cicada. Soon the open woods, tree-lined roads, and backyards will be reverberating with the sounds of hundreds of these large, harmless insects. Often erroneously called locusts (which are grasshoppers), these robust, 2-inch cicadas are really related to the aphids and leafhoppers. They emerge from round holes in the ground—where they have spent several years feeding on the sap of plant roots—as wingless, brown nymphs. The nymphs then climb up trees with their thick, clawlike front legs and, usually under the cover of darkness, undergo a metamorphosis almost as miraculous as that of a butterfly. Each nymph's shell splits down the back, and out emerges a pale green cicada with soft, creamy white wings covering its back. By morning the cicada's skin has hardened and has turned black on top and chalky white on the underside, with a few dark green patches. The huge wings have become transparent and stiff, allowing the adult cicadas to fly into the treetops leaving dozens of empty nymph shells clinging to the tree trunks.

The cicada is the percussionist of the insect orchestra. The male possesses a pair of membranous tymbals, or "drums," on his belly, one on each side at the base of the abdomen and concealed by a pair of large, oval plates. Each drum is stretched out over its own sound chamber and attached to powerful muscles that can contract with great rapidity. With each muscular contraction the drums are drawn inward and then released to create the cicada's characteristic rattling sound, which becomes a loud buzz when the muscles contract up to four hundred times per second. Females are attracted to the males' calls (a cicada's "ears" are located on each side of its abdomen), and after mating they deposit their eggs into slits that they cut into twigs. The adult annual cicada only lives about two weeks, but the nymphs that hatch from the eggs and drop to the ground may live and grow beneath the earth for five or more years before they reemerge into the summer sun and undergo their metamorphosis. The closely related periodical cicada spends seventeen years as an underground nymph (thirteen years in the southern states), and all the adults of this species emerge in the same spring in a specific region after this extremely long immature existence. The annual cicada, on the other hand, is not characterized by this extreme synchronization, and adults emerge every year during the hot days of summer.

Many of our common locusts—or "short-horned" grasshoppers—possess short, stiff antennae and make their raspy sounds by rubbing the spines, or pegs, of their long, jumping, hind legs across a stiff, thick vein on the outer surface of their forewings. Others, including the familiar Carolina locust with its butterflylike black-and-

————*Observations*————

yellow-banded wings, produce crackling or rattling sounds when they fly by rubbing their hard outer and soft inner wings together. As with cicadas, the ears of these grasshoppers are located on each side of the bottom of the abdomen.

The songs of the male long-horned grasshoppers (their threadlike antennae are as long as or longer than their bodies) have much more of a pattern and rhythm than those of their short-horned relatives. Their method of sound production, or stridulation, is also quite different, with the two front wings (the hard outer "shell" that covers and protects the folded membranous inner wings used in flight) specially modified to create a sound characteristic of each species. Near the base of the right front wing there is a "scraper," or thick, hard ridge, next to a "mirror," a circular, veinless area of the wing. On the underside of the base of the left front wing there is a "file," a thickened crossvein with a row of transverse ridges, much like the teeth of a comb. When the teeth of the file are rubbed across the sharp edge of the scraper, it is set into vibration, with the mirror acting as a resonator to magnify the sound. In some of these species, interestingly enough, the female also stridulates, but only during the very limited time when she is ready to mate with a male, and her sound is rarely heard or recognized by humans.

Common in the tall grass and shrubs of marshes, meadows, and roadsides, the bush katydids, round-headed katydids, angular-winged katydids, and cone-headed grasshoppers are all large, greenish members of the long-horned family. Their sounds usually consist of high-pitched "ticks," sharp "zicks," or "tsip-tsip-tsip" notes, produced in an interrupted series in some species and a continuous, powerful buzz in others. They are often heard ticking outside window screens on warm, sultry summer evenings and buzzing from the vegetation along rural roads. The closely related but smaller meadow grasshoppers are found in grassy areas near ponds, streams, marshes, and wet meadows, and their songs consist of relatively long buzzes separated by several sharp "zips."

The most famous member of the long-horned grass-hopper family is the true katydid, a large (almost 2 inches), broadly oval insect, which usually begins to produce its well-known "katy-did, katy-didn't" song from the oak trees during the last week of July. The katydid chorus increases in intensity through August, when it gets so loud that all other evening sounds are obscured. It ends with the arrival of cold, autumn weather, although some lone katydids can still be heard during mild spells in November when, curiously enough, they switch from nocturnal to daytime singing.

Soon after depositing her eggs inside plant stems slit open with her sharp, swordlike ovipositor, the female katydid dies.

The crickets are usually regarded as the most accomplished, aesthetically pleasing songsters among the insects. Close relatives of the katydids, they produce their songs in a similar fashion. In most cricket species the chirping sounds result from the scraper on the left wing being drawn across the file on the underside of the overlapping right wing, setting these two outer wings into vibration. The membranes of these wings also function as sounding boards, and by changing the angle at which they are lifted up over its body during stridulation, the cricket can dramatically change the volume of its sound. It can even become a ventriloquist.

A cricket's ears, like a katydid's, are two disklike spots, one on each front leg. Only male crickets can sing, however, and they may change the quality of their song according to the situation. Once a female is attracted to his common, characteristic call, the male often switches to a second, quieter, high-pitched courtship trill to induce her to mate. A third type of song is used to intimidate an aggressive male that enters his territory, and rival males may even sing duets. If one male fails to retreat, serious fights often ensue. In some species of crickets (as with bullfrogs, see chapter 12), including the common field cricket, "satellite males" may quietly hide in the territory of a singing male and attempt to intercept females attracted to his song. These males may not mate with as many females as one that successfully defends a territory, but neither are they as exposed to predators or parasites attracted to the calling crickets.

Day and night the small ground crickets of meadows and lawns produce soft, high-pitched pulsating trills, sometimes resembling the metallic tinkling of miniature bells. The large black field crickets and the yellowish brown house crickets (a species introduced to our region from Europe) sing in a series of triple chirps and are often found beneath rocks and debris. The pale, delicate tree crickets are perhaps the best singers of all, with most species producing high, pulsating, continuous trills from trees, shrubs, and tall weeds. The snowy tree cricket, however, sings in separate, repetitive chirps at a very regular rate—so regular, in fact, that it can be used to estimate the air temperature. (Crickets, like all insects, increase the rates of their activities as temperatures warm up.) Adding the number of chirps produced in fourteen seconds to forty gives a very close approximation of the temperature in degrees Fahrenheit. Snowy tree crickets often call in unison, and on some evenings the air seems to throb with their regular, pulsating chirps—a pleasantly hypnotic sound to drift asleep to on warm, still, late summer nights.

21

The Wings of August

Millions of shorebirds head south

―――――*Observations*―――――

It hardly seems possible when the first sandpipers appear along the coast at the beginning of August. Wasn't it only a few weeks ago that millions of these shorebirds were making their spectacular migratory journeys through our region en route to their Arctic breeding grounds? How can they have already finished raising their young and started their long trip back to South America in such a short span of time?

Shorebirds—sandpipers, plovers, phalaropes, and their relatives—live in the fast lane. Their hurried, abbreviated life-styles are legendary. In fact, the last of the northbound migrants that leave their staging areas along Delaware Bay in early June (see chapter 11) have barely arrived in their Arctic breeding sites when the first groups to finish nesting there are already beginning to return to South America. This hectic schedule is necessary, given the extreme brevity of the Arctic summer and the restricted period when insects reach their peak abundance. In order to take advantage of this enormous output of insects in late June and early July, shorebirds have dispensed with many of the rituals practiced by birds in more hospitable, giving environments.

Many species arrive in the Arctic already paired, and those that aren't exhibit very brief courtship displays (wing-tilting, song-flights, and so forth) and then get right to the matter at hand. Some species don't even bother constructing a nest, merely laying the four eggs characteristic of almost all these species right on the tundra ground. Incubation is usually shared by both parents and lasts about three weeks. Then, only a few days after the young are born, one parent (usually the female) begins the southward migration, having spent a scant four or five weeks on the breeding grounds. But all young shorebirds are precocial, capable of leaving the nest within a few hours and running after their first insects by the next day. Only for their first few days of life do baby shorebirds need a parent, not for food but for warmth and protection. The second parent usually leaves them even before they learn how to fly, which occurs about two and a half weeks after hatching. Then the young shorebirds are on their own, just two weeks after learning to fly, to make that miraculous jour-

ney down along the Atlantic to South America without
guidance. It's a journey they've never made before, yet
they reach the same wintering grounds as their parents,
which left weeks before them.

There are about thirty different species of shorebirds
that pass through our region during migration. Almost all
of these birds nest outside of our area in the Arctic tundra
or prairie wetlands of Canada (the killdeer and spotted
sandpiper, which nest around inland lakes, marshes, and
fields in our region, are two notable exceptions, as are the
rare upland sandpiper and the piping plover). Similarly,
most of these species spend the winter outside of our locality as well, flying down to South America or perhaps the
coastal areas of the southern United States. Sanderlings,
purple sandpipers, dunlins, greater yellowlegs, and knots
can be seen in some numbers in winter along our northeastern coast, but by and large the shorebird is a migratory phenomenon in our region.

During the early part of August the first fall movement
of shorebirds through our region reaches a peak. These are
the adult birds that have left the tundra weeks before their
offspring. Solitary sandpipers on the first leg of their
southward trek begin to appear along the shores of our inland lakes and ponds as early as mid-July, and the beaches
and mudflats along the coast are visited soon afterwards.
From the Bay of Fundy to Cape Cod to Long Island to Cape
May the sandpipers, turnstones, plovers, and other shorebirds make their annual pilgrimages in August, filling up on
marine worms, mollusks, small shrimp and other crustaceans, and insects before they leave and continue southward. Later in September the young birds replace the
adults along these same shores, and by the end of the
month the food supply is exhausted and the beaches and
mudflats are comparatively deserted.

Just as the Delaware Bay functions as a critical staging
area where these birds can gorge themselves with food before resuming their northward migrations in spring, the
Bay of Fundy in New Brunswick and Maine plays a similar
role in August. Because of its enormous tides (a rise and
fall of 50 feet occurs on the northern edge of the bay), vast
expanses of mudflats are periodically exposed, and un-

————*Observations*————

———*Observations*———

believable numbers of shorebirds flock to these flats to feast on small clams, snails, shrimp, worms, and other creatures. It is estimated that 900,000 semipalmated sandpipers (North America's most abundant shorebird) crowd the shorelines and mudflats of the Bay of Fundy each season to put on body fat. Then in August the adults and in September the young ones take off for a nonstop flight all the way to Suriname on the northern coast of South America! Because of the importance of the Bay of Fundy to these and other shorebirds, efforts are under way to protect it from development, and in 1987 the Canadian government declared Mary's Point, New Brunswick, a Western Hemisphere Shorebird Reserve.

Radar studies of the shorebird migration in Cape Cod have revealed some fascinating information about this annual event. Many of the shorebirds begin their journey at night, after a cold-front weather system has moved across the North American coast and the resulting northwest winds provide favorable tail winds. One contingent follows the Atlantic coast southward—these are the ones we see at our beaches in late summer and early fall—but a great number of them take an overwater route, flying as high as 3,000 to 6,000 feet over the Atlantic Ocean and covering as much as two hundred and fifty to five hundred miles per day. When they reach the vicinity of the Sargasso Sea, the northeast trade winds take over and begin to push these birds closer inland. By the time they reach the West Indies, some of these shorebirds may be flying as high as 20,000 feet before they begin a gradual descent toward their ultimate destination, perhaps several thousand miles from where they just spent their brief summer feeding on insects on the tundra.

22

Webs Everywhere

The orbs, domes, sheets, and nursery webs of spiders

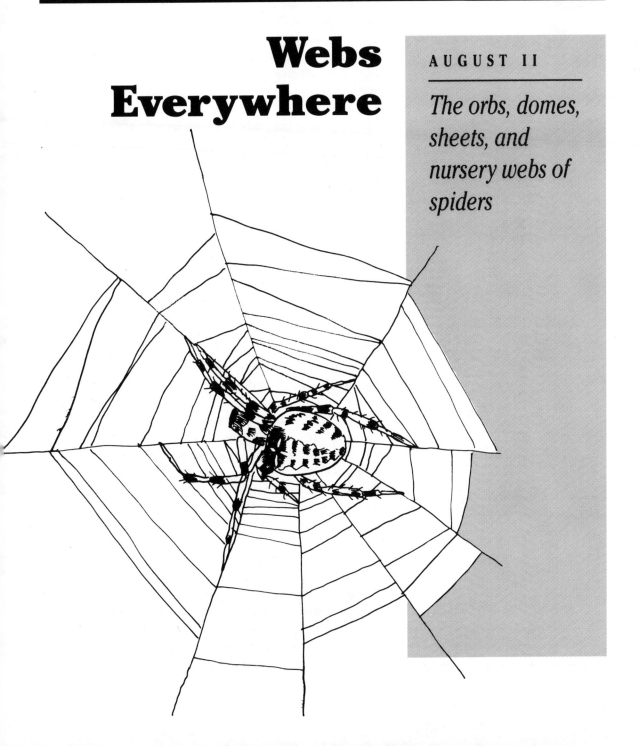

————*Observations*————

Glistening with dew as the sun rises over a meadow on a warm August morning, spider webs seem to stretch between the stems of every weed and cover every open patch of grass. There may be thousands of webs per acre, and the number of insects consumed by these master predators is unimaginable. In most cases the owners of these webs are not visible now that dawn has broken and the eyes of hungry predators search the meadow for food—the spiders are hiding nearby in a rolled-up leaf or piece of loose bark connected to the web with strands of silk. The struggles of an insect caught in the web will send vibrations along these strands to the spiders' hiding places. Only then will they risk coming out into the light, and only as long as it takes to secure their meals.

Spiders are active all during the warmer months, but since most of our species (especially those that build webs) don't emerge from their egg sacs until spring, they don't really become very noticeable until late summer when they and their webs have finally reached their full sizes. Then they seem to be everywhere—forests, fields, yards, lakeshores, front porches, and even inside buildings. Many people become quite concerned about spiders during this season, but there really is no need to be alarmed. Although all of the hundreds of different kinds of spiders found in the northeastern United States possess venom glands with which they subdue their prey, there is only one—the black widow—that is dangerous to humans. And this infamous spider (whose bite may be very painful but rarely fatal) is rare in our region, becoming more common in vacant lots and landfills in the southern edges of our area and in the southern states, where our country's only other dangerous species—the brown recluse—is also found.

Not all spiders capture their prey in webs. There are several large groups that actively hunt for prey or wait in ambush for insects. Like the web-making species, these hunting spiders also become mature and more noticeable to humans in August, after several months of eating, growing, and undergoing a number of skin molts to accommodate their increasing size. (Spiders do not experience metamorphosis like the insects.) Once a spider is full grown, molting stops, and finding a mate (usually the job of the male) and laying eggs (the job of the female) now become the most important concerns. Their increased courtship and reproductive activities at this season also render spiders more visible.

One group of hunting spiders that becomes very prominent in late summer is the fishing spiders, which include our largest species. A few species of *Dolomedes* are greater than 1 inch in body size and have thick legs spreading more than 4 inches. They are usually found on or under large stones, boat docks, and shoreline vegetation around lakes, ponds, or rivers, where they feed mostly on insects but have the strength and size to pull very small fish, tadpoles, and salamanders out of the water. Although these huge spiders can swim across the water's surface with ease, their buoyancy prevents them from submerging unless they grasp onto emergent aquatic vegetation. A female fishing spider encases her several hundred eggs in a large silken sac that she then grasps beneath her body in her sharp chelicerae, or "fangs," forcing her to walk up off the ground on her tiptoes. When the babies are ready to emerge from the sac, the mother constructs a silken tent, or "nursery web," in the top of a plant and stands guard over her offspring for several days until they undergo their first molt and disperse on their own. Shortly after this the female dies; the young will spend their first winter beneath stones or wood.

Closely related to the fishing spiders are the somewhat smaller wolf spiders, the females of which also exhibit an unusual degree of parental care. In this group of mostly nocturnal, stout-legged, ground-hunting spiders the females attach their round egg sacs to their spinnerets (the spigotlike structures through which the silk emerges) at the tips of their abdomens. It is not uncommon in late summer to see wolf spiders running through the grass or across stones with their white egg sacs trailing behind them. Once the babies emerge, they crowd onto the top of the mother's abdomen, where they remain in her protective custody for a week or two. Like the fishing spiders, the wolf spiders possess keen senses of touch and vision, and

————Observations————

————Observations————

their eight eyes reflect the beam of a flashlight shined on them as they hunt for insects at night.

In late August crab spiders lie patiently in wait for their prey on the flowers of black-eyed Susan, yarrow, Queen Anne's lace, early goldenrod, and other plants that color the meadows and roadsides. Sitting motionless with legs stretched out crablike, they are ready to ambush hover flies, bees, moths, small butterflies, and other insects that visit these blossoms for nectar or pollen. They have the element of camouflage on their side. Not only are they colored the same shades of white, yellow, brown, or even pink as the flowers upon which they hide, but some species can actually change their coloration if they switch their hiding places to differently colored flowers. Crab spiders even run backwards and sideways like their namesakes, but most often they simply prefer to sit still and blend invisibly into their backgrounds.

Also commonly found on meadow flowers are the jumping spiders, a widespread group of small, stocky, short-legged, colorful species that possess the best vision of any spiders. Two of the jumping spider's eight eyes are huge and owllike and are situated right on the front of the face to give it binocular vision. A moving insect can be seen from several inches away, and the jumping spider often approaches its prey in catlike fashion, running a few steps, stopping to reassess its next move, moving a little closer in slow motion, then pouncing on the insect. Jumping spiders can accurately leap upon an insect that is as far as 10 inches away, but if they miss, they are left supported in midair by a silk thread, which they always secure to their perch before jumping.

Among the web-making spiders is a group whose members, with their thick legs, brownish coloration, and quick movements, closely resemble the wolf spiders. The funnel-web spiders, or grass spiders, are very common in meadows, woodland clearings, and yards, where their flat, sheetlike webs are very conspicuous when they are covered with dew on late summer mornings. In some areas literally hundreds of these "gossamer" webs may cover a single large yard or field. The webs narrow at one end into a tubular silken retreat where the spider hides, giving the web its general resemblance to a funnel. When an insect falls onto the sheet (often by first flying into a tangled mass of silken strands directly above the sheet), its movements alert the spider, which then dashes out with great speed, grabs the victim, and pulls it into the retreat. Females of these spiders lay their eggs in disc-shaped sacs later in fall, usually beneath the loose bark of a dead tree, and often die right on top of the sac.

Also seen in great abundance on dewy August mornings are the sheet-web spiders, small species with slender legs and wavy black-and-white patterns on their abdomens. These spiders are named after the shapes of the sheetlike webs that they build—hammock spider, dome spider, and bowl spider being three of the more common northeastern species. They hang upside down beneath their webs, ready to bite insects that get caught and pull them through the silk. A maze of silken threads is often built above and below the hammock, bowl, or dome, both to break the flight of passing insects and as protection from predators. These spiders are unusual in that both the male and female are often found hanging upside down from the same web for several days. In most spiders the male remains with the larger female for only as long as it takes to mate and then swiftly makes his getaway before she decides to make him her next meal.

The web that attracts the most attention, and the one universally used to characterize spiders in films, books, and magazines, is the orb web. This geometrically beautiful, wheel-shaped structure is considered to be the most efficient web because, given all the spaces between the radiating spokes and concentric circles, it uses the least amount of silk to cover a specific area. Many different spiders construct their own variations of the general orb shape, and because their vision is very poor, the web functions as their chief source of information and connection to the outside world. Some of these orb-weavers live around homes and gardens, where their engineering skills easily can be observed each evening (or morning, depending on the species) when a brand new web is constructed with silk that is recycled from eating the old webs. A very common location for these webs is around outdoor porch lights, where the spider rests in the center of its orb waiting to trap moths attracted to the lights.

Certain orb webs may stretch several feet between tree trunks across woodland paths. Spiders often bridge such wide gaps by simply standing on tree trunks with their abdomens pointing into the air and letting the breezes carry their sticky silk across. (Spider silk, with a greater tensile strength than steel, begins as liquid protein droplets that are transformed first into liquid crystals and then fibers as they are stretched out by the spider.) In the centers of these woodland webs rest the strangest looking of all our orb-weavers, the spiny-bellied spiders, looking more like tiny conch shells or white, irregular bird droppings than spiders.

Canoeists often encounter another unusually shaped orb-weaver along the shores of ponds and rivers or beneath bridges. The long-jawed orb-weaver's web is slanted toward the horizontal, unlike the vertical orbs of most other species. The slender, elongated spider is extremely well camouflaged as it presses its body and extends its very long legs along the stems of weeds and bushes connected to the web. These spiders often fall into canoes that brush against their hiding places and then clumsily attempt to run up the sides with their long, gangly legs. Like most web-making spiders, they are much more agile in their webs than on the ground.

The largest and most attractive of our orb-weavers are the two *Argiopes*, which construct their huge, tough webs in grassy meadows, marshes, and the weedy borders of roads and ponds. The banded *Argiope*, with its 1-inch-long body decorated with black-and-silver bands, is impressive enough, but its close cousin the black-and-yellow *Argiope* is our region's largest and most recognizable web-making spider. With legs stretching as much as 3 inches as it hangs head downward in the center of its orb, this huge, colorful, heavy-bodied spider is very conspicuous, and it makes itself even more noticeable when disturbed by repeatedly pulling its entire web back and forth like a vibrating, vertical trampoline. Both of these *Argiopes* feed on grasshoppers, katydids, bees, beetles, and any other insects that become entangled in their sticky snares, and their speed and agility at twirling their victims around as they "mummify" them in a shroud of silk must be seen to be believed.

Scientists believe that the *Argiopes* employ their bright colors, diurnal habits, and the thick, silken "zigzag" lines that they spin down the centers of their webs to make themselves visible to birds so they will avoid the sticky webs as they fly over the meadows. In this way *Argiopes* are spared the necessity of rebuilding their webs every day like most other orb-weavers. In addition, some recent studies have suggested that the zigzag lines actually reflect certain light frequencies that attract insects, thus increasing the web's success at trapping prey.

Around farms, meadows, sunny woodland clearings, and yards members of the *Araneus* genus of orb-weavers construct their webs and hide off to one side in tentlike shelters built of leaves rolled up with silk. Insects trapped in the web transmit vibrations to these shelters via signal lines of silk, and the spiders rush out to bite and wrap up their prey. Often called garden spiders, these species have fairly large (3/4 inch), fat bodies decorated with colorful patterns. One common species, the shamrock spider, has three-leaf-clover markings on its abdomen and banded legs and may come in several distinct colors—brown, maroon, or white. Another, the marbled spider, also appears in color variations, including a beautiful, bright orange.

Several *Araneus* species typically construct their webs around the outside of buildings and in basements. The largest of these, the hairy, grayish brown barn spider, was the central character in E. B. White's famous children's book *Charlotte's Web*. Like Charlotte, all of these orb-weavers that become so conspicuous in late summer usually die sometime in September, although a few may linger on until the first hard frosts of autumn. Males (much smaller than females) die soon after mating. Females construct thick, silken sacs for their several hundred eggs, attach the sacs to plants, and then die, never seeing the spiderlings that emerge to begin a new generation the following spring.

23

The Magic of Mushrooms

Late summer rains bring up mushrooms overnight

————Observations————

For the better part of two decades I enjoyed late summer vacations in New York's Adirondack Preserve, taking off sometime during the latter part of August for one or two glorious weeks in the mountains. Indelibly etched in my memory are certain sensory experiences from days spent out in those great north woods: the fragrant scents of pines and balsam firs; the cheerful songs of goldfinches and the nasal calls of red-breasted nuthatches; the beautiful appearance of orb webs outlined with morning dew across meadows of goldenrods and asters, where monarch butterflies flitted about after the sun warmed the air. Some of my most vivid recollections are of the remarkable variety of mushrooms that were growing in the cool, shaded forests. Every conceivable shape and color was present on fallen logs, tree stumps, and leaf litter. Their diversity added immeasurably to the enjoyment of hiking the trails, and each year I looked forward to seeing and photographing additional species of these unusual living things.

Besides their attractive colors and shapes, mushrooms have additional features that have been responsible for their prominent roles in human folklore, cults, and superstitions over the centuries. Many species literally pop up overnight after a rainfall and may just as mysteriously wither or "melt" away a couple of days later. The dependence of many species on decomposing leaves and wood has strengthened their association in human minds with death. Perhaps most importantly, however, mushrooms have assumed such a high profile because of their long history of human use. Some species are not only edible but almost fanatically sought as valuable delicacies. Others, because of their hallucinogenic properties, are used in a ritualistic or hedonistic manner. And, of course, some species are famous for their very deadly nature: Every year there are a few victims of mushroom poisoning, and these stories are given much emphasis in the press.

The terms *mushroom* and *toadstool* are very general, inexact names given to the fruiting bodies of various fungi. Once all grouped together as "nonflowering plants," fungi have now been given their own kingdom (Fungi), completely separate from the green plants due to their lack of chlorophyll, their reproduction by spores, and other unique anatomical characteristics. What we recognize as a mushroom, puffball, or shelf-fungus are all fruiting bodies produced by the more extensive, hidden part of the fungus. Known as the mycelium, this growth is a branching network of threadlike strands called hyphae, which grow in soil, dead wood, leaf litter, or other organic matter. The mycelium is the actual spreading, feeding part of the fungus, secreting chemicals to digest organic matter. If environmental conditions are right (slightly cooler weather and a recent rainfall that moistens the earth—which often happens in middle to late August and September in the Northeast), the mycelium produces above-ground fruiting bodies of various forms, depending on the species. These fruiting bodies ripen and release thousands (or billions in some cases) of microscopic spores into the environment. Given the right conditions, a spore may grow into a tiny, threadlike hypha that branches out into leaf litter or wood to form another mycelium.

Fungi may pursue three completely different life-styles. Some species are parasitic, penetrating their hosts (usually the roots of trees) to take nourishment, eventually weakening or killing the trees. Many others are saprophytes, subsisting entirely on dead organic matter. These species are among nature's most valuable recyclers, decomposing dead material and releasing nutrients back into the soil. During the past decade, scientific studies have revealed that some of these wood-eating fungi supplement their diets by preying upon tiny roundworms, amoebas, rotifiers, bacteria, and other microscopic creatures that they capture with a remarkable array of weapons, including miniature lassos, harpoons, sticky nets, hooks, invasive spores, and paralytic toxins, all produced by their hyphae.

Much scientific research today concerns a third life-style of fungi: the mycorrhiza. Many of our most common and easily recognized mushrooms—*Amanita, Russula,* and *Boletus* species, for example—form an intimate, symbiotic relationship with the roots of many green plants. Their underground hyphae intertwine, ensheathe, and penetrate the rootlets of trees, shrubs, and smaller plants to form a dual association called a mycorrhiza, or "fungus-root."

-----*Observations*-----

From the roots the fungal hyphae derive water and nourishment (sugars manufactured by the above-ground green leaves and passed down to the roots) without harming the plants. This nourishment is stored by the fungi all spring and summer to enable them to produce the beautiful mushrooms we admire in late summer and fall. So dependent are some species of fungi on their mycorrhizal associations that they can't survive on their own, and many will form these relationships with only one specific kind of green plant.

In return for their nourishment the mycorrhizal fungi assist the green plants in taking up nitrogen, phosphorus, potassium, and other nutrients from the soil, mainly by creating a much more extensive surface area for mineral absorption via their branching hyphae. This is especially valuable for green plants growing in nutrient-poor soils like peat bogs as well as for seedlings trying to get established amidst larger, more competitive trees and shrubs in a forest. The fungal hyphae also protect the roots from drought and invasion by nematodes, parasitic fungi, and other harmful organisms. They even secrete auxins and other natural plant growth substances that help to promote the root growth.

Without mycorrhizal associations in their roots, many trees and shrubs grow much more slowly and are unable to compete favorably with other plants that enjoy the benefits of fungal hyphae enmeshing their roots. In fact, conifer trees cannot survive without mycorrhizae. Many species of orchids are so dependent on mycorrhizae that they can't nourish themselves as seedlings without the specific fungal hyphae in the soil, and even transplanting mature orchid plants to other locations jeopardizes their survival if the fungal partner is absent. In some forests it has been found that hyphae from some trees and shrubs extend into the roots of other plants, and the nourishment may be shared by many different species of green plants and fungi in a vast, complex, underground mycorrhizal web.

Based upon the shapes and reproductive features of their fruiting bodies, fungi can be classified into several groups. Commonly considered "true mushrooms" are the gilled fungi, most of which exhibit the typical mushroom shape: a flat or rounded cap, borne like an umbrella on an upright stalk and containing on its underside a series of spokelike gills radiating outward from the stalk. The spores are shed from these gills. Resembling this group are the boletes in which the gills beneath the cap are replaced by numerous open pores, which are the open ends of closely packed tubes that produce the spores. In another group, the teeth fungi, the spores are shed from distinctive, spinelike teeth that hang from beneath the cap. Morels (which only occur in spring) also have central stalks and caps, but the spores are produced from pockets in the very wrinkled, pitted, spongelike cap.

Resembling tiny reefs from the ocean floor, the colorful coral fungi comprise another very distinctive group. Some species are highly branched, while others contain just a few erect "fingers." At the opposite extreme are the puffballs, some resembling golf balls, others looking like giant, white basketballs lying on the ground with little or no stalk. Included in this group are the earthstars, in which the outer skin peels back from the round puffball in several pointed sections to resemble a star on the bare ground. The puffball fungi produce millions or even billions of spores when, at the touch of an animal or even a rain drop, the top breaks open and releases them like clouds of dust. Closely related to the puffballs are the stinkhorns—in which the spores coat the surface of a slimy, smelly cap borne atop a chambered stalk—and the tiny birds' nest fungi, in which the fruiting bodies look just like miniature bird eggs inside an open stalkless, nestlike cap usually sitting on a dead branch.

Among the most prominent fungi to appear at this season is the polypore family, often resembling woody shelves or brackets protruding from tree trunks. Many species grow in overlapping layers, while others exist as individual shelves that grow larger each year. One of the largest species, the "artist's conch," has a white underside and was once used as a surface for sketching or painting pictures. All the polypores contain numerous pores beneath their fleshy or woody surfaces from which the dustlike spores fall to the ground or get carried away by the breezes.

————*Observations*————

─────*Observations*─────

There are also rubbery, colorful, jelly fungi, which are found on wood; small, stalkless, brightly colored cup fungi; and unusual, upright "earth tongues" and "dead man's fingers," which protrude from the ground. Their infinite variety make mushrooms and other fungi one of nature's most fascinating groups of living things. The propensity of many species to grow only at specific seasons, in specific habitats, and even on specific kinds of living or dead material, only adds to their mystique. But their most widespread source of interest is their edibility or inedibility. There are approximately one thousand species of mushrooms and other fungi in the Northeast, and many of these not only are delicious but also are good sources of vitamin B, iron, potassium, and protein. Examples of the more readily identifiable, edible kinds are the morels, puffballs, shaggy mane and other ink-cap mushrooms, oyster mushrooms (*Pleurotus*), chantarelles, honey mushrooms ("shoestring" fungi), and the large, orange-and-yellow sulphur polypore (or chicken mushroom).

However, about one hundred of these northeastern fungi are considered poisonous, of which fifteen can be fatal. These include the bright orange jack-o'-lantern, the false morels, a few of the *Lepiotas*, and several of the *Amanitas*. In fact, only two ounces of the death cap or destroying angel (two *Amanita* species) can be fatal to a human.

Some groups of mushrooms, like *Russula* and *Boletus*, contain both edible and poisonous varieties. There is absolutely no general rule of thumb, no single test to differentiate between edible and inedible mushrooms. It is safe to sample the edible kinds *only* if you have learned how to identify each species without a doubt. But even so-called experts are occasionally fooled (with some mushrooms there is no room for error . . . and no second chance). The safest way to enjoy mushrooms is to purchase them in a store. All the beautiful kinds that pop up in our woods after late summer rains can be enjoyed, too, but by nonconsumptive means like photography, field-guide identification, or simply admiring their diverse forms, colors, and habitats.

24

Den Mothers

Rattlesnakes, copperheads, and other snakes give birth

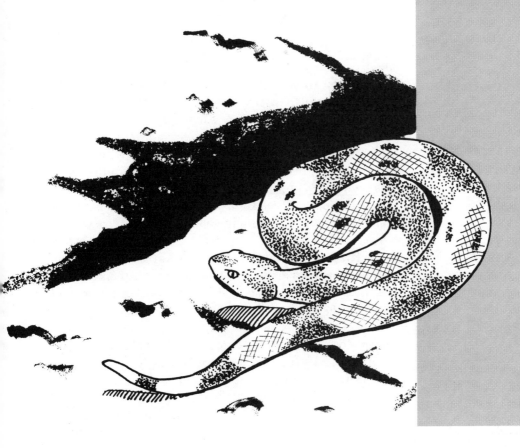

──Observations──

The days are now growing shorter and the nights cooler. The hot, hazy days of summer are on the decline, and there is a crispness and clarity in the morning air that belongs more to autumn than to August. Warbler species from Canada reappear for the first time in our region since last spring, this time in their drab autumn colors as they head for the Tropics. Some of the leaves on the sour gum trees and blueberry bushes may even begin to show the blazing reds that will paint our landscape in another month. Summer is ending in the northeastern United States.

For snakes this season marks the culmination of their year and the most important period in their annual cycle—the time when a new generation is born. Baby snakes of about twenty northeastern species make their appearance in late August and September. Numbers of newborn snakes per clutch vary from as few as two to as many as eighty-five, depending on the species, and they are completely independent from the moment of birth. None receives any food, care, or guidance from the mother, and some go into hibernation soon after being born, not even taking their first meals until they reawaken next spring.

Many of these baby snakes hatch from clusters of eggs deposited in midsummer by their mothers in rotting stumps or logs, piles of sawdust or decaying leaves, or under stones, places where moisture and warmth hasten the incubation process. Some of these sites may be used by several different snakes as communal nests. The eggs of snakes are white or creamy yellowish in color, and their shells are soft but tough, leathery, or parchmentlike in texture. The size of an egg ranges from less than 1 inch for the smaller species like the worm snake to more than 2 inches for the big black rat snake. The number of eggs produced by a female snake is also roughly proportional to her size, with the worm snakes and ring-necked snakes laying two to eight eggs and the black racer and rat snakes depositing over two dozen (the medium-sized hognose snake may lay up to sixty eggs in an underground cavity).

The incubation period varies according to the temperature, but for most species in the Northeast it is about two months. Eggs of the smooth green snake may hatch in less than two weeks, while those of the black rat snake may take as long as four months. At any rate, most of these baby snakes come into the world sometime in late summer or early fall, usually at the end of August or the beginning of September in our region. A hatchling black rat snake may be as long as 16 inches (it may someday exceed 7 feet), while a baby worm snake is only 3 or 4 inches, but this is already almost half its adult size.

Not all of our local snakes lay eggs. Many are live bearers, giving birth to babies encased in a soft, moist membrane that they break through very soon after leaving their mother's body. Examples include the small, 12-inch red-bellied and northern brown snakes, which each produce about ten tiny, 3- to 4-inch live babies in late August or September; the large, thick-bodied northern water snake and the slender eastern ribbon snake, which each give birth to fifteen to thirty babies during the same season; and the common eastern garter snake, which has been known to produce as many as eighty-five live young at a time and as late in the year as October.

Our three closely related venomous snakes also bear live young in late summer. Barely extending its midwestern range into our region in extreme northeastern Pennsylvania and isolated spots in central New York, the massasauga, or swamp rattlesnake, gives birth to about a dozen babies, each one 6 to 9 inches long. Our other two poisonous snakes are much more widespread. The copperhead is found from central Massachusetts and southern New York southward; it is absent from New Hampshire, Vermont, and Maine but common in Pennsylvania, Connecticut, eastern New York, and New Jersey. The timber rattlesnake is found only in the extreme southwestern part of Maine and in the southern portions of Vermont and New Hampshire, but it is found in most of Connecticut, Massachusetts, Pennsylvania, and New York (except the higher Adirondack Mountains north of Lake George), and in both the northwestern hills and southern pinelands of New Jersey.

Both the copperhead and the timber rattlesnake return to their winter dens in late summer before giving birth to their live young. These dens, often shared by both

————Observations————

species as well as by black rat snakes and black racers, are usually located in rock outcrops on a hillside with southern or eastern exposure. The dens are often associated with rock ledges where the snakes can bask in the autumn (and spring) sun to elevate their body temperatures and below which they can take shelter from the midday sun and potential predators. But the most important prerequisite for a snake den is the presence of a crevice or hole that leads deep enough into the rocks to enable the snakes to escape the penetration of winter's freezing weather while they hibernate for six or seven months.

A good snake den is thus a very specific place, and not just any rocky hillside will fill all the necessary criteria. A den may be occupied by hundreds of snakes and is used by successive generations of snakes for centuries. A knowledge of their locations is extremely important to these snakes from the time of their birth. This is why the copperhead and timber rattlesnake wait until they return to their dens at the end of summer to give birth to their six to twelve babies, so the memory of the site will be imprinted on the newborn snakes. Unfortunately, humans have exploited the dependability of these snakes in returning to their ancestral dens by visiting these areas in late summer and fall to kill or collect the serpents. Rattlesnakes and copperheads have been wiped out of many areas of the Northeast by mass killings at their dens, and they are on the decline in many others.

Because of its endangered or threatened status, the timber rattlesnake is now protected in New York, New Jersey, Massachusetts, and Connecticut. Even in Pennsylvania, its last real stronghold in the Northeast, the traditional "rattlesnake roundups," with their field hunts, exhibitions, and various snake-handling contests, are now regulated by state laws designed to ensure the safety and ultimate release of the timber rattlesnakes. But careless and rough handling, release into the wrong areas (where dens are absent), and illegal killings at dens still go on throughout this reptile's range.

Though potentially dangerous, both the timber rattlesnake and the copperhead are very shy and reclusive, preferring to live their lives far from human habitations and reluctant to strike unless in immediate danger of being stepped on or touched. It is certainly a tragedy that so many of these unique, fascinating, and beautiful reptiles are persecuted each year at this season, when they and their newborn young congregate and prepare to retire ahead of the first frosts of fall.

———*Observations*———

25

September's Songbirds

SEPTEMBER I

Billions of small birds begin their annual journey to the tropics

——————*Observations*——————

There are few, if any, areas of natural history more fascinating and mysterious than the annual migration of birds. The fact that tiny, featherweight creatures are capable of flying vast distances each fall over unfamiliar territory and then returning to the same breeding areas months later has piqued the curiosity and fueled the imagination of humans for centuries. Today it may be easy to laugh at ancient theories that attempted to explain the annual disappearance of summer's birds by suggesting that they hibernated beneath the mud like amphibians or even flew straight to the moon. But the answers that modern scientists are coming up with may seem even more unbelievable. Based on reliable observations, at least one of the old bits of Indian and early American folklore traditionally scoffed at in scientific circles has now actually been accepted as truth by many naturalists: hummingbirds and other small birds do, at least occasionally, hitch rides inside the feathers of geese and swans during their long migrations!

The autumn migration begins for some species of shorebirds (see chapter 21) and early warblers (yellow, blue-winged, and Louisiana waterthrush) as early as the end of July in the Northeast. Then, in late August the swallows and nighthawks leave our area for South America, sometimes migrating in spectacular numbers. But the real peak of the fall passage doesn't begin until September, when most of the warblers, vireos, thrushes, tanagers, orioles, and other songbirds fly through our region to their tropical wintering homes in southern Mexico, Central America, South America, and the Caribbean Islands. At this time it is possible to see over one hundred different species of birds, including twenty-five to thirty species of warblers, in a single day as they hurry through our area. This movement continues in somewhat less dramatic fashion into October, when it is gradually replaced by the migrations of the sparrows, juncos, and several members of the blackbird family (red-wing, grackle, cowbird) that migrate much shorter distances (to the more southern states) than their predecessors.

Scientists estimate that at least 20 billion birds take part in this annual fall migration in North America, approximately double the spring total because autumn's numbers include the young of the year, many of which die over the next few months and fail to return. In our northeastern region about 75 percent of our species of birds leave each fall. The feats accomplished by some of these migrants have become legendary. The arctic tern flies from the Arctic to the Antarctic each fall and then back again in spring—over twenty-two thousand miles round-trip. The tiny blackpoll and other warblers fly two thousand miles nonstop over the ocean from Canada and New England to the Caribbean in three or four days. The migrants fly at altitudes of several thousand feet, some even exceeding 20,000 feet in frigid, oxygen-deficient atmospheric conditions.

Their navigational abilities during this long journey are even more extraordinary. Various species from swallows and sparrows to shearwaters and pigeons have been kept in dark containers and experimentally flown hundreds or even thousands of miles from their nests. Then, released in totally strange surroundings under completely overcast skies, they have returned to their homes a few days later—sometimes even ahead of the scientists who transported them! How do birds (including young ones that are flying for the first time) accomplish such long journeys twice a year, reaching the same ancestral winter and summer homes thousands of miles apart?

Many birds possess not only some kind of internal, biological clock that keeps track of the passing seasons (and which, together with autumn's decreasing daylength, or photoperiod, acts on their hormones and causes them to go without sleep and restlessly fatten themselves up for their long trips) but also a daily clock that tells them the time of day. It has been demonstrated in many species of birds that this daily clock is used in conjunction with the bird's observance of the sun's position and movement across the sky to figure out directions. In other words, the sun is used by birds as a compass in choosing their bearings. Under completely overcast skies some species of birds have demonstrated an ability to ascertain the sun's position in the sky by seeing its ultraviolet radiation or the plane of polarized light that reveals its hidden location.

————*Observations*————

——Observations——

Even more amazing, however, is the ability of many birds to successfully navigate at night, perhaps using the glow of the sunset as their directional cue at takeoff and then using the positions of the moon and the constellations to guide them as they migrate. Thrushes, warblers, vireos, and other small songbirds may fly hundreds of miles in this way, using the same celestial clues that guided the ancient mariners. These birds are picked up as countless dots by radar screens in fall, and humans can actually hear their high-pitched chirps and squeaks on cool, clear autumn nights as they pass overhead.

But birds can successfully migrate even on completely overcast nights when views of the sky are obliterated. Some of these species have been shown in carefully controlled experiments to possess an innate directional sense: They are born with the ability to determine north, south, east, and west, and they take the appropriate flight direction dictated by their seasonal rhythms. This may explain part of the puzzle. But how do birds fly in cloudy weather to the same region, sometimes the same woodlot or backyard, around the same dates each fall and spring? A directional compass alone cannot adequately explain these miraculous accomplishments. Only some kind of complicated map sense can explain their success in reaching an exact destination—an ability to know where they are relative to "home" and to figure out the correct route to get there.

The environmental cues used by birds during their astonishing navigations is now one of the most active fields of ornithological research throughout the world. The more this phenomenon is studied, the more complicated and enigmatic it becomes. Some of the findings that have come out of these investigations have suggested that birds may possess sensory capacities previously thought impossible, and that they may call upon certain ones only when necessary. For example, just as daytime migrants can use visual landmarks like coastlines, mountain ranges, and other topographical features as guidelines, some birds migrating at night or under overcast skies, when celestial cues are unavailable, may switch to a magnetic sense—the ability to navigate by using the varying strengths of the earth's magnetic fields. Some species, like homing pigeons, even possess tiny deposits of magnetite in their brains, which react to the earth's changing fields.

Recent studies have shown that some birds are born with an innate magnetic compass sense that they then use in their early weeks as a reference in calibrating their own celestial system of navigation. Other studies have shown that birds can extract from their environments certain sensory stimuli like infrasounds (the roar of the ocean surf, the winds across the mountains) or wind-carried odors (marsh vegetation, meadow flowers) coming from various directions and then construct their own maps for navigation, which they learn and use from year to year. Among the other environmental variables being studied for their possible roles in bird navigation are changes in barometric pressure and the earth's gravitational forces. Scientists now believe that birds may possess several different orientational and navigational strategies, including primary modes that they were born with or learned from their environments soon after hatching and backup systems used when the preferred ones are blocked.

In addition to all of these seemingly impossible sensory abilities, it has been shown that many of our birds take full advantage of the season's prevailing weather conditions to make their long journeys easier. Just after the passage of a cold front across our region, when blasts of air from the northwest provide tail winds, millions of birds leave the northeastern United States and Canada at night. (Up to 12 million per night are detected on radar screens in September!) Their flight speeds are accelerated by these winds as they are carried to the southeast over the coast or the open ocean waters. Many are then moved inland by the northeast trade winds that prevail around the Sargasso Sea south of Bermuda. Thus, they are brought to their destinations in the Caribbean, Central America, and South America.

Why bother with this long, dangerous journey at all? Almost without exception the inevitable shortage of food that follows autumn is the reason migration has evolved. The swallows, swifts, nighthawks, and small songbirds would certainly starve after the caterpillars, flies, moths,

—————*Observations*—————

beetles, and other insects that they depend on succumb to the cold weather, just as waterfowl would die after the ponds and lakes freeze over and lock up their aquatic plants. By traveling to the Tropics, where insect prey is abundant, and then returning to the Northeast in spring to raise their families on the millions of insects emerging during the warmer months (without the competition from the tropical resident birds or the danger from more numerous predators), these birds take advantage of environments thousands of miles apart.

The dangers, of course, are vastly multiplied by such journeys. Negative circumstances on their breeding grounds, wintering homes, and en route stopovers can have drastic consequences on their numbers (see chapter 15). The miracle of bird migration still retains many of its secrets. Unlocking these fascinating riddles depends in large measure on preventing the destruction of the forests, fields, and wetlands to which these birds are mysteriously guided during their long annual journeys.

26

Hundreds of Hawks

The spectacular fall migration of the raptors

—————Observations—————

The air is crisp and clear, and the mid-September sun warms the rocks on the mountaintop vista where people patiently await the arrival of the first hawks of the day. The maples in the lower valleys are beginning to turn red and gold, and the chirps of crickets and the cheeps of migrating songbirds emanate from the surrounding oak forests. What a glorious day to be outdoors! Someone calls attention to a distant speck floating in the blue sky to the north, and as it gradually draws closer to the lookout, it assumes the unmistakable shape of a hawk. Suddenly, many more specks are seen trailing the first and coming this way. Soon the skies above the lookout are filled with broad-winged hawks, hundreds of them soaring in circles higher and higher and then gliding rapidly past the lookout only to be replaced by hundreds more. Over 1,000 hawks pass by in a few minutes, and then the awestruck observers notice hundreds more coming from the same direction. By the end of the day the count totals over 5,000 broad-winged hawks, and the hawk-watchers descend the trails from the mountain, deeply satisfied with an autumn day well spent in the outdoors and anticipating what the next day will bring.

Such an experience has become an annual occurrence at many outdoor areas throughout the northeastern United States as the sport and science of hawk watching has grown in popularity over the past two decades. Lookouts along the Appalachian Mountains, Atlantic coast, Great Lakes shorelines, and many other hilltops throughout our region are manned by people from late August through November to record the progression of raptors moving to the south. Their observations have resulted in a wealth of information about the mysteries and mechanics of autumn hawk migration, perhaps the most spectacular and dramatic of all of nature's annual events in the Northeast.

The second and third weeks of September are traditionally the best times to see great numbers of raptors, for this is always the peak of the migration of broad-winged hawks, our most abundant species. (See chapters 2 and 7 for descriptions of all these raptors.) Tens of thousands are occasionally seen in a *single day*! On the other hand, only a handful may pass by on the preceding and succeeding days. Likewise, one lookout may record great numbers one day, while another site only a few miles away may record hardly any. The next day or week the situation may be reversed. Such are the vagaries of this annual phenomenon, and the reasons behind these discrepancies usually relate to the weather, as revealed by an analysis of the vast data accumulated over many years by the hawk-watchers.

Hawks seek to conserve energy during their long migratory flights by utilizing various weather conditions and air movements. One important aid is the thermal—a mass of warm, buoyant air that can rise up from the ground as fast as 20 feet per second, and which is used by soaring hawks as a "hot air balloon" to gain altitude. Thermals are formed wherever differential heating of the earth's surfaces (a farm bordered by shaded woods, a boulder field surrounded by cool forest) results in the cooler air rushing in to replace the lighter, less dense air being heated by the sun, causing it to break away and float up like a huge bubble. The peak season for thermal formation in our region is September, just when the broad-winged hawks migrate.

Once they reach a few thousand feet (strong thermals may lift hawks beyond the visual limit of unaided human eyes), the hawks stop circling, break away from the now-weakening thermal, and glide up to 10 miles on locked wings down to the next thermal at speeds ranging from 25 to 40 miles per hour—an excellent way to cover up to 250 miles in a day without beating a wing.

Another migratory aid is the updraft—wind deflected off mountain ridges or other obstructions and used by hawks to obtain free rides. During the fall, when prevailing winds are often from the northwest, excellent updrafts are formed along the ridges of the Appalachian Mountain range, whose northeast-to-southwest orientation across the eastern United States is perfect for deflecting winds from this direction. Hawks often follow these ridges for long distances.

An examination of all the record-breaking hawk flights at lookouts across our region has confirmed a definite correlation with the recent passage of a low-pressure weather

———*Observations*———

system across the northern United States and Canada. When a low (with its counterclockwise air movement) moves across this region from the west, the warm flow of southerly, moist air is followed by winds from the north. Then with the advance of a cold front (the boundary between a low- and a high-pressure air mass) and the approach of a high (with its clockwise air rotation) from the west, the northerly flow of clear, cool air is reinforced. Hawks use these air movements as tail winds when they take off on their migrations from Canada and the northern states.

On September 13, 1978, when a low was centered to the northeast and a high to the northwest, creating a strong flow of air from the north, over 10,000 broad-winged hawks flew over Wachusett Mountain in eastern Massachusetts. In 1983, on the same date and under the exact weather conditions, 20,000 broad-wings (as many as 5,000 in a single, soaring mass, or "kettle") migrated past this same lookout. On September 14, 1986, following the passage of a cold front and under strong northwest winds, 14,000 broad-wings were counted at the Montclair Quarry lookout in northern New Jersey. But this total was dwarfed on that same day when a new eastern record was set at Quaker Ridge in Greenwich, Connecticut: 30,535 broad-winged hawks, over 17,000 in a single hour! There is something magical about those days in mid-September.

If northwest winds are too strong, however, many of the lighter-weight raptors, like the broad-winged and sharp-shinned hawks, are blown toward the coast, and the more inland lookouts may see very few. For example, in 1984, during an autumn dominated by strong northwest winds, the phenomenal total of 61,180 sharp-shinned hawks (almost twice the average annual total) were counted at Cape May on New Jersey's southern coast, and in 1981 strong northwest winds gave the Cape May lookouts a seasonal count of 14,000 broad-winged hawks, while unusually low numbers were recorded at most inland lookouts.

The reverse situation occurred in 1989, when warm weather and southerly winds at Cape May brought extremely low numbers of sharp-shins and only 822 broad-winged hawks, while some inland lookouts broke new records for this species.

Once a high-pressure system becomes stationed over the Northeast and calm, sunny, mild weather takes over, hawks no longer concentrate along the ridges but may migrate in a broad front, drifting all across the landscape using the strong thermals generated under such conditions. Then they may be seen just about anywhere, even from suburban backyards. There is still much to be learned about hawk migration, and parts of the puzzle will continue to be solved and a more complete migratory map can be drawn as more lookouts fill in the gaps throughout our region.

Not all of the fifteen species of raptors regularly seen migrating through our region react to these weather conditions in the same way. For example, broad-winged hawks and, to a lesser extent, red-shouldered hawks excel at soaring on thermals, while sharp-shinned hawks and the heavy red-tailed hawks are more apt to use updrafts to carry them along. The most consistent difference occurs between the falcons and the buteos. Buteos (red-tailed, red-shouldered, broad-winged, and rough-legged hawks), with their wide, fanned tails and extensive wing surfaces, are built for soaring and floating on updrafts and thermals. They are more likely to migrate inland along the ridges than along the open coast. On the other hand, the slim, streamlined, and extremely fast falcons (kestrels, merlins, and peregrines), with powerful, pointed wings that carry them like bullets across the open country they prefer, do not depend as much on wind and weather aids and are more likely to be found along the beaches and sand dunes on the coast. There they hunt for shorebirds and other migrating birds as they move south (some peregrines fly all the way down to Patagonia for winter). Some merlins and peregrines may even migrate right over the open waters of the Atlantic Ocean, bypassing the coast except when easterly winds cause them to drift landward.

Of Hawk Mountain's average annual total of 22,400 migrating hawks, almost 13,000 are buteos and only 600 falcons. At Cape May, where annual totals average an amazing 60,000 raptors, about 15,000 of these are falcons

————*Observations*————

(mostly kestrels) and only 6,000 buteos. Coastal sites see more falcons in a single day than inland lookouts record all year: Cape May had 25,000 kestrels on October 16, 1970, and 157 peregrines on October 3, 1989. On barrier beaches and outer islands these falcon/buteo differences are even more striking. In the fall of 1989 on New York's Fire Island 5,377 hawks were counted, including 2,244 kestrels, 1,362 merlins, 196 peregrines, and none of the buteos. At nearby Robert Moses State Park a 1987 total of 5,896 raptors included 3,245 kestrels, 1,181 merlins, 169 peregrines, and no buteos. Sharp-shinned hawks are also curiously absent from these island hawk stations, indicating the tendency of this small raptor to cling to the coast rather than cross open water.

As already implied, there are certain places in our region that, by virtue of their topographical features or strategic locations along the migratory routes, have become famous for their large concentrations of hawks in the fall. Two sites on the northern shore of Lake Erie across our border in Ontario must be mentioned due to their incomparable totals. Hawk Cliff, rising 100 feet near Port Stanley, occasionally records over 56,000 migrating hawks, the majority being broad-wings. Holiday Beach, at the western end of Lake Erie, owns the record: 141,636 hawks in 1984! This remarkable total included 110,000 broad-wings—95,000 on a single memorable September 15, with 54,000 of those in eighteen minutes! The other raptors are also seen here in great numbers: up to 9,000 red-tailed, 1,400 red-shouldered, 300 rough-legged, 18,000 sharp-shinned, and 900 Cooper's hawks; 1,600 harriers; 5,700 kestrels; and 12,500 turkey vultures. The reason for these unbelievable concentrations is the same one that explains the high numbers of northward-moving hawks seen on the lake's southern shores in spring—the reluctance of these raptors to cross vast expanses of cold waters, which provide hardly any thermal lift. Upon reaching Lake Erie's north or west shores, Canadian hawks usually follow it west-southwest until they can continue south. As they reach the end of these detours, their numbers have been augmented by others continually joining them from the north and by those funneling down from the north shores of nearby Lake Ontario. The result: a sky filled and boiling with circling, gliding hawks.

Another major topographical feature that concentrates migrating hawks is the Appalachian Mountains, especially that section running through New York, New Jersey, and Pennsylvania known as the Kittatinny. Raptors glide southward on updrafts created when northwest winds strike these ridges. Excellent thermals are also generated from the farms and rock fields surrounding the range. Mohonk Preserve in New York and Sunrise and Scott's mountains and Raccoon Ridge (which often records over 20,000 migrating hawks) in northwestern New Jersey are those states' best-known Kittatinny lookouts, while Bake Oven Knob, Waggoner's Gap, Tuscarora Summit, and Hawk Mountain (the oldest and most famous lookout of all) lie along the Pennsylvania section of the ridge. Hawk Mountain, near Kempton, is the southeasternmost point on the Kittatinny and is the last source of updrafts for migrating raptors, which cling to it rather than fly over the open valleys beyond the ridge. In addition, several smaller mountains to the north bend southward toward Hawk Mountain and funnel raptors to its bare, rocky, exposed summits, where views of the hawks are outstanding. Annual totals of all species often exceed 30,000, including 4,000 red-tailed, 300 red-shouldered, 7,000 sharp-shinned, and 500 Cooper's hawks; 500 kestrels; 550 ospreys; 350 harriers; 40 bald eagles; 80 goshawks; and 55 golden eagles (all average figures). On September 14, 1978, Hawk Mountain experienced its own record-breaking day when 21,000 broad-winged hawks passed overhead.

Throughout New England there are many hawk lookouts where totals don't approach those of the Kittatinny and Great Lakes lookouts but are invaluable in mapping the routes taken by these migrants. Mount Agamenticus near York, Maine; South Harpswell, a rocky peninsula off Maine's southern coast; New Hampshire's Little Round Top (in Bristol) and Gap Mountain (in Troy); southeastern Vermont's Putney Mountain; Granville in western Massachusetts and Mount Tom near Holyoke—each of these lookouts records between 2,000 and 10,000 migrating hawks per year. Even higher numbers (up to 20,000 per

————*Observations*————

year) are seen at Wachusett Mountain in Princeton, Massachusetts, and southern Connecticut's Quaker Ridge and Lighthouse Point.

Hawks continuing their migrations down from these New England lookouts have been followed by glider planes and by observers stationed at interception lines of sight along their routes. Upon reaching Long Island Sound (where great concentrations may occur under strong northwest winds), the hawks veer west and continue flying in a broad front into southern New York and northeastern New Jersey before turning south again near the Kittatinny Ridge. Some lookouts in this "middle ground" between the coast and the mountains are very productive hawk-watching stations. Bear Mountain, Butler Sanctuary, and Hook Mountain in southeastern New York occasionally record between 15,000 and 25,000 hawks (mostly broad-wings) in a single season. Rifle Camp Park, Skyline Ridge, and Boonton in northern New Jersey are three other popular hawk lookouts. But a lookout atop an old quarry in Montclair, New Jersey, has gradually proven to be one of the most productive of all northeastern hawk-watching sites. In 1986, 52,418 hawks were counted there, including 43,460 broad-wings, 5,300 sharp-shins, 1,350 red-tails, and 837 ospreys.

Finally, the Atlantic coast functions as yet another migration corridor for hawks, with New Jersey's Cape May peninsula the most famous coastal lookout of all. As migratory raptors reach this long, narrow southern extension of New Jersey's coastal plain and are confronted with Delaware Bay and the Atlantic Ocean, their flight is diverted and they become concentrated in the skies above the cape. Great flights are experienced when strong northwest winds blow inland raptors to the coast. Cape May Point State Park and Higbee Beach are two of the most popular vantage points here. Seasonal totals at Cape May often exceed 80,000 hawks, with up to 50 percent of these (occasionally more) being sharp-shinned hawks, 25 percent falcons, and 10 percent (or less) buteos. No other lookout in the United States can match Cape May's seasonal records for osprey (5,400), harrier (3,118), kestrel (30,268), merlin

(2,876), peregrine (702), sharp-shinned hawk (61,180), or Cooper's hawk (2,950).

As in the spring, each of the fifteen or sixteen species of raptors (the southernmost sites see a few black vultures almost every year) regularly seen at all these lookouts has its own migration timetable (see chapter 7). In the fall, however, the order is reversed, with the last birds of the spring now being the first to appear at the lookouts. As early as mid-August the lookouts begin recording a few ospreys, harriers, broad-wings, and kestrels on their way south, as well as Florida bald eagles that have spent the summer up north (Hawk Mountain had 14 bald eagles in August 1989).

September, of course, is the biggest month as far as numbers are concerned, since the abundant broad-winged hawk peaks at this time. But by the end of the month or the first week in October, all the broad-wings from Canada and the northern states have finished migrating through our area, and soon they will arrive at their winter homes in Central America or South America. Some travel up to 4,500 miles to Peru or Bolivia. By the time they near their destinations, their numbers may be incredible. On October 3 and 4, 1977, between 750,000 and 1,000,000 broad-winged hawks were seen over Corpus Christi, Texas—probably the largest concentration of hawks ever witnessed.

Also peaking in September is the osprey, with over 100 per day sometimes passing Hawk Mountain toward the end of the month and up to 1,000 per day at Cape May. These large fish-eating raptors spend the winter from Florida and the West Indies down to northern South America. From mid-September to early October the sharp-shinned hawk, its larger but rarer cousin the Cooper's hawk, and the three falcons begin to reach their peaks. The harrier, or marsh hawk, has the longest migration period of any raptor. Immature birds begin traveling south in August and September, followed by adult females in October and adult males in late October and November. At that time the raptor migration has experienced a change of cast. Gone are the broad-winged hawks, ospreys, and most of the falcons, Cooper's hawks, and sharp-shinned hawks. Now appearing

————Observations————

————Observations————

in peak numbers are the three big buteos (red-tailed, rough-legged, and red-shouldered hawks), turkey vultures, the rare goshawks, golden eagles, and bald eagles from Canada that bring the autumn migration to a close (see chapter 33).

There was a time when many of these hawk lookouts were visited by a different brand of birder. Familiar with the tendency of hawks to concentrate along the ridges each autumn when winds blew from the north, people armed with guns would hike to these spots and shoot great numbers of raptors year after year. The purchase of Hawk Mountain in 1934 and its conversion into a pioneering sanctuary and outdoor laboratory for the study of raptors stopped the slaughter of hawks that took place from its lookouts each fall. Today, birds of prey are recognized as valuable members of our natural communities, and they are all protected by law.

But in the 1950s and 1960s more insidious dangers began to take a toll on hawk populations. DDT and other pesticides sprayed all over the landscape began to show up as residues in the tissues of bald eagles, ospreys, and peregrine falcons, causing them to lay thin-shelled eggs that cracked beneath the weight of the incubating females. Widespread reproductive failure resulted and populations plummeted. By about 1970 the peregrine was extinct as a breeding bird in the eastern United States. Numbers seen at Hawk Mountain each fall dropped from as many as 45 in the 1940s to as few as 10, and these were all from the Canadian wilderness. Likewise, annual bald eagle counts at Hawk Mountain decreased from 100 per year in the 1930s, 1940s, and 1950s (142 in 1950) to only 20 to 50 by the 1970s. At Cape May ospreys fell from 706 in 1935 to 90 in 1965.

Then, in 1972 DDT was banned in our country, and efforts to bring these raptors back from endangered status were initiated by wildlife agencies throughout our region. Captive breeding and releasing, habitat preservation, and more stringent law enforcement gradually brought their numbers back up. By the late 1980s lookouts were once again recording numbers of migrating bald eagles very close to pre-DDT levels, and new seasonal records for peregrines, merlins, ospreys, and harriers were being set at lookouts from Hawk Mountain to Cape May to the Great Lakes. At the same time, an unprecedented interest in birds of prey and their preservation took hold of the public. Hawks, eagles, and falcons became extremely popular, even revered creatures, and hordes of people flocked to an increasing number of lookouts like Hawk Mountain each autumn to glimpse these majestic, powerful masters of the sky soaring, gliding, and flapping their way from northern wildernesses to tropical forests. Binoculars have replaced guns, and now the excited calls and cheers of hawk-watchers echo into the valleys from lookouts where once the sounds of bullets filled the autumn air.

The data accumulated over the years from all these lookouts have proven invaluable in tracking the population trends of the raptors and warning of possible problems as well as cheering the recoveries. Sitting at a lookout on a gorgeous September day, however, is much more than just counting hawks. It is an opportunity to watch some of nature's wildest, most elusive creatures at close range during one of the year's most spectacular pageants as they use autumn's air currents to carry them far beyond our horizons.

27

Migration of the Monarch

Our best-known butterfly flies to Mexico

—————Observations—————

As incredible as the journeys and the amazing feats accomplished by migratory birds may seem, there is another creature participating in an even more unbelievable migration this month. Starting soon after Labor Day, peaking during the latter half of September, and continuing until the cold weather of late October, the monarch—America's most familiar butterfly—experiences its own odyssey to a destination beyond our country's borders.

For many years it was known that these large, beautiful, orange-and-black butterflies fly southward each autumn. Great numbers of monarchs are seen in September throughout the northeastern United States, where they visit the asters, goldenrods, and other fall flowers to sip nectar. Scores of them may congregate in a sunny meadow, producing a dazzling display of color as their fluttering orange wings contrast with the yellows, purples, and whites of the blossoms. At hawk lookouts hundreds are seen against deep blue skies moving southward with the broad-winged hawks, kestrels, and other raptors. The largest numbers are seen along the Atlantic coast's beaches and sand dunes and the shores of the Great Lakes. Thousands of orange wings flap along these shorelines, stopping periodically to feed on sunflowers, goldenrods, and joe-pye weed, then continuing their movements and sometimes assembling in great numbers toward dusk to rest in pine trees and other nighttime roosts. At places like Cape May, New Jersey, these assemblages create quite a spectacle, and the monarchs here may still be numerous into the end of October because of the milder temperatures.

Like the birds, these $1/15$-ounce butterflies take advantage of moving air currents to save energy during migration. Floating along on the breezes, monarchs may cover eighty miles a day at speeds ranging from ten to thirty miles per hour. It appears that their migratory flights are triggered by the approach of a cold front—perhaps they can sense a fall in barometric pressure. Once they take off, they follow a route that they have never traveled before, but one that countless previous generations of monarchs have taken to a winter home.

In the western United States monarchs end their migratory journey at California's Monterey Peninsula, where the town of Pacific Grove has named itself "Butterfly City, U.S.A." after the millions of monarchs that assemble there in the pine trees all winter. But the destination of all the monarchs from Canada and the United States east of the Rocky Mountains long remained a stubborn mystery. Except for what appears to be a small resident and overwintering population in Florida, the migrant butterflies seemed to disappear beyond our country's borders.

For thirty-nine years Dr. Fred Urquhart of the University of Toronto sought the answer to the monarch's migratory riddle. He devised an ingenious way to apply tiny gummed labels onto the butterflies' wings, tagging them like birds in order to follow their travels. With the help of hundreds of volunteers who spotted these tagged monarchs and relayed the information back to him, Dr. Urquhart was able to plot the monarch's migratory route down to Texas, but there the butterflies once again seemed to disappear.

Finally in 1975, after 300,000 butterflies had been tagged, a call came from an excited American named Kenneth Brugger who was working in Mexico and had heard about Dr. Urquhart's request for clues to the monarch's mysterious winter home. Up in the Sierra Madre, at 9,500 feet above sea level in the state of Michoacán, Brugger came upon a sight that must have taken his breath away in the thin mountain air. There in the towering fir trees were tens of millions of monarch butterflies clinging to the trunks and branches. With butterfly densities approaching 4 million per acre, the evergreen forest was colored orange instead of green, and large limbs occasionally crashed to the ground from the weight of all the insects. After almost four decades of searching, the winter home of the monarch butterfly had at last been found, and Dr. Urquhart was able to witness the grandest insect spectacle on earth.

Although a few other butterflies, like the buckeye, painted lady, and the sulphurs, may move southward in autumn to the warmer states, the monarch is the only insect in the world to conduct a regular, annual mass migration in which every individual in the population takes part in

———Observations———

traveling a predictable route to a specific destination. Year after year every monarch butterfly east of the Rockies flies down to the same trees in the mountains of Central Mexico, arriving in November and December to about fifteen hidden valleys each only a few acres in size. Here, with air temperatures hovering just above freezing, over 200 million monarchs remain semidormant in the dense trees for four or five months—perfect conditions for conserving precious energy. Some scientists believe the monarch's migration strategy evolved after the Ice Ages, when this tropical butterfly began to disperse northward, following the spread of its only food plant, the milkweed, into the United States from Mexico and Central America. Unable to survive freezing temperatures, however, the monarch was forced to retreat back to its southern homeland each fall, thus giving rise to an annual migration pattern.

The overwintering monarchs occasionally leave their communal roosts to take moisture from streams and wet ground, especially toward the end of winter when warming temperatures begin to stir them for their return journey. In March they reawaken, mate, and begin to fly north to the United States. Males die soon after mating, but females begin to lay from four hundred to eight hundred eggs on milkweed plants as they travel. By June or July a few faded, tattered female monarchs make it back to the northern states and Canada, completing what may have been a three-thousand-mile round-trip odyssey.

It appears that most of the overwintering butterflies fail to return, however, and the fresh monarchs seen in early summer are their offspring, which have continued the northward journey to the homeland of their exhausted parents. This summer generation only lives about a month, but it gives birth to the late-summer monarchs, which will live nine to twelve months after navigating hundreds of miles over unknown terrain to secluded, mountainous forests they have never visited before. The owners of these forests and the Mexican government have agreed to preserve these sites as "monarch sanctuaries," ensuring that the king of butterflies will always find a safe winter haven.

28

Fall Flowers

Asters, goldenrods, and witch hazel

———*Observations*———

With the arrival of the autumnal equinox, summer is now officially over, and the nights once again are longer than the days. The so-called short-day plants have been gradually dominating the woods, fields, and roadsides with their flowers as daylength has been decreasing, and by now the sunnier, more open habitats portray a dazzling display of colors. As a preliminary exhibition to the annual fall foliage transformation that will shortly follow, the landscape is now covered with various shades of yellow, gold, purple, pink, and white from plants that open their flowers in response to the waning days of summer.

The majority of fall flowers belong to one of nature's most successful and widespread families of plants, the composites. The chief characteristic of these plants is the massing together and fusion of numerous tiny flowers into a central flower head. What appears to be a single daisy or sunflower is actually an aggregation of tiny "florets" clumped onto a common receptacle. The petals of the individual flowers have been fused together to form the florets, and a single "petal" of a daisy is actually an entire flower with several petals fused together and a full array of reproductive parts at its base.

These petallike flowers are called ray florets, and a few of the more familiar composites that possess only this arrangement are dandelion, chicory, and hawkweed. Other composites also contain so-called disk florets compressed into a cone or buttonlike mass in the central portion of the flower head, with the ray florets resembling petals encircling the margin. Composites that possess both disk and ray florets include asters, sunflowers, goldenrods, daisies, and black-eyed Susan. A third group of composites possesses only disk florets, sometimes compressed so tightly together that the plant portrays no open-headed flower appearance. Examples of these discoid composites are the thistles, burdocks, joe-pye weeds, white snakeroot, and ragweed. In most species of composites the disk florets produce the pollen and seeds while the rays function as colorful attractants for insect pollinators.

More than any other fall flowers, two groups stand out as the most abundant and diversified throughout the

Northeast: the asters and the goldenrods. More than fifty species of each of these composites exist in our region, and from late August through October they completely dominate the meadows, open woodlands, roadsides, and shores. A few species of goldenrods, like lance-leaved, early, and sweet, begin to flower in late July, but the real peak of the goldenrod explosion is around early September in the Adirondacks and northern New England, late September in southern New England, New York, and most of Pennsylvania, and lasting well into October in southern New Jersey. Some of the more familiar species (which can be identified with a good wildflower field guide like *Newcomb's Wildflower Guide* or Peterson's *A Field Guide to Wildflowers* on the basis of their leaves and the shapes of their flower heads) are Canada, blue-stemmed, rough-stemmed, gray, zigzag, tall, and late goldenrods. The most common coastal species is the large, attractive, somewhat succulent seaside goldenrod. There is even a white species (the rays are whitish and the disks pale yellow) known as silverrod. Perhaps the most attractive species of all is the bright golden, showy goldenrod, which brings the progression to a close throughout our region in October.

Although goldenrods have often been associated with hay fever (the real culprit is usually ragweed, which blooms at the same time), scientists now know that their pollen grains are too heavy and sticky to float in the wind. Instead, these plants are adapted to be pollinated by insects, and few, if any, flowers in our region attract as many species—over one thousand some naturalists claim. The rich supplies of pollen and nectar in goldenrods, advertised by their bright colors and sweet fragrances, are gathered by monarch and sulphur butterflies, white-faced hornets, paper wasps, yellow jackets, blister and soldier beetles, locust borers, honeybees and bumblebees, and syrphid flies, among the more easily recognized species. Well-camouflaged crab spiders and ambush bugs hide inside the flowers and patiently await their prey, and large *Argiope* and *Araneus* spiders (see chapter 22) string their orb webs among the plants to capture some of the pollinators. Goldfinches, which occasionally nest as late as September in our region, often construct their cup-shaped nests in goldenrod stems. Several species of flies and moths lay eggs in parts of the goldenrod, causing the plant to produce odd-looking swellings around the eggs and the larvae that soon hatch from them. Goldenrods are veritable zoos of living creatures in autumn, each one directly or indirectly relying on the flowers' bountiful resources.

The asters generally do not begin to compete with the goldenrods until later in summer, although at least one species, the violet colored large-leaf aster, blooms at the end of July, and the extremely common white wood aster dominates open woods in August. Not until later in September, however, do most of the other asters produce their flowers, and then, because this group of composites portrays a much more varied palette than the almost uniform goldenrods, there is a veritable burst of colors. Many asters are white (calico, panicled, heath, flat-topped, and small white), while others are lilac or blue-violet (New York, heart-leaved, and wavy-leaved), and a few of the largest and showiest, like the New England aster, are deep purple. This last species is extremely attractive to butterflies, especially the monarch, which uses its nectar as fuel during the first trek of its long journey to Mexico.

When the autumn flowers begin to pass their peak display and the forest trees begin to turn color, one final plant opens its buds and signals an end to the flowering season. Not until the very end of September or beginning of October does witch hazel produce the last flowers in the northeastern United States, and often the long, narrow, ribbonlike yellow petals do not appear on some of these plants until almost Halloween. With its small size and horizontal, zigzag branches, this twisted, multitrunked shrub is scarcely ever noticed in the shade of the towering oaks and maples. It rarely exceeds 15 feet in height (although some extraordinary specimens reach 40 feet and 5 inches in diameter). But the late appearance of its flowers and their lingering on the branches until well after the last of the forest's leaves have fallen to the ground suddenly make witch hazel a very conspicuous member of the autumn woods.

At the same time that its flowers appear, the fruits from last autumn's blossoms mature, having taken a year to fully ripen. These two-chambered, nutlike capsules have a unique way of dispersing their two shiny black seeds. As each fruit dries during autumn's Indian-summer days, it shrinks and contracts, slowly splitting open and forcing its slippery seeds out like bullets between its moist halves. Some seeds are ejected as far as 50 feet away from the shrub with loud snapping noises, leaving the empty, open fruit capsules to remain on the branches all winter.

The Onondaga Indians of New York are credited with teaching the white settlers how to extract the sap from witch hazel by boiling the leaves, twigs, and bark. When added to alcohol, it was once a very popular hair tonic, liniment for aching muscles, and rubbing solution for skin discomforts and inflammations. Today, its pleasant aroma and soothing feel are mostly memories of the past, although it continues to be manufactured in Connecticut, and bottles may still be seen in some barbershops and drugstores.

Witch hazel's most unusual use, which probably gave it its name, was as a "divining" or "witching rod" to find water or precious metals beneath the ground. According to folklore, a gifted individual can locate such commodities by holding a Y-shaped witch-hazel branch with a point held in each hand and the stem pointing forward and walking until it is mysteriously pulled downward by the force of underground water or buried gold. Even without this magical property (which has never been scientifically proven), witch hazel's jet-propelled seeds and spidery, Halloween blossoms make it a remarkable plant.

29

The Autumn Harvest

*Fruits and nuts
are gathered
by squirrels and
other wildlife*

————*Observations*————

For both humans and wildlife autumn is rightfully the season of plenty and the time of the harvest. As pumpkins ripen on the ground and delicious apples are picked off the trees, many kinds of wild fruits also mature in the woodlands. From fleshy fruits on low shrubs to hard nuts growing on the branches of the tallest trees, these fruits of fall are extremely valuable commodities for wildlife at this season of preparation. Birds strip berries off the branches to fuel their long migratory journeys; black bears fatten themselves on acorns before their winter sleep; animals such as the white-tailed deer and wild turkeys gorge themselves before the upcoming lean months; and mice, chipmunks, and squirrels store nuts at a feverish rate before the snow flies. Competition for autumn's fruits is intense, and there is no time to relax while the weather is still pleasant—chipmunks make over one hundred trips a day bringing food into their underground dens, and black bears have been known to feed up to twenty hours a day during this season of plenty.

Unlike the fruits of summer (see chapter 19), which are high in sugar content, autumn's berries are generally rich in lipids, which have twice the energy content of carbohydrates and are much more valuable than sweets to migratory birds at this season. High-lipid fruits include those of sassafras, spicebush, arrowwood (a viburnum), and several species of dogwood (flowering dogwood and several smaller shrubs like the red osier, silky, gray-stemmed, and round-leaf dogwoods). Migrating songbirds flock to these fruits in autumn on their way south, aiding in their dispersal when the seeds come out in their droppings miles away from the parent plants.

Berries that are low in lipids (less than 15 percent dry weight), like mountain ash, winterberry holly, greenbrier, highbush cranberry, maple-leaf viburnum, and the sumacs are often left to dry up on the branches where they are later used as winter foods by the birds that stay in the North. Interestingly, just as some of the summer-fruiting plants like blueberries and blackberries may advertise to birds the readiness of their fruits by passing through several bright colors as they ripen, the fall fruits are accompanied by similar attention-grabbing "flags" in their leaves, which are often among the earliest and brightest of the fall foliage displays (for example, black gum, or tupelo, Virginia creeper vine, poison ivy, and dogwoods).

By the end of September and beginning of October all the nut trees in our region are either bearing their ripe fruits on their branches or dropping them to the ground. Up until the early part of the twentieth century, one of the most prevalent and valuable of these species was the American chestnut, but a fungus "blight" accidentally introduced into this country from Europe spread rapidly throughout this tree's range and wiped it out in an unprecedented episode of exotic invasion and destruction. Today sprouts still pop up from the old root systems, and some even survive a few decades before succumbing to the fungus, but the chestnut is essentially gone from our region. Other nut trees have filled in the gaps in the forest and taken over a greater role in feeding wildlife.

Among the easiest nuts to notice are the black walnuts, since they ripen into large, green, limelike fruits that remain on the branches after the leaves drop off in early October. Once they fall to the ground, their pulpy green husks turn brown and mushy, and a strong, dark dye can be made from them. Black walnut is one of our most valuable trees because of its beautiful, strong, brown wood, which is used in fine furniture, but it is no longer as common along the floodplains and fertile valleys it once dominated. A smaller, more upland relative, butternut, bears similar fruits that are more ovoid in shape and covered with sticky hairs.

Closely related to the walnuts are the hickories, four species of which grow in the Northeast. In drier upland situations the mockernut and pignut hickories often become important elements of the mixed-oak forests. Pignut's husk is very thin, while mockernut's is thick, but both species contain very little meat in their nuts. In swamps, river floodplains, and other moist habitats, bitternut and shagbark hickories often grow side by side, the former with tight, smooth, striated bark and small, thin, bitter nuts, the latter with very distinctive, shaggy bark and large, thick, four-parted husks containing delicious, meaty nuts. Shagbark's nuts contain twice as many calories as

——Observations——

acorns and are always quickly gathered by squirrels, which remove the fragrant husks before burying them.

With its smooth, tight, silvery gray bark, one of the most beautiful and distinctive trees in our forests is the American beech. Closely related to the chestnut tree, the beech bears small burrlike fruits that are covered with weak, curved spines and split open into four parts to reveal a pair (sometimes three) of triangular nuts inside. In some years these delicious nuts are produced by the thousands and are eaten by almost every species of wildlife, but in other autumns the trees and the forest floor are empty of beechnuts.

Of all of nature's autumn bounty, none is more valuable to wildlife than the acorn. Rich in both fats and carbohydrates, these fruits of the oak trees are often responsible for the winter survival of many animals as well as their breeding success the following spring. Eight species of oaks are common in our northeastern region (white, red, black, scarlet, swamp white, pin, scrub, and chestnut), while an additional ten species barely enter our area from the west (bur and chinquapin oaks) and from the southern New Jersey pinelands and Long Island (post, swamp-chestnut, southern red, blackjack, willow, dwarf chinquapin, shingle, and water oaks).

Oaks belong to the same family as beech and chestnut, and they are usually divided into two separate groups based on the time it takes for their acorns to mature: the white oak group (including white, swamp white, bur, post, the chinquapins, and the two chestnut oaks), which takes only a single year for the acorns to mature and fall, and the red oak group, which requires two years for the acorns to mature (and both immature one-year acorns and ripe ones may occur simultaneously on the same tree). As a rule the white oak acorns are sweeter since they contain less tannic acid than those of the red oaks.

Wood ducks, wild turkeys, and ruffed grouse swallow acorns whole, allowing their gizzards to grind them up with the pebbles and other grit they contain. Grouse may swallow six to twelve whole acorns in a single meal. Blue jays store hundreds of acorns in hollow trees, and during autumns when oaks fail to produce many acorns, the jays migrate by the thousands. Black bears devour countless acorns, crunching them up with their powerful, flat-topped grinding molars as they consume up to twenty thousand calories per day during their autumn feeding binges. Acorns are also eaten by a variety of wildlife from crows to raccoons, and in the fall the white-tailed deer's diet may be 80 percent acorns. White-footed mice store them beneath stones and in empty bird nests and boxes, while flying squirrels stuff them into hollow trees and chipmunks hoard them in their underground hibernation burrows.

The one animal associated with acorns more than any other, however, is the ubiquitous gray squirrel. So dependent is this animal on acorns that over the past two centuries mass migrations involving millions of squirrels have been witnessed by naturalists in the East at irregular intervals whenever the oaks failed to produce acorns, probably as a result of late spring frosts killing the flower buds. Not as prevalent or as dramatic in the past few decades, a large migration of gray squirrels nevertheless occurred along the East Coast as recently as 1968.

Gray squirrels may rely on stored acorns for over half of each year, and they must replenish their supply annually since, unlike the pine and spruce cones stored by their cousins the red squirrels, buried acorns germinate within a year into oak seedlings. Each acorn is buried individually (again, unlike the red squirrel's habit of piling all its cones and nuts in a big "cache") in a hole, which is then refilled with soil by the squirrel and carefully covered with dead leaves. Even captive squirrels instinctively try to bury acorns indoors.

Experiments at Princeton University's woods have finally settled the argument about how gray squirrels find these acorns in winter. Their sense of smell is extremely acute, and they can detect buried acorns even beneath the snow. But when the snow cover is too deep for the acorn's odor to be sensed, the gray squirrel can rely on its memory. Over 90 percent of the acorns and nuts buried each fall are subsequently uncovered and eaten, but not necessarily by the same squirrels that buried them—they may "pirate" the caches of other gray squirrels, red squirrels, chipmunks, and even blue jays. Enough nuts are left forgotten and undetected, however, to germinate and sprout into the beeches, oaks, and hickories of tomorrow's forests.

30

Flaming Fall Foliage

The colors peak

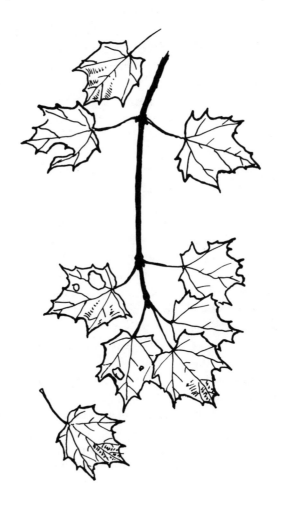

Observations

Long before autumn officially arrives, the subtle transformation of the forest begins in the Northeast. As early as Labor Day weekend the leaves of the red maple, highbush blueberry, and sour gum start to turn reddish, and vines such as Virginia creeper and poison ivy suddenly become highly visible as their leaves change to brilliant shades of red against the dark trunks and green foliage of their hosts. But now, during the first weeks of October, the weather changes, and with it comes one of nature's most electrifying transformations: green gradually giving way to an incredible array of other colors.

The peak of this display varies throughout our northeastern region, generally occurring by the end of the first week of October in the Adirondacks and the mountainous areas of New England; by mid-October in Pennsylvania, central and western New York, and southern New England; and the last week in October in New Jersey and southern New York, where the late-changing oaks dominate the woodlands. "Leaf-peekers" travel by the thousands to the more scenic, rural landscapes throughout the Northeast to follow autumn's progression, contributing greatly to the local economies. This breathtaking show of color is without a doubt enjoyed by more spectators than any other natural event of the year.

No other area of the world presents such an exciting annual display of colorful foliage. There are some forests in eastern China, parts of Japan, and small areas in southwestern Europe and southern South America where the leaves turn color, but nowhere does it match the intensity, variety, and vastness found in our northeastern forests. Even the transformations of the aspens and oaks in the western United States pale in comparison with the kaleidoscope of color seen on a New England mountainside or Adirondack lakeshore in early October. Almost every imaginable color is present in the forest and reflected off the clear, still waters.

What makes our region so unique in this respect? One reason is the great diversity of trees and shrubs growing here—as many species as in all of Europe. But, more important, the season of autumn arrives here much more suddenly than in Europe. No sooner does the summer vacation end and another school year begin than the balmy, warm weather of summer gives way to the cool, crisp, clear weather of autumn. The fall colors depend very much on this typical northeastern autumn weather, and in areas of the world where the seasons merge into one another much more gradually and imperceptibly, the colorful phenomenon is just not as striking.

The annual autumn display is ultimately rooted in the deciduous habit of most species of northeastern trees. Farther north, in the evergreen spruce-fir forests of Canada, and in the Southeast, where pines and evergreen oaks dominate, there is very little color transformation. In the temperate-zone forests of our latitudes, however, most trees and shrubs experience an annual loss of leaves in preparation for winter. This is an adaptation to protect the plants against desiccation rather than cold weather. The broad, thin leaves of oaks, maples, hickories, and other species lose a tremendous amount of moisture to the air by transpiration during the summer months, and this water is constantly being replaced from the ground. During the winter months, when the air is much drier and the ground water frozen into ice, these leaves would experience excessive drying as well as damage to their cells by constant freezing and thawing. Thus, to prevent the destruction of their leaves, deciduous trees and shrubs simply shed them each fall and replace them during the following growing season. Starting at the end of the summer, layers of spongy, corky cells form at the base of each leaf stalk. Then, just above these cells there forms an additional "abscission," or separation layer of cells, which finally breaks the leaf's connection with the twig and causes it to fall off in the wind or rain, leaving the corky layers to function as protective scar tissue over the dry winter months.

Fortunately for the hordes of tourists flocking into the Northeast every autumn, this separation of leaves is preceded by another annual transformation. As temperatures get cooler and days become shorter in September and October, chlorophyll (the chemical that plays a major role in photosynthesis for all green plants), begins to disappear from the leaves. Normally replaced by the plant on a regular basis throughout the summer, chlorophyll is now no

————Observations————

longer manufactured, and whatever is left in the leaves begins to break down. This change may be related to a "salvage operation" being initiated at this time by the tree or shrub in response to the shorter, cooler days of autumn. Useful materials like carbohydrates are transformed into simpler substances (sugars) and then transported from the leaves to the roots, where they will be stored until needed again next spring. It is thought that an accumulation of sugars in the leaf during cooler weather is responsible for the decay of chlorophyll.

Once the chlorophyll disappears, other pigments that have always been present in the leaves in much smaller amounts begin to show up. Like the chlorophyll pigments, carotenes (oranges and yellows) and xanthophylls (pale yellows and tans) are present all summer in special pigment cells called plastids, but they are masked by the much more abundant green pigment until it disappears in fall. In certain trees and shrubs other pigments called anthocyanins also begin to form at this time in the cell sap in response to the sugars accumulating in the leaves. The higher the sugar content, the more anthocyanins are produced. These new pigments are water soluble and very sensitive to the pH of the sap: purplish colors result when the sap is neutral or slightly alkaline, while reds form in acid sap. There are also chemicals called tannins that are responsible for many of the tans and bronzes in the oaks and beeches, and which eventually turn all leaves brown after they fall to the ground.

Different species of trees and shrubs exhibit different combinations of pigments each fall, which contributes to the variety of colors in the autumn landscape. Some trees—like the tulip tree, cottonwood, witch hazel, striped maple, birches, aspens, and hickories—always turn yellow or gold in autumn, showing hardly any variance from year to year. The sumacs, blueberries, sour gums, and scarlet oaks almost always turn a vivid, solid red, the result of anthocyanin pigments and a low pH (acidic) sap. Other species exhibit more of a variety from year to year, even during the same year among different individuals of the same species in the same area. Red maple, for example, can turn red, orange, or yellow in the same forest, and some white oaks and white ashes may display beautiful burgundy or dark maroon foliage, while others simply turn brown. A single sassafras tree may have pink, red, orange, and yellow leaves, while the beautiful sweet gum often adds purple to these four colors on a single branch, especially if the sap in the leaves has a neutral pH. The most beautiful and famous autumn tree of all, however, is the sugar maple. Its flaming, golden orange and red foliage, resulting from a combination of xanthophyll and anthocyanin pigments, is responsible for more autumn snapshots, New England postcards and calendars, and picturesque regional "coffee-table books" than any other northeastern tree.

There is also a certain sequence exhibited by the trees and shrubs as they change color each year. Sour gum (also called tupelo or black gum) is usually the first to turn color, followed through September by red maple, sumac, Virginia creeper, and poison ivy. Black, yellow, and white birch, sugar maple, and sassafras are also rather early. Among the later species are the tulip tree, the aspens, and huckleberry, while the oaks are generally the last hardwoods to turn brown and lose their leaves. The fall foliage display ends during the last days of October when tamarack, or American larch—the only deciduous conifer in the North—begins to drop its feathery needles after they've turned a brilliant gold amidst the dark green spruces of boreal bogs.

With all these variables—sap pH, sugar content, pigment type, tree species—coming into play, it's not surprising that autumn's painted landscape is never the same from year to year. The biggest factor determining the brilliance of fall's foliage, however, is the weather. Cool, clear nights and bright, dry, sunny days usually bring on the most fabulous colors since these conditions cause a more rapid and complete breakdown of chlorophyll and a higher concentration of sugars trapped in the leaves. A prolonged Indian summer, with abnormally warm weather, will result in more subdued colors or in the fading away of colors already present on the trees. Strong winds and rain will knock off the leaves before their colors can be enjoyed, and a hard frost often causes leaves to fall off before

——Observations——

——Observations——

they've even had a chance to turn color. Fortunately, northeastern autumns are usually characterized by at least several spells of this cool, bright weather. In some years when winds, heavy rains, and hard frosts are absent, the colorful leaves may remain on the branches into late October—or even November in New Jersey and Long Island—providing for an extended enjoyment of nature's most attractive annual display.

31

Hibernating Herptiles

Snakes, turtles, frogs, and salamanders retreat underground

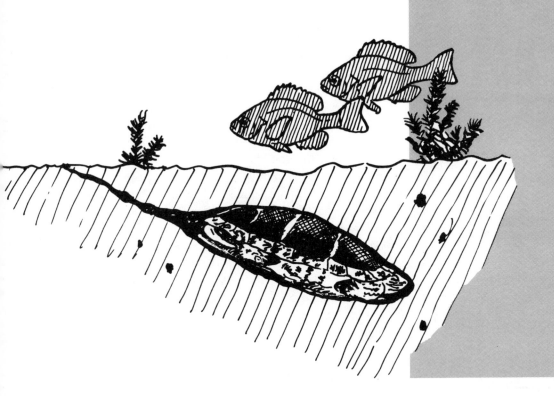

——————*Observations*——————

Nights are much cooler now, and the sun spends less time warming the earth in the Northern Hemisphere as it sets earlier with each passing day. Some Indian-summer days may interrupt this cooling trend when warm breezes blow from the south, but these offer just a temporary respite from the frosty weather that will soon arrive and take hold of all living things for the next five or six months. Mammals continue to gorge themselves on autumn's bounty or to store seeds and nuts in underground burrows to prepare for the approaching lean months, and late migrating birds like sparrows, blackbirds, ducks, geese, and some hawks continue to forsake the Northeast for more southern refuges.

For some species of wildlife, however, once the cold weather arrives there is no other choice but to retreat to some protected burrow or den and to lapse into a state of dormancy. The cold-blooded vertebrates—fish, amphibians, and reptiles—have no wings with which to migrate to warmer climates. Nor do they have the ability to internally regulate their body temperatures like the warm-blooded birds and mammals and remain warm and active through the winter. As environmental temperatures drop, so do their body temperatures, bringing about a drastic reduction of their metabolic rates, a sudden slowdown of their activities, and the danger of being left out in the potentially lethal cold. The choices are very limited: either find some place to hibernate where the freezing temperatures can't reach them or somehow survive the winter in a frozen state until spring arrives. By late October the days of activity for these animals quickly dwindle down to a precious few.

Although, as many ice fishermen can attest, some fish, like the yellow perch, pickerel, and trout, remain somewhat active throughout the winter months, others like the carp, sunfish, and bass sink down to the lower depths of the lakes and ponds and become dormant for most of the winter. The snapping, musk, painted, and other aquatic turtles likewise sink into the mud at the bottom of ponds and enter a state of suspended animation, as does the diamondback terrapin of the Atlantic coastal estuaries—the only turtle capable of hibernating in both fresh and salt water. A painted turtle's heartbeat may decrease to as low as once every ten minutes (less than 1 percent of its summer rate), and breathing may cease entirely, although blood vessels in the anal opening may function like a gill in taking in some oxygen. Bullfrogs and green frogs also spend the winter in the bottom muck, taking in what little oxygen they need during hibernation directly through their skins.

A few aquatic herptiles actually may remain semi-active beneath the ice during the winter by becoming "cold tolerant," that is, by adjusting their metabolic rates upward after being in cold water for a certain amount of time. Ice skaters are sometimes surprised to see the salamanders known as red-spotted newts slowly wiggling in the frigid waters beneath the ice. This amphibian is one of the first to reproduce in spring, males and females beginning to pair off as soon as the ice melts away from the lakes and ponds. Wood turtles also occasionally leave their winter dens in muskrat burrows or holes beneath the banks of streams and ponds in winter, and they, too, have been seen swimming beneath the ice during the cold months. Stream salamanders like the two-lined and northern red salamanders spend the winter beneath stones and gravel in the icy flowing waters, where they may be active (but sluggish) in water temperatures as low as 35 degrees Fahrenheit. Another brook species, the dusky salamander, goes into hibernation under stones in the deeper pools and, like most northern amphibians, doesn't become active again until spring.

Terrestrial reptiles and amphibians can't simply sink down into the soft mud and await the return of warmer spring weather. They must somehow dig down into the soil or find ready-made burrows or rock crevices extending down deeply enough to escape the subfreezing temperatures that would turn their blood and body fluids to ice. Some salamanders, like the ubiquitous red-backed salamander and the large, subterranean spotted salamander, dig down as deep as 15 inches below the forest's leaf litter. The American toad may burrow as far as 18 inches below the woodland floor, and a more northern cousin, the Manitoba toad, has been known to dig 4 feet down into gopher

—————*Observations*—————

mounds to escape the deadly Canadian freezing weather. Eastern box turtles may retreat into underground chambers 3 feet deep and then tightly close their shells until the ground warms up again in April or May.

For snakes the problem of finding a winter retreat is even more critical. Lacking claws and limbs, they are incapable of burrowing into hard or stony soils to escape the frost. The northern water snake may hibernate beneath the overhanging banks of a pond or stream or even under a few inches of water in a spring where temperatures remain above freezing. Garter snakes have also occasionally been seen hibernating in large groups underwater in cisterns, and scientists believe that, like aquatic frogs, their skins function as gills in straining from the water what little oxygen they need for their hearts to beat only once or twice a minute during hibernation.

Most garter snakes, however, prefer to hibernate in drier dens on land, and it is to these sites that they and other snakes are sometimes drawn en masse during the cooler days of October. On October 12, 1989, I uncovered 22 eastern milk snakes, 6 red-bellied snakes, and 2 northern ring-necked snakes getting ready to retire for the winter beneath a pile of small rocks no larger in area than a small room. The following autumn I returned to find 27 milk snakes in the same rock pile.

Other naturalists have come across even more spectacular aggregations of serpents in winter dens: 75 northern brown snakes and 10 garter snakes in an old rodent burrow; 148 smooth green snakes and 8 garter snakes in the same anthill; and seven different species of snakes, a toad, a frog, and a salamander all hibernating together in one circular ant mound. A scarcity of good, safe winter dens certainly results in strange bedfellows! These sites are used year after year by the same snakes and their offspring, especially in the case of rattlesnakes, copperheads, and black snakes, which require deeper crevices and rock cavities (see chapter 24).

In recent years some remarkable new details about the winter-survival adaptations of some reptiles and amphibians in our region have been discovered. Instead of digging down deep below the frost line, a few species merely retreat below a rotten log or stump or cover themselves with a few inches of leaf litter for the duration of the winter. Somehow these creatures manage to survive the cold months even though they are reached by the subfreezing temperatures. Like many overwintering insects, these herptiles are capable of "supercooling"—lowering the freezing point of their body fluids below 32 degrees Fahrenheit by eliminating plasma proteins, foreign bacteria, food particles, and other "nuclei," or "seed crystals," around which ice would form. In effect they stabilize the liquid state of their body fluids at temperatures that would normally freeze them solid. Some species also have been found to load their body fluids with glycerol, an antifreeze compound that further lowers their freezing point—just like it does in an automobile's radiator during winter—allowing the temperature of their internal fluids to fall well below 32 degrees Fahrenheit without turning into ice.

Still more amazing is the discovery of four species of northeastern frogs and at least one turtle that routinely survive the winter frozen solid like ice cubes! Instead of fighting the cold or resisting the deep freeze, these creatures turn into ice until the spring thaw. The wood frog, spring peeper, gray treefrog, and striped chorus frog all apparently have the ability to spend the winter with up to 65 percent of their body water as ice. Baby painted turtles, after hatching from their eggs in nests 3 or 4 inches below the ground in September, may not emerge until the following May. During that seven- or eight-month period they may experience freezing and thawing episodes several times without injury. In their frozen state these frogs and turtles are characterized by no movement, breathing, blood circulation, or heartbeat—truly a state of suspended animation!

Research during the late 1980s and early 1990s has revealed some of the secrets of the seemingly impossible ability of these creatures to survive being frozen alive. Of crucial importance is limiting the formation of ice outside the cells to eliminate possible cell damage and death. By forming proteins ("seed crystals") in the fluids outside the cells (extracellular spaces, blood plasma, abdominal cavity), these frogs and baby turtles control the formation of

————*Observations*————

ice in the parts where it won't cause cellular injury and keep harmful ice crystals from growing inside the cells.

Furthermore, to prevent the rupture or collapse of the cell membranes from their contents leaking out into the extracellular ice, these animals flood their bodies with massive quantities of glucose (or glycerol in the case of the gray treefrog) as soon as their skins begin to freeze in winter. Protected by these "cryopreservatives," these herptiles remain dormant until the spring, with metabolic rates only 1 to 10 percent of normal levels. Then, as the snow melts and the ground thaws out, so do their body fluids, and they miraculously travel to the ponds and wetlands to begin another season.

32

Flying in Formation

OCTOBER IV

Ducks and geese move southward

Observations

There is something about a flock of migrating Canada geese in October that stirs the spirit of any onlooker. Flying in unison, usually in a V formation, their approach is first noticed by their distant honking as members of the flock communicate their positions to each other. The honking becomes louder and louder until that group of distant dots coming from the north grows into hundreds of flapping geese passing overhead in the late autumn sky. This breathtaking sight exerts a profound effect on the onlooker's imagination: Where have these symbols of the wild come from, and what is their destination? How do they find their direction during their long annual journeys? Unlike the small songbirds, migrating waterfowl are highly visible, and their movements are much easier to follow. Upon seeing their passage through the autumn skies, one can't help but wonder about the magic and mysteries of nature's seasonal events.

Canada geese are the most noticeable and familiar of over thirty species of waterfowl (ducks, geese, and swans) that migrate through our region along the Atlantic Flyway each year. Flocks may begin passing overhead in early October, but their peak numbers are reached near the end of the month when thousands thunder out of the northern skies en route to wintering areas from New Jersey to North Carolina, especially the Chesapeake Bay and Delmarva peninsula. At the end of October and early November two other geese, the snow goose and the smaller brant, join these Canada geese in their wintering areas. New Jersey's coastal wildlife refuges—like Brigantine—offer great opportunities to see tens of thousands of these three geese through the winter months.

Over twenty-five species of ducks also migrate along the Atlantic coast each autumn. The most familiar are the nine species of "puddle ducks," or "dabblers," which feed on lakes, ponds, and marshes by dabbling near the surface with their bills or upending their bodies to reach down a little deeper for aquatic vegetation. This group includes the mallard, wood duck, black duck, pintail, shoveler, gadwall, widgeon, and the blue-winged and green-winged teal. Swamps of the Deep South become the winter homes for tremendous numbers of these ducks, but stragglers of many species can be seen throughout the winter, especially near our coastal regions.

The rest of our ducks are divers, completely submerging their bodies beneath the water and swimming after aquatic vegetation, mollusks, insects, crustaceans, or fish. Groups of these ducks periodically disappear from view below the surface (often in unison), and then reappear as if by magic a short distance away. Of the divers, the so-called sea and bay ducks make up the largest subfamily, with fifteen different species showing up in our region. Besides their diving behavior, these ducks can be differentiated from the puddle ducks by their method of leaving the water: They run and patter their feet along the surface before taking to the air, whereas the puddle ducks take off directly into the air. Most of the ducks in this group breed far to the north in the tundra pools, marshes, and coastal estuaries of Canada, although a few—like the lesser scaup, common goldeneye, and ring-necked duck—enter extreme northern United States, and the canvasback and redhead extend their ranges into the midwestern prairie potholes. During the winter the Atlantic coastal waters are home to the three scoters (surf, white-winged, and black), the oldsquaw, and the greater scaup. The harlequin duck, king eider, and common eider overwinter mainly along the New England coast, where they are seen diving into the ocean for food. The common goldeneye, canvasback, and redhead spend the winter mainly in coastal bays but are also found on some of the larger inland lakes and rivers. This is even more true for the lesser scaup, bufflehead, and ring-necked duck, which often spend the winter on the inland lakes, ponds, and marshes of the southern states.

Another subfamily of diving ducks includes the three mergansers—common, red-breasted, and hooded. These fish-eating ducks have sawtoothed edges on their bills for holding slippery fish and are somewhat similar to loons in profile. The red-breasted merganser spends the winter along our Atlantic coast after breeding in Canada, and the common merganser is often the only duck to remain on our New England and Adirondack rivers during the cold months (the hooded merganser leaves the ponds and lakes of our northeastern woods for the southern states in win-

———*Observations*———

ter). Finally, the small, squat ruddy duck leaves its midwestern and Canadian wetlands to spend the winter in the southern states and the salt bays along our Atlantic coast.

Like the geese, the ducks migrate mainly in October, often flying in formations similar to their larger relatives. These may be tight, symmetrical Vs or long, undulating, diagonal lines. It is thought that the leaders of these formations are generally the older, more experienced geese and ducks that are familiar with the migratory route. These leaders expend more energy by breaking into the wind, and they will occasionally exchange places with other more rested birds that have been encountering less resistance by trailing in line, or "drafting."

Waterfowl migrate both day and night, landing when they are tired, feeding for a while, and then taking off again to continue their journey. Some species, however, are capable of some unbelievable flight records. Snow geese may fly as far as eighteen hundred miles nonstop to their wintering areas, and brant may actually fly twice that distance without stopping in just two and a half days, maintaining an average speed of fifty or sixty miles per hour! Blue-winged teal have been known to migrate as much as four thousand miles to their winter homes, stopping at several resting areas along the way. In clear skies snow geese and Canada geese may fly over a mile high, but heavy cloud cover may bring them down to just a few hundred feet so they can better scan their surroundings and guideposts. In such conditions they often become much more vocal, possibly to remain aware of each other's positions, and the honking of flocks of low-flying geese can easily be heard by humans walking below, even though the birds are invisible in the thick clouds.

Many of our waterfowl species are in deep trouble. Their numbers have been declining greatly over the past thirty to forty years, as verified by counts recorded by the United States Fish and Wildlife Service. Totals for all species throughout the country have fallen from 45 million in 1975 to just 31 million at the end of the 1980s. A comparison between counts taken by the Service in 1956 and 1988 showed declines of 25 percent for the blue-winged teal and over 50 percent for pintail, mallard, and black duck. Scaup and canvasback populations are also way down. In New Jersey, where 30 percent of all the black ducks in the Atlantic Flyway spend the winter, decreases have been as much as 60 percent since 1950.

Scientists all agree on two factors as the most probable causes for these serious declines in our duck populations. Both at the national level and along the Atlantic coast, where a great many waterfowl have traditionally spent the winter, the loss of wetlands has been staggering. Over 50 percent of our historic total acreages of swamps, marshes, bogs, and other wetlands valued by waterfowl for both breeding and wintering habitats have been lost to development—drained, filled in, or otherwise destroyed for agriculture, second homes, industrial sites, highways, or shopping malls.

The second probable cause is the loss of productivity in our remaining wetlands, ponds, and lakes from pollution and acid rain. The population declines noted for the various species of waterfowl since 1955 have a definite correlation in time with the increased industrial emissions responsible for acid rain. Acidified lakes and ponds throughout the Northeast have become biological "deserts," with hardly any insects or other invertebrates capable of surviving in the low pH waters. Thus fewer and fewer fish manage to find enough food. All waterfowl require high-protein diets (insects, crustaceans) during their first weeks, and many continue to include insects and fish in their diets when they are mature. When these organisms disappear from their habitats, so do the waterfowl.

Wetlands are now protected by law, both at the federal level and by many states, and in 1990 the new Clean Air Act included key provisions to reduce acid rain. In 1986 the North American Waterfowl Management Plan was formulated by both Canada and the United States, with the aim of preserving wetlands and maintaining minimum populations of both breeding and migratory waterfowl of fifteen different species. The plan recommends the protection of a million acres of waterfowl habitat in both countries, and during the last few years joint ventures among federal, state (or provincial), and private conservation groups have already initiated land-preservation projects designed

—————*Observations*—————

to reverse the downward population trends in many of our ducks.

As an example of how an animal can stage a comeback if given sufficient and protected habitat, one need look no farther than the familiar Canada goose. In the early 1900s the goose was down to very low numbers due mainly to market hunting. Today it has increased so remarkably (between $1^1/_2$ and 2 million along the Atlantic Flyway alone) that it is actually considered to be a pest around golf courses, lawns, parks, beaches, and lakes, where its prodigious droppings foul the grounds and waters.

The establishment of numerous wildlife refuges throughout the East is probably a chief cause in the goose's exploding numbers. Geese quickly populated these thousands of acres of new habitat extensively managed and planted with food crops, and many became nonmigratory, breeding residents, choosing to remain all year rather than fly back north in spring. These resident geese in turn attracted other migrants, which also remained. Soon there was a shift in the breeding, migratory, and wintering locations of Canada geese along the Atlantic Flyway. Although the majority of these geese still breed in the arctic and subarctic areas of Canada west to Alaska, now a substantial number stay in the mid-Atlantic and northeastern regions all year long. Until the 1950s the main wintering areas were in North Carolina, but there has been a northward shift to the Chesapeake Bay, Delmarva area, and even New Jersey and New York. Up to eighty thousand Canada geese now spend the winter in central New York's Cayuga Lake!

The surplus goose populations from these new habitats have now dispersed to urban and town parks, where they are fed and encouraged to remain by people and where they are free from predators and hunting. Nearby farms provide them with ample food in the form of corn, soybeans, wheat, rye, barley, and other grain, but this has only increased their status as a pest in many areas. Some estimates of the numbers of "urban geese" in our country run into the hundreds of thousands. Solutions have ranged from destroying eggs to sterilizing the males to transporting hundreds of geese to other areas of Canada and the

United States where their numbers are still low, but Canada geese remain a problem in some northeastern communities. Like white-tailed deer, wild turkeys, and a few other very successful animals, the Canada goose serves as a reminder that wildlife species are capable of extraordinary comebacks if given a helping hand and ample habitat.

—————*Observations*—————

33

On Northwest Winds

NOVEMBER I

The last and biggest raptors make their appearances

————Observations————

By the end of October the magnificent migration of birds of prey through our region has experienced a change of cast (see chapter 26). Gone are the broad-winged hawks, the ospreys, and the three falcons, and the flights of sharp-shinned and Cooper's hawks have dwindled down to just a handful of birds per day. Now appearing in greater numbers and gradually peaking in November are the turkey vulture, the three big buteos (red-tailed, red-shouldered, and rough-legged hawks), the rare goshawk, and the biggest raptors of all, the bald and golden eagles. Gone also are the big crowds of hawk-watchers now that September's warmth, October's flaming foliage, and daily flights of thousands of broad-wings are recent memories. But the thrill of seeing the huge, powerful raptors of November still draws people to the hawk lookouts to brave the frigid weather and northwest winds.

One earlier hawk that continues to migrate in November is the harrier, or marsh hawk, but now, instead of mostly immature and female birds, the majority of those passing the lookouts are adult males. These beautiful birds are easily recognized by their silver gray backs, white underparts, long, narrow tails, very long, narrow wings with jet black wing tips, and white rumps that show up when the harriers tilt and rock back and forth in flight. (Females and immatures are much darker above and below.) At Hawk Mountain and other Appalachian vistas male harriers peak at the end of October and early November, when 20 or 30 per day are seen. As many as 50 per day migrate over Cape May in November, and two or three times that number have been counted on peak days in mid-November at lookouts on the northern shore of Lake Erie.

Turkey vultures make their biggest flights during this same period—somewhat earlier around the Great Lakes than along the coast and inland ridges. These huge, dark raptors may spend the winter months as far away as South America, although in recent years a few have been wintering in New Jersey and southern Pennsylvania. Tremendous numbers are sometimes observed migrating through Central America in late October. On October 28, 1967, over 100,000 vultures flew over Panama in a single day! Turkey vultures have been expanding their range northward in the past few decades, and in 1989 new seasonal records for this raptor were set at Cape May (1,033) and Holiday Beach (over 12,500).

The most erratic of all raptors is the goshawk, the biggest and most powerful of our area's three accipiter hawks. A big female stands 27 inches high, weighs over 3 pounds, has a wingspread of almost 4 feet, and will even attack humans who happen to come too close to her nest. Mostly Canadian in their breeding distribution, goshawks periodically "invade" the United States in late fall and winter in great numbers when their food supplies (rabbits, hares, grouse, and other birds) are insufficient in Canada. These movements were particularly noticeable during 1962–64 and 1972–74, when unusually high numbers of goshawks were counted at the hawk lookouts. Cape May, which usually averages about 10 goshawks per year, counted over 100 in 1973, and Hawk Mountain recorded 428 in 1972, well over their average annual total of 80. Following such unusual peak years, goshawk numbers suddenly fall down to 5 or 20 birds per year for a while before hitting another "irruption" perhaps a decade later. There is still much to be learned about the population dynamics of the goshawk.

The rarest of the three big buteos in November is the rough-legged hawk, a large, strikingly patterned, black-and-white hawk from northern Canada, which comes in both light and dark color phases. Many inland sites see only 5 or 10 of these rare raptors each year, and even Hawk Mountain's annual average total is only 15. The Great Lakes region substantially exceeds these numbers, since lookouts there are closer to the rough-legged hawk's Canadian homeland. Hawk Cliff and Holiday Beach, both on the northern shore of Lake Erie, average 43 and 138 rough-legged hawks, respectively, with the best daily flights occurring throughout November.

The smaller red-shouldered hawk—a handsome, reddish brown buteo with narrow black-and-white bands across its tail—is counted in numbers approaching 30 or 40 per day at Hawk Mountain in late October and early

———Observations———

November, with annual totals averaging about 300. Cape May's annual average is 500, while Holiday Beach almost doubles that number, recording as many as 1,400 in 1987.

Of all the raptors, the one species that truly owns the month of November is the red-tailed hawk, the only species to sometimes reach four digits in its daily total at this time. At Cape May, Hawk Mountain, Raccoon Ridge, Holiday Beach, and most other prominent hawk lookouts, red-tailed hawks reach their peak from about November 5 to 15. No other species can fill the cold, windy November skies but this one, and its ability to master the strong updrafts rebounding off the ridges during its migration is a pleasure to behold. On calmer days the red-tail soars in wide circles, showing its white underparts, dark belly band, and wide, reddish brown tail against the clear blue sky.

Up to 500 red-tails per day are counted in early November at Hawk Mountain, where annual totals average 4,000. At Cape May, where it peaks a little later in the month, up to 400 have been seen on days following sustained northerly winds, which tend to blow them closer to the coast. Waggoner's Gap, southwest of Hawk Mountain, had 748 red-tailed hawks on November 1, 1987, and New Jersey's Raccoon Ridge counted 951 on November 12, 1989. As with the other buteos, however, the records belong to the Lake Erie lookouts, where up to 1,500 red-tails pass by in a single day in November and where in 1987 over 9,000 red-tails were counted at Holiday Beach.

Finally, there are the eagles, a single sighting of which can make any hawk-watcher's day a memorable one. In November bald eagles from Canada pass this way, en route to overwintering destinations on northern lakes, rivers, reservoirs, and coastal estuaries. Eight of these Canadian eagles were seen at Raccoon Ridge on November 12, 1989. On that same day 7 migrating golden eagles were seen at Montclair Quarry for the second day in a row!

Until the 1930s, when Hawk Mountain began counting migrating raptors, the presence of the golden eagle (a common raptor in the western United States) in the East was thought to be mostly accidental. But when low numbers of this huge, most powerful American raptor were counted there each year, a resident eastern breeding population was suspected and later verified in the wilds of New England, the Adirondack Mountains, and eastern Canada. In 1987 Hawk Mountain broke their annual golden eagle record with 98—and 14 were counted on a single day, November 12 (Raccoon Ridge counted 17 that day). In that same year nearby Waggoner's Gap set a new golden eagle record with 123, including 12, 16, and 16 counted on November 5, 6, and 14, respectively. What a glorious way to bring an end to another migration season!

———*Observations*———

34

The Shredders and Decomposers

————Observations————

At the end of each autumn residents of the northern United States witness one of nature's most complete transformations: the annual fall of leaves onto the forest floor. It has been estimated that up to 10 million leaves fall from the trees each autumn on every acre of ground in a northeastern deciduous forest, suddenly leaving bare and gray a forest that was ablaze with fall colors just a few days before. These dead leaves, together with branches, nuts, and other organic debris, may amount to as much as $1^1/_2$ to 2 tons added to each acre of forest every year. It seems miraculous that the forest isn't buried in its own wastes, but another profound transformation that follows the annual leaf fall prevents this from happening.

This second event occurs largely without notice or fanfare, hidden from view within the forest litter and humus, but its importance to the life of the forest is unmatched by any other process during the year. Once the dead leaves are delivered to the forest floor at the end of fall, it becomes a natural recycling center that shreds, disintegrates, softens, and decomposes the forest's wastes and remains. Billions of organisms in this lowest layer of the forest digest the dead organic matter and break it down into simpler components that can be reused by the living trees, shrubs, ferns, and wildflowers. In this way nitrogen, carbon, and other elements present in the dead matter are recycled back into the soil. Thus, the forest floor is directly or indirectly responsible for the continuation of all life in the community, since without its recycling organisms, essential nutrients would remain locked up in the forest's organic matter.

The time required for this breakdown varies from plant to plant. Some leaves, like those of the tulip tree and birch, may completely decompose in a year; others, like oak and beech, require at least two years; while pine needles may take three or four years to fully return to the soil.

Each square foot of forest soil and leaf litter contains literally billions of organisms in just the top 2 or 3 inches. Most of these are microscopic fungi and bacteria, by far the most important agents of decomposition in a forest. In the humid, stable environment beneath the leaf litter these invisible organisms quietly work on the forest's remains, secreting enzymes that render the dead leaves and wood soft and spongy. Then this partially decomposed organic matter is shredded apart and further utilized by other larger soil organisms like millipedes, sowbugs, pillbugs (small, hard terrestrial crustaceans that can roll up into an armored ball like an armadillo), slugs, snails, mites, and springtails.

These last creatures are tiny, very primitive, wingless insects that can leap several inches by releasing a forked, taillike appendage bent under their bodies. Springtails (also known as collembola) may number two thousand per square foot of forest soil, and by parting the leaf litter they can be seen jumping and running about. Soil mites may outnumber the springtails by seven to one and, like the other soil animals, they feed on both the partially decayed plant matter and the bacteria and fungi that coat these soft, dead leaves.

One of the most valuable members of the soil community is the earthworm, a half million of which may inhabit each acre of forest. Worms increase the soil's productivity not only by shredding and eating dead leaves and converting them to rich feces ("castings") but also by mixing different layers of soil, aerating it, and allowing water to penetrate via their extensive tunnel systems.

The soil decomposer organisms are eaten by other small animals in the leaf litter as part of a very complex food web. Predatory mites, tiny pseudoscorpions, spiders, ground beetles, ants, and centipedes feed on the smaller soil animals like springtails, sowbugs, and worms; and they in turn are eaten by moles, shrews, salamanders, toads, and birds. Larger predators like weasels, hawks, snakes, owls, and foxes comprise still another level. For all these creatures, from the tiniest to the largest, the end is the same: decomposition by the soil organisms and a return of their elements to the ground.

After the leaves fall each November, there is another theater where the act of decomposition is carried on in a vigorous way. Countless dead leaves wind up in the streams, rivers, and ponds, either by falling directly into these waters or by being swept in by wind or rain. Just as in the forest soil, there are numerous tiny underwater organisms waiting for this valuable source of energy found in the leaves' organic carbon. In fact, recent research in New York, New Hampshire, and other states has found that some streams derive almost all of their energy from leaves and other organic matter that come into them from the land.

Again, bacteria and fungi prepare the way by coating the dead leaves and softening them as they break them down. Then, larger aquatic creatures like stonefly nymphs, crane fly larvae, caddisfly larvae, and isopods (freshwater relatives of the sowbugs) shred apart the leaves and consume both their bits and pieces and the fungi and bacteria coating them. Other aquatic insects like mayfly nymphs, blackfly and midge larvae, and other species of stoneflies and crane flies, which have smaller, less powerful mouthparts than the "shredders," filter out smaller leaf fragments as well as shredder feces from the water for their sources of food.

These decomposer animals are often victims of predators just like their terrestrial counterparts. Dragonfly nymphs, water bugs, diving beetles, hellgrammites (fierce, large dobsonfly larvae with powerful biting mouthparts), stream salamanders, turtles, and, above all, trout and other fish prey upon the aquatic nymphs and larvae. These underwater food webs are somewhat simpler than those in a forest, but, like all food webs, their continuity depends on the lowly organisms of decay that are nature's original recyclers.

35

The Season of the Rut

The white-tailed deer breed

———*Observations*———

The woods are now bare and gray; stillness and silence prevail since the great majority of birds have forsaken their northern breeding grounds for the warmer climates of the south. Frogs, turtles, snakes, and insects are invisible in their underground or underwater hiding places, and the mammals have just about completed their food hoarding and feeding binges in preparation for the winter months—which will arrive very soon. Sportsmen throughout the country, however, anxiously await the opening day of another deer season and soon 13 million of them will enter the woods in search of their quarry. In contrast to most of the other creatures with which it shares its habitat, the white-tailed deer now reaches the peak of its annual life cycle.

The quintessential big game animal of our country, the white-tailed deer is found in all of the lower forty-eight contiguous states (and in South America). At least thirty-five different subspecies or geographical races exist, from the tiny Florida key deer, which weighs as little as 50 pounds, to the huge northern whitetail, which may exceed 300 pounds. In Pennsylvania, where it is the official state mammal, an average buck weighs about 150 pounds, stands 32 to 35 inches at the shoulder, and is about 70 inches long excluding the tail. Throughout the country the whitetail is extremely adaptable in both its diet and habitat: Over one thousand different plants have been listed in its menu, and it thrives in habitat from steamy, southern cypress swamps to frigid, snowy northern spruce forests.

In the early years of this country's European colonization it is estimated that there were 35 to 40 million white-tailed deer. By the end of the nineteenth century, due to excessive clear-cutting of trees by the lumber industry and unrestricted hunting, both for the market and for individual consumption, their numbers dropped to perhaps 300,000 nationwide. In many northern states, including Pennsylvania, New Jersey, Ohio, Illinois, and most of New York, the deer disappeared entirely by the early 1900s. Today, due to forest regeneration, farm abandonments and their regrowth into young woodlands, restocking by state agencies, extirpation of predators (wolves and mountain lions), and strong restrictions on hunting, the white-tailed deer has made the most successful comeback of any animal in this nation's history. Many individual states now have more deer than were present in the entire country in 1890. Pennsylvania alone has over 1 million whitetails, and small, densely populated New Jersey has over 160,000. With their soaring numbers have also come inevitable problems of the destruction of crops, ornamental shrubbery, and even their own forest habitat by overbrowsing. Thus, state wildlife agencies are relying on hunting as the chief means of controlling the numbers of white-tailed deer and keeping the population of this beautiful, adaptable animal in balance with its food supply.

For much of the year deer travel in small family groups composed of a mature doe, several generations of her daughters, and their young fawns of both sexes. Does become solitary in late spring when they have their own fawns, but they regroup in autumn and spend the winter together in the family group again. Larger congregations of deer often come together during feeding in winter; these are not organized "herds" but rather several different family bands that happen to be feeding in the same area. When yearling bucks mature in their second autumn, they leave their family groups and may become solitary or join small groups of other young bucks. In any given area there is one dominant buck, usually the biggest one, to which all the other bucks are submissive. These subordinate bucks are allowed to share the dominant male's range, but during the fall breeding season he alone impregnates most of the mature does in his area, chasing away the other males during this season of heightened activity and aggression.

The whitetail's peak breeding season in the Northeast occurs during the second and third weeks of November. For months, however, the deer have been unconsciously preparing for this time. Back in April the remarkable process of antler growth in the males began. On each side of the top of the head two platforms of bone called pedicels are attached to the skull. On these pedicels fuzzy "buttons" begin to grow into antlers—living, solid bone (without marrow) that may grow out of the skull as much as 1 inch per day by late summer. This process is initiated by photoperiod (the increasing length of the day in spring

———*Observations*———

—————Observations—————

causes the brain's pineal gland, which acts like an internal clock, to release hormones responsible for these profound physical and physiological changes).

A soft, mosslike skin called "velvet" covers the developing antlers and actually lays down the bone material. The velvet contains a rich supply of blood vessels that transport calcium, phosphorus, and other salts from the buck's bones and deposits them on the antlers, where they gradually harden and grow faster than any other bone material known to science. The young, velvety antlers are very sensitive in their early stages and easily deformed, but after a few months another hormonal change occurs in the buck. In September and October rising levels of the male hormone testosterone (in response to the decreasing daylengths of summer) cause the antlers to mature and harden. Suddenly the blood vessels in the velvet begin to constrict, cutting off the blood supply and causing the skin covering on the antlers to dry up and peel off. Much of this covering falls away or is rubbed off on tree trunks, but some is eaten by the buck since it is such a rich source of minerals.

A typical set of deer antlers consists of two main beams that curve gracefully up and back and then forward again. Each beam may have several tines, or points, and the number and arrangement of these depend on many different factors, including genetics, age, health, and nutrition. Generally the number and arrangement of a buck's points depend on the genes he was born with, but the size and massiveness of his rack depend a lot on his nutrition. Bucks as young as one and one-half years (the age at which they are sexually mature) may sport eight-point racks if they have benefited from an excellent food supply, while others with poor diets may possess a pair of tiny spikes or no antlers at all. With sufficient food a buck's antlers may get bigger each year, but since the habitat's food supply may vary from year to year (and antlers, unlike the horns of sheep, goats, and rhinos, are shed and regrown every year), the size of a buck's rack is not a reliable estimation of his age. It may, however, be an indication of his ability to survive the winter. A large percentage of mature bucks with no antlers or short, three-inch spikes fail to survive the winter because their habitats have inadequate food to support them.

Antlers serve as status symbols for the bucks, advertising to both sexes their strength, fitness, virility, and social status or rank. They also serve as weapons when two bucks contest each other's rank. Starting in September the biggest dominant males in an area begin to rub and polish their antlers on saplings, "attacking" these small trees and testing their strength as a prelude to the coming breeding season. In the process the rest of the velvet is rubbed off the antlers, but this is incidental to the practicing and sparring activities of the buck. Other, lower ranking, males begin to rub in October. There is another important function of this rubbing behavior: Special glands in the buck's forehead deposit a scent on the saplings as they are being rubbed, and these small trees then become signposts that advertise the presence and rank of the buck. Most buck rubs in any given area are made by the highest ranking males, and although these bucks don't defend a strictly delineated territory, they are never far from their signposts during the breeding season.

Bucks also create another curious type of advertisement during this season. Known as scrapes, these are areas where the buck paws away the leaf litter to expose the bare soil. Generally beginning in September, soon after the start of the buck rubs (later in October for the yearling males), scraping is commonly concentrated in an open part of the forest with little shrub cover, and the same sites may be used by the buck year after year. A buck may urinate or defecate on or near the scrape, and the area may be raked of its leaf litter by the antlers. It is thought that each scrape is "anointed" with scent from the buck's interdigital glands (between the toes). The strangest activity of all, however, is the buck's habit of biting off or breaking with his antlers the tips of a branch or cluster of branches hanging over the scrape. Scientists believe that this is another form of scent-marking, in which the deer deposits chemicals from its forehead glands, nasal secretions, or even tarsal glands (transferred first to its tongue by licking its legs) onto the twigs after fraying their edges. Even though the white-tailed deer is the most researched animal in the country, with thousands of scholarly papers and books written about it, much remains to be learned about some of its strange mannerisms.

Like the buck rubs, the scrapes function to communicate information to both the males and females about the buck's presence, readiness to breed, and possibly even his strength, fitness, and social rank. Females visit these visual and olfactory signposts during the breeding season, which starts in late September or October in the northeastern United States but peaks in mid-November when more than 50 percent of the does breed. Does come into heat every twenty-eight days at this time, but for only a twenty-four-hour period, and their readiness is advertised by chemical scent secretions. During this time the buck's testosterone levels also peak, resulting in an increase in his rubbing, scraping, and aggressive temperament. His neck has become thick and swollen, increasing by as much as 10 inches in circumference, and his antlers are full grown and polished. In short, he is "in rut," or at the peak of his sexual desire. In this condition a buck attempts to test his strength and prowess, and he reacts to another's presence by pawing the ground, snorting, lowering his head and antlers, and charging. Some battles may be quite serious, and injuries or even death may result from antlers being locked together inseparably, but most often the bucks have a pushing contest with the weaker or more submissive combatant leaving the area. The dominant male is then free to mate with the females in his area and, although no "harem" is maintained, he may breed with as many as seven does.

After the mid-November peak most breeding is completed by late December, although a few deer may mate into late January or even February. At this time, however, the rutting season is over and the bucks' antlers drop off in response to falling levels of testosterone. Some bucks retain their antlers into March, but most are shed suddenly after the breeding season in late December or January as the cells at the base of the antlers break down. On the ground the antlers become important sources of calcium for mice, squirrels, porcupines, and other mammals, and they quickly disappear. The bucks, weakened from a strenuous rutting season and as much as 25 percent leaner than in early fall, must now concentrate on surviving through the winter. As for the does that have been impregnated—and in habitats with excellent food over half the seven-month-old fawns may breed—they must find enough food to nourish themselves and the twin fawns that develop within them for two hundred days and come into the world the following May or June.

————Observations————

36

Invaders from Canada

NOVEMBER IV

Finches, owls, and other winter birds visit from the far north

————Observations————

Late autumn can be one of the most boring and frustrating times of the year for birders. The regular migration season is over, and the excitement of the annual Christmas Bird Count is still several weeks away. The woods and fields seem to be empty of all movement and sound. Bird feeders are visited by the local chickadees, nuthatches, juncos, and woodpeckers, but the variety that was present during the September–October migration is absent. Birders with binoculars scan the trees, bushes, windswept fields, and lake shores hoping to glimpse some new shapes and colors belonging to a different feathered creature to brighten their gray November days. Their efforts may be rewarded—in some years a hundredfold—when our northern states are invaded by the birds of the Far North that sometimes arrive at this time to spend the winter.

A few of these November arrivals are fairly regular in the timing and magnitude of their annual occurrences. The tree sparrow and fox sparrow, for example, are both Canadian breeders that migrate to our northern region of the United States every year and are reliable visitors to bird feeders. The solitary fox sparrow is often heard in the woods before it is seen, and its habit of noisily scratching away the leaf litter to look for seeds makes this large, handsome, rusty brown sparrow sound much bigger than it is. Tree sparrows travel down from the Arctic in flocks, the greatest numbers occurring during severely cold or snowy winters. In our region they spend the winter months eating the seeds of weeds and grasses in brushy meadows and old overgrown fields, and their musical, tinkling notes are among winter's most cheerful natural sounds.

Also occurring in our northeastern region every year, but in much more irregular and unpredictable numbers, is the purple finch. Although this attractive, rose red finch (females are brownish and heavily streaked) nests throughout New England, northern Pennsylvania, and upstate New York (and it is the state bird of New Hampshire), its numbers greatly increase throughout our entire region during some winters when it is seen at countless bird feeders. But these movements may occur at a much lower level in succeeding years, and the sight of a purple finch may not be an everyday thing in those winters. Similarly, the snow bunting often migrates by the thousands down to our area from the Arctic tundra in late autumn. Flocks of these white-and-brown, sparrowlike birds frequent open fields, farmlands, and sand dunes, often swirling together into the air like snowflakes over a winter field. Horned larks and Lapland longspurs—two other winter visitors that inhabit the open country—sometimes join these flocks, which may contain hundreds of buntings one year but only dozens the next.

Perhaps the most exciting winter birds that begin to arrive here in late November are the "erratics," or irruptive invaders. These species are northern birds that may visit our region in great numbers one winter but then remain rare or completely absent for several succeeding years. In most cases the underlying cause of their irruptions is the failure of trees and shrubs to produce sufficient seeds, fruits, or buds in Canada, thus creating a shortage of food. This may in turn be related to some weather variable like an unusually late spring cold spell that damaged the buds or perhaps to a summer insect infestation that weakened the trees. In years when food is abundant these birds may remain in Canada all year, and hardly a one is seen in our region.

Some of these erratic visitors are really present as breeders in our region (at least the more northern areas) in summer, so it is not entirely accurate to call them winter invaders. But their low numbers in the summer woods suddenly multiply explosively during their irruptive years, and they become some of the most abundant winter birds, even in the southern parts of our region like New Jersey and Long Island where they are absent as summer breeders. Among these species are the red crossbill, the white-winged crossbill, the evening grosbeak, and the pine siskin, all of which breed regularly in northern New England and northern New York.

In some years, starting in late November, these birds invade our region from Canada by the millions. The large, striking, yellow-and-black evening grosbeak becomes a common visitor to bird feeders in these years, but it also feeds on the seeds and buds of box elder, sugar maple, and

—————*Observations*—————

other trees. The small, yellow-streaked siskin visits ever-green forests as well as alder and birch thickets for the seeds found in cones and catkins, and after a particularly heavy invasion year (such as 1987, when tens of millions ir-rupted from Canada) some pine siskins may remain to nest far south of their customary breeding range. The two crossbills are perhaps the most erratic of all the winter visitors, with several years going by without a single one being seen throughout most of our region. These small birds inhabit the northern evergreen forests, where they extract seeds from the cones of pine, spruce, and hemlock with their unique, crossed, scissorlike mandibles.

Among the winter visitors that nest beyond the north-ern limits of our region are two Canadian finches well known for the cyclic nature of their invasions. Every five or six years the pine grosbeak (our largest finch at 10 inches in length) shows up in the northeastern United States. Males are rose red in color and females are olive gray, and they feed on the fruits of sumac and crab apple, as well as grit and salt from the roadsides. Much smaller (5 inches) is the redpoll, which sports a bright red cap on its forehead. Its irruptions are often nine or ten years apart (1978, 1987) and when they occur, it is usually in great numbers, mixed in with pine siskins and goldfinches. Between their inva-sion years they are generally very rare or absent from our region. Birders should closely inspect flocks of redpolls for a much rarer but very similar relative, the hoary redpoll (a "frostier" bird with a white rump), which may occasionally join them in their cyclic flights from the Arctic (just as the extremely rare Bohemian waxwing occasionally shows up in winter flocks of the abundant cedar waxwing).

Not all of these winter invaders are small songbirds. Our region is also visited every few years by birds of prey: hawks, owls, and even a robin-sized, predatory songbird, the northern shrike, which is famous for its habit of impal-ing small birds and mice on thorns or barbed wire. Like the erratic songbirds, the reason for the invasions of these predators is a shortage of food—mice, lemmings, grouse, rabbits, hares, or other animals that often experience "boom and bust" population cycles in the North. Already mentioned in chapter 33 are our two winter hawks from

Canada: the rough-legged hawk, which inhabits our open marshes and fields in varying numbers every winter, and the goshawk, whose periodic mass invasions are legendary among birders. (The goshawk is also becoming an increasingly common breeder in our region.) The most exciting of all the winter visitors, however, are the owls, news of which spreads rapidly throughout the birding community via the local Audubon Society's "hotline" telephone message service, or "rare-bird alert."

Some of these winter owls, like a few of the winter finches, are present in our region year-round as rare breeders. The saw-whet, short-eared, and long-eared owls are three examples. But every few years great congregations of one or more of these fly down from the North in November and overwinter in areas where there are lots of mice. In the winter of 1975 I watched over twenty crow-sized short-eared owls flapping like huge moths in the late afternoon over an overgrown, abandoned airfield in New York's Hudson Valley. A few years later I stared in disbelief at twenty-one long-eared owls roosting in a single spruce tree in urban Lyndhurst, New Jersey (near a landfill infested with mice)!

Every four years or so, coinciding with the cyclic decline in the numbers of lemmings, the great snowy owl moves down into the United States from the Arctic tundra in large numbers, creating quite a stir among people not used to seeing a huge, white owl perched on a sand dune, fence post, or landfill. An even rarer visitor is the great gray owl of the Canadian boreal forest, our largest owl at 2 feet high and with a 5-foot wingspread. Over 300 were recorded in 1979 in New York, New England, Quebec, and southern Ontario—the biggest invasion since 1890. Another irruption occurred in 1983. Nothing causes as much excitement among the local birding community as the appearance of one of these owl species from the Far North. When they visit our region, they bring with them an aura of wildness and freedom from their pristine northern homes, untamed as yet by human civilization. Their sudden appearance on a gray, cold day in late November is certain to provide just the spark needed to look forward to the coming winter months.

————*Observations*————

37

Facing the Freeze

Coping with ice and snow

Observations

Weeks before the official start of winter, its approach is heralded by the first snowflakes drifting across the landscape and the appearance of the first glaze of ice over our smaller ponds and wetlands. These initial frosty signatures of winter may last only a few hours, but as the sun sinks lower in the sky and drops below the horizon earlier with each passing day, there comes a time in late November or early December when snow and ice are here to stay. The season of winter has arrived, the landscape becomes frozen for the next three or four months, and wildlife adjusts to a new set of environmental conditions.

Even plants respond to the freezing weather in some remarkable ways. Once the ground becomes frozen, the absorption of water by roots is impossible, so photosynthesis shuts down for the season. Deciduous trees have already lost their leaves in preparation for this dry season (see chapter 30). This is also true for evergreen trees, which, contrary to popular belief, do not photosynthesize during winter. They do, however, carry on photosynthesis much longer in autumn after the deciduous trees drop their leaves, as well as much earlier in the spring before the other trees get their new foliage. This "evergreen advantage" enables them to survive in harsh, bitterly cold environments where the frost-free season is minimal. Since they don't have to grow a completely new set of leaves each year, evergreens conserve precious nutrients and energy in the Far North and on alpine summits where growing conditions are so hostile and nutrients so limited. A few deciduous trees, like the paper birch, aspen, and tamarack, compete with the evergreens in these habitats, and one adaptation that increases their odds of survival is the ability to carry on some photosynthesis during winter thaws via chlorophyll present in their bark.

Just like some animals (see chapter 31), plants have evolved ways of surviving winter temperatures that plummet to below freezing. Northern trees are capable of supercooling, where, by getting rid of seed crystals or nuclei around which ice would form, their fluids remain liquid at temperatures well below the freezing point of water. Some trees that have the most northern ranges, such as arborvitae, balsam fir, tamarack, jack pine, white spruce, black spruce, trembling aspen, paper birch, and balsam poplar, are also capable of extracellular cooling, in which the cell liquids ooze out into the extracellular spaces and freeze there, thus preventing cellular damage. Such strategies enable these trees to survive temperatures as low as 80 degrees Fahrenheit below zero. Acquiring this amazing resistance to freezing, or "cold acclimation," occurs in a series of stages beginning in autumn in response to both the decreasing amounts of daylight and the first exposures to freezing temperatures.

More than any other natural event, that first lasting snowfall of the season signals the arrival of winter. To some people the white stuff is simply a nuisance to shovel from driveways and plow away from slippery roads. To others snow is the very essence of winter—a pristine blanket that whitens and softens the landscape and enables them to plummet downhill on skis or sleds at breakneck speeds or glide easily cross-country through quiet, beautiful woods and fields. To children "thinking snow" means igloos, snowball fights, snowmen, and possibly an unexpected day off from school. A snow-covered environment presents both hardships and advantages for northern plants and animals, too.

A heavy snowfall can add tremendous weight to the tree branches, bending and deforming saplings or snapping off small trunks and limbs from even the largest trees (the flexible boughs and spire shapes of conifers help them shed snow more easily). For some animals snow makes it more difficult to find food. Acorns and pine cones are harder for squirrels to retrieve, while predators like foxes and bobcats are forced to rely more on their senses of smell and hearing to detect prey scurrying beneath the white surface. Deep snow slows down deer, causing them to expend much more energy in their daily travels and rendering them weaker and more vulnerable to their predators. Snow also has a profound cooling effect at night, radiating into the atmosphere much of the heat absorbed by the earth during winter's short days (especially on calm, clear, cloudless nights). At night the coldest part of the winter environment is right at the surface of the snow.

——————Observations——————

But wildlife has had millions of years to evolve adaptations to winter's snowy landscape. Most dramatically, a few species, such as weasels and snowshoe hares, shed their brown summer coats and turn white in winter, which enables them to blend in with the snowy surroundings and, say some scientists, possibly to stay warmer since the unpigmented, hollow white hairs trap air against the skin for added insulation. The snowshoe hare has another winter feature: broad, densely furred feet that travel across the snow without sinking through. The coyote also grows hair on the soles of its feet in winter. Another animal that grows "snowshoes" in winter is the ruffed grouse. A fringe of scales grows out from the sides of each toe, enabling the grouse to trek over the snow as well as grip onto icy aspen branches when it fills up on buds.

Many animals use the snow to their advantage. Rabbits stand on high snow banks to reach additional twigs and buds, while branches weighed down by fresh snow bring new forage to hungry deer. Small mammals gnaw on roots and the lower trunks of trees and shrubs beneath the safety of the snow, hidden from the eyes of predators. Weasels and minks often enter the tunnels of rodents to capture a meal beneath the snow. Most of all, however, snow provides wildlife with a blanket during the cold winter. Several inches of snow insulate the ground from changes in the air temperature, saving wildlife and plant roots from widely fluctuating temperatures above the surface. Ground temperatures beneath 20 inches of snow remain almost constant. The mass of snowflakes traps the dead air in countless spaces between the snow crystals, acting much like a thick blanket or down jacket. The looser and less packed together the snowflakes are, the higher the insulative value of the snow cover.

The temperature on the ground beneath 2 feet of snow may be as much as fifty degrees higher than the air temperature above the surface on very cold nights. If the snow has a hard upper crust, a "greenhouse effect" is created with even greater temperature differences. Without a snow blanket the winter frost line would extend much deeper into the ground, and both underground plant parts and dormant animals would experience greater mortality.

Indeed, this sometimes happens if the ground freezes before the first good snowfall. Small mammals that remain active throughout the winter, like moles, shrews, voles, and mice, rely on snow's insulating value as they tunnel and burrow beneath it searching for food. On a subfreezing winter night, a mouse loses more than three times as much energy per minute on the exposed snow surface as in an insulated tunnel. Some normally solitary species of small rodents and shrews (sometimes even two different species) congregate in temporary groups beneath the snow, huddling together in nests to share body warmth. Their tunnels, holes, and runways are easy to see in late winter once the snow melts down to their depths. When traveling across the snow surface, some mice create "warming huts"—shallow burrows just beneath the surface where they briefly rest to rewarm their bodies before venturing out again.

The most unusual way of utilizing snow's warmth is the habit of ruffed grouse and snow buntings of actually diving headfirst into deep snow and waiting out the most frigid weather. Hikers are sometimes startled when grouse suddenly burst out of a snowbank in the middle of a quiet winter woods. If a hard crust forms over these temporary shelters, the birds may become helplessly entombed and die of suffocation or hunger.

Perhaps no other part of the winter landscape appears so lifeless as a frozen, snow-covered lake or pond. Yet, as any ice fisherman can attest to, here life also exists beneath the surface. Many frogs and turtles are dormant in the mud at the bottom (see chapter 31), but some fish continue to swim and feed all winter long. What saves these animals from freezing to death is a unique property of water. Like most liquids, water becomes denser as it cools, but once it reaches about 39 degrees Fahrenheit, it is at its maximum density. As it continues to cool and finally turns to ice at 32 degrees, water becomes lighter, unlike other liquids.

Thus, in autumn a lake or pond loses heat as the weather gets cooler, and the water near the surface sinks and is replaced by warmer (and lighter) water from below the surface. By late November or early December, however, when the surface waters reach 39 degrees, further cooling causes the top water to remain at the surface, since it becomes less dense as its temperature falls to the freezing point. Finally there comes a cool, still night with subfreezing temperatures, and a layer of ice forms over the pond or lake. Since a body of water freezes from the top rather than from the bottom, aquatic life below this ceiling of ice is safe in a stable, undisturbed environment until the spring thaw in March or April. The icy crust may become thicker all winter, but as long as the lake or pond is deep enough, aquatic animals are not likely to freeze to death.

The real danger to aquatic animals in winter is suffocation since the ice sheet shuts off the water's oxygen supply from the air. Whatever oxygen is present below the surface is used up by both animals and plants in their respiration, and the decomposition of dead plants and animals in the mud contributes heavily to the oxygen depletion. By the end of a long winter—and winter usually lags on longer for aquatic organisms than for land dwellers since the ice cover on a pond may not melt away for weeks after the disappearance of snow on the ground in spring—there may be a substantial die-off of fish and tadpoles due to oxygen depletion in the water. But it's precisely at that time that the yellow perch start to lay eggs in the shallows, and the first frogs and salamanders begin to reawaken and breed in the waters to reproduce a new generation after a long northern winter.

38

The "False Hibernators"

The shallow winter sleep of skunks, raccoons, and black bears

————Observations————

Among the most fascinating of our wild creatures are those that have developed the seemingly impossible ability to simply shut themselves down for the winter and await the spring in a state of dormancy. Living without food and water for weeks or even months is an adaptation at which humans have marveled for centuries. It's amazing enough when exhibited by such creatures as frogs, snakes, and insects, but this ability to suspend life's requirements seems even more remarkable when practiced by the larger mammals like bears, raccoons, skunks, and woodchucks. How can these warm, furry animals—so similar in many ways to pet dogs and cats—go without the bare necessities for such long periods of time in their frigid winter dens?

A few of these mammals—woodchucks, chipmunks, jumping mice, and some bats—are true hibernators that lower their body temperatures almost to the freezing point and spend the winter in a near-lifeless state with drastically reduced metabolic rates. This feat is examined in chapter 45. Others are sometimes called "false hibernators," alluding to the fact that their winter sleep is characterized by a nearly normal body temperature and a much less reduced metabolism. The three northeastern mammals that exhibit varying degrees of this so-called winter dormancy, or "carnivorean lethargy" (they all belong to the carnivore order), are the striped skunk, raccoon, and black bear.

After feeding heavily in the fall to acquire a thick layer of body fat, a striped skunk may retire to an old woodchuck burrow (or dig its own den) for up to three months, from early December to late February or early March. This is especially true for female and young skunks during cold or snowy winters, but they may emerge for short excursions on unseasonably warm nights. Adult males may remain active in all but the coldest weather, and they begin to seek mates after mid-February no matter how cold it is. The body temperature of a dormant skunk in its winter den (which it may share with several others) is about 96 degrees Fahrenheit, a drop of only three degrees from its normal level.

Raccoons most commonly utilize hollow logs or trees as their winter dens, and one large den tree may house several females and young at the same time. They usually remain asleep if the outside temperature falls more than a few degrees below freezing, but warm winter nights may bring them out to search for food along the banks of streams and ponds or in farm fields. By February males are out looking for mates as long as temperatures stay above 20 degrees Fahrenheit or so.

Like the skunk and raccoon, the most famous hibernator of all is really a "false hibernator," but the black bear's winter sleep is one of nature's most miraculous accomplishments. After feeding up to twenty hours a day in autumn and consuming up to twenty thousand calories worth of food daily, a black bear may have put on 5 inches of body fat and gained over 100 pounds by the time it is ready to retire for the winter. At the same time, its fur more than doubles its insulative value. Then feeding suddenly stops, and the bear seeks a sheltered place to spend the next several months. What brings on this sudden change of behavior remains a mystery. It may be the season's decreasing daylength, colder weather, gradual scarcity of food, or the bear's own internal clock that triggers the hormonal releases that cause it to retire. In any case, to conserve energy during the approaching stressful months of winter, a bear assumes a long period of dormancy. Pregnant females and mothers with last year's cubs retire the earliest (late November or early December), followed by solitary, barren females, and then finally males by middle to late December. A serious scarcity of autumn foods (acorns, beechnuts, and other mast) may cause bears to retire as early as mid-October.

Once inside its winter den (see chapter 42 for a description of a typical bear den in the Northeast), a black bear usually remains there for the next four or five months (as long as seven months in northern Minnesota). During this time it goes completely without food and water and eliminates no body wastes. Curled up with its head against the ground and its nose near its tail to minimize its body's exposure to the cold air and to reduce heat loss (the temperature of its den may be well below zero), the bear remains quiet and still, awakening briefly once or twice a day and then drifting back to sleep. Its heart rate drops to as low as eight beats per minute from a normal sleeping rate of forty, and it may breathe only a handful of times each minute. Nevertheless, it maintains a high body temperature—between 90 and 96 degrees Fahrenheit, a drop of only a few degrees from its normal 98 to 100 degrees during summer. In this respect a bear (like the skunk and raccoon) differs greatly from the "true hibernators," which go through the winter in a state of suspended animation with body temperatures close to freezing. A hibernating woodchuck, for instance, is in a stiff, cold, deathlike state from which it cannot easily be awakened, whereas a sleeping bear can be aroused in its winter den by the slightest noise.

During its winter sleep a black bear relies strictly on its body fat for energy, burning about four thousand calories a day. Since it burns fat rather than protein, its production of urea (a waste product of protein metabolism) is minimal, and this is broken down and recycled into new proteins. A dormant bear's manufacture and breakdown of protein increases five fold without increasing the amount of protein in its body. So efficient is a bear at conserving its protein and water that no excess urea is produced, and blood samples taken from dormant bears have the same concentrations of urea, ammonia, uric acid, and proteins, and the same water content in the plasma and red cells as active bears. The kidneys produce just a trickle of urine, which is reabsorbed into the blood through the bladder's walls, thus making urination unnecessary. Without urination or defecation the bear's only water loss is through its shallow breathing, and this loss is also replaced from its fat stores.

The black bear pays a price for maintaining its high body temperature during its long winter sleep. To keep warm it needs to burn fat, and so it continually loses weight in its den. By the time it emerges in the spring, it may have lost from 15 to 40 percent of its weight, and this is not replaced until the summer when berries and other foods become abundant. Emergence from the winter den usually starts in late March with the males, followed by barren females and those with yearling cubs in early April, and then mothers with new cubs in middle to late April.

Perhaps the most wonderful aspect of all in the remarkable story of the black bear's annual dormancy is the birth of tiny, helpless babies to a lethargic mother in the dead of winter and their emergence three months later as active cubs weighing more than five times their birth weight. But this part of the story is yet another one of nature's annual events to be covered next month.

————Observations————

39

The Birds of Winter

The Christmas Bird Count

————Observations————

Every year since 1900, on a day during the two-week period centered around Christmas, people throughout the country have participated in a competition that has been called the country's biggest sporting event: the Christmas Bird Count. In 1990 more than 40,000 people took part, at about 1,500 sites across the continent, making it the world's largest and oldest wildlife survey. Each site is covered by a group of people—mostly amateur bird-watchers but often including professional naturalists and scientists—for a twenty-four-hour period, and the goal is to count all the birds they see (or hear, in the case of nocturnal owls) on that day. This is a friendly but spirited competition, both among the various teams and at the individual team level to see the most species of birds and to break their own records from previous years.

The Christmas Bird Count was initiated in 1900 by Frank Chapman, a professional ornithologist and editor of National Audubon Society's *Bird Lore*, who proposed it as an alternative to the then-popular Christmas "side-hunt," an outrageously cruel and wasteful annual competition in which teams of hunters set out to shoot as many birds and small mammals as possible on Christmas Day. Since then not only has the Christmas Bird Count grown tremendously in popularity, its results have become increasingly valuable to scientists in charting the population trends and ranges of native birds. The National Audubon Society or one of its regional chapters assigns each team to a specific "count circle" 15 miles in diameter. Team captains then usually divide the group into smaller parties to cover their 177-square mile circle in the twenty-four-hour period and then report back at the end of the day. Data recorded include the number of different species, total numbers of each species, miles traveled by foot or car, hours spent afield or at feeders, number of participants per party, and habitat descriptions. Detailed accounts and corroborations are often required for very rare species.

After nine decades of Christmas Bird Counts the National Audubon Society has accumulated an enormous amount of information, and the annual reports (published as an issue of *American Birds*) are over five hundred pages long. This is a unique opportunity for scientists to use data gathered by thousands of volunteers at the same time every year. Christmas Bird Counts have provided valuable insights into the gradual range extensions of certain species (such as the northward spread of the cardinal and mockingbird), the geographic and habitat preferences of various species in early winter, and population fluctuations over the years. Periodic irruptions, or "invasions," by goshawks, snowy owls, and Canadian finches have been documented (see chapter 36), as well as long-term declines in species like the black duck and subsequent recoveries of birds like the bald eagle (see chapter 41).

But most of all the Christmas Bird Count is a convenient excuse to go outdoors during this invigorating season. The spirit of competition helps add to the excitement, especially among neighboring count circles with a long tradition of Christmas Bird Counts. At most inland areas throughout the northeastern United States somewhere between thirty and seventy-five species can be expected to be recorded, depending on the weather and the number of birders. Over one hundred are counted each year in coastal regions like Long Island, and up to one hundred and fifty at Cape May, New Jersey, where coastal marshes, ponds, sand dunes, woods, and the open sea combine to produce a great variety of habitats. In the entire country the most productive sites are Santa Barbara, California, and Freeport, Texas, two warm and diversified areas that each record about two hundred different species on the Christmas Bird Count. In contrast, the Yukon region usually sees only one—the common raven!

Bundled up against the cold, with numb fingers attempting to manipulate binoculars and frostbitten toes, birders in the Northeast participating in this annual event can't help but wonder how their quarry manages to remain warm, active, and even seemingly cheerful in the face of frigid temperatures and biting winds. But birds possess the best-known natural insulation—feathers—and species like redpolls, goldfinches, and white-throated sparrows, which remain in the North for winter, may grow and add up to 50 percent more feathers to their bodies to increase their resistance to the cold. To further add to the thickness of their insulation, birds fluff out their feathers, which

——Observations——

traps more air near their skin and prevents their body warmth from escaping. Some species, like juncos, also add 15 percent more fat to their bodies before winter in order to stay warmer.

Birds will draw up one leg beneath their feathers when they are perched in order to reduce the exposure of these featherless extremities to the cold air. At night birds seek out sheltered areas like evergreen groves, tree cavities, thickets, or shrubs planted around homes in which to spend the coldest hours, often in company with others of their kind in order to share body warmth. Ruffed grouse and snow buntings even dive into snowbanks, where temperatures may be over forty degrees warmer than the frigid air and where windchill is not a factor. Recent studies have shown that goldfinches and other winter residents shiver constantly all night long while they sleep in order to generate enough body warmth by burning their fat to make it to the morning, when they can resume normal muscular activity. But the most remarkable adaptation to winter belongs to that most familiar and popular winter resident in the Northeast, the black-capped chickadee. In order to save precious energy the chickadee "lowers its thermostat" by up to twenty degrees each winter night, dropping from a normal body temperature of 108 degrees to as low as 88 degrees Fahrenheit—a controlled state of hypothermia, or torpor, and an extreme example among the birds of winter energy conservation.

Without food, however, birds would succumb to the cold regardless of their insulation. In winter, as soon as dawn breaks, birds begin their search for energy-rich foods—the seeds of weeds, conifers, alders, birches, and tulip trees; the fruits of crab apple, holly, sumac, barberry, and wild rose (the planting of ornamental multiflora rose bushes, which provide fruits all winter long, has been credited with the successful northward spread of the mockingbird); the buds of aspen, willow, and maple; and acorns hidden beneath the snow and leaf litter by squirrels or within tree cavities by blue jays and nuthatches.

At dusk ruffed grouse and winter finches may fill up their crops with aspen buds and seeds, respectively, in order to derive fuel during the overnight digestive process.

Great horned owls have been known to cache unfinished prey during winter and then thaw it out later by sitting on the frozen carcass! And, finally, there are bird feeders, which may play an important role in the survival of birds during extremely cold and snowy winters. Studies have shown a twofold survival rate among chickadees that frequent feeders during such winters versus those that rely on natural foods (small birds must have a twentyfold increase in the time they spend feeding during very cold winters compared to summer). Even during mild winters, however, when feeders don't contribute to the actual survival rates of our winter birds, their success at drawing these delightful visitors to windowsills, porches, and yards adds immeasurably to the enjoyment of the winter season.

————*Observations*————

40

Day Conquers Night

———*Observations*———

The holiday season evokes many cheerful and optimistic images, memories acquired over the years from giving gifts, decorating rooms, listening to joyful carols, and enjoying the holiday meal with beloved family members. Outdoors there are snow-covered evergreens, smoke rising from chimneys, and colorful lights strung across front porches, doorways, and ornamental shrubs. It's easy to get into the holiday spirit and eagerly look forward to this happy season year after year.

There's another reason why this time of the year is so festive. On December 21 or 22 the winter solstice occurs—that day when the earth's northern polar end leans as far as it ever does away from the sun. Because the earth's axis has a permanent tilt (twenty-three and one-half degrees from the vertical) as it rotates around the sun, it experiences the four seasons. In our summer the northern hemisphere points toward the sun and thus receives more hours of sunlight, while the opposite occurs in the southern hemisphere. On the winter solstice the sun remains twenty-three and one-half degrees below the horizon at the north pole for the entire day and, of course, there is no sunrise or sunset. Throughout most of our northeastern region there are about nine hours of daylight and fifteen of night on that day.

Why should the winter solstice—the shortest day of the year and the first official day of winter—be reason to celebrate? For the past six months, ever since the first day of summer, the days have been getting shorter. Now, finally, the trend has reversed and the days will once again start to lengthen for the next six months. This may not be very noticeable at first, but there will surely come a time during the next month when children playing outdoors and commuters bound for home will realize that darkness descends later and later.

Humans were once much more attuned to the seasonal changes in daylength, or photoperiod. Ancient cultures kept track of the sunsets and sunrises, and some based their lives and annual rhythms around elaborately contrived sundials and calendars that recorded changes in daylength. There were celebrations marking the annual solstices and equinoxes that have now been largely lost in today's indoor-oriented and artificially lighted societies.

But plants and animals continue to be greatly influenced by photoperiod. Their responses to the changing daylengths over the course of each year are extremely important in controlling their activities. Wildflowers, for example, bloom in response to certain photoperiods, and they can be classified as short-day, long-day, or day-neutral plants, depending upon how many hours of light stimulate them to blossom (see chapter 8). The buds of trees and shrubs respond to spring's increasing daylengths by opening their scales and extending their leaves for a new growing season (see chapter 8).

Many species of insects enter a state of diapause (their equivalent of hibernation) in response to the shortening days of late summer and fall, and this spell of suspended animation in many cases remains unbroken until the days get longer again in spring. Some species respond to a certain critical daylength, while others are stimulated merely by the trend toward longer days and the end of winter. Insects can be "fooled" into entering diapause by experiencing artificially shortened periods of light in the laboratory.

Photoperiod is also an overriding environmental factor responsible for the phenomenon of bird migration each autumn. The shortening days stimulate the birds' pituitary glands, and hormones consequently cause them to experience "migratory restlessness," a state characterized by increased appetite, acquisition of body fat, and a strong urge to fly southward. In spring it is the increasing hours of daylight that cause birds to start singing, establishing their nesting territories and other breeding activities.

In many mammals photoperiod is also an important factor in their reproductive cycles, such as the growth of antlers and regulation of testosterone levels in buck white-tailed deer (see chapter 35). The change of color in a snowshoe hare's coat from brown in summer to white in winter is controlled by photoperiod, as are the seasonal changes in eating habits and food storage behavior in wildlife such as the gray squirrel.

————Observations————

Even humans are affected by the earth's movements and seasonal changes in daylength more than is commonly realized. Like many other mammals, humans tend to gain weight and become more lethargic in winter—adaptations that would have been very critical to the conservation of energy and survival of our forebears during the lean months. Recently doctors have recognized a psychological depression experienced by many humans, especially in the northern climates, that occurs as the days grow shorter in autumn. The depression is treated by administering increasing doses of artificial light to the patient.

Just as surely as the earth turns and revolves around the sun, the days are now getting longer. Photoperiod is a reliable environmental signal that, unlike the weather, is a completely dependable cue upon which plants and animals can base their annual cycles. Soon, as they have for millennia, they will begin to respond to the increasing amounts of light in their own innate ways. Looking for signs of these responses during the coming months can make the cold, long (but shortening) winter nights much more bearable.

41

Regal Visitors from the North

Bald eagles overwinter on lakes, rivers, and reservoirs

Observations

It was a frigid January morning in 1975 as I drove to a series of large reservoirs in a remote section of Sullivan County in upstate New York. For some years I had heard about the presence of a wintering population of bald eagles on these reservoirs, and I was very eager to finally get a look at these rare and majestic birds. When I arrived at the reservoirs, about eight miles south of Monticello near the small town of Forrestburg, the air was clear and still, the temperature about 10 degrees Fahrenheit, and the ground covered with snow. Immense white pines, sycamores, and hemlocks rose from the shores of the reservoirs, the waters of which were kept unfrozen by their movement through turbines to generate electric power during certain periods of winter.

Not a sound disturbed the silence of the area, and I remember thinking that I could have been in some frozen, faraway wilderness of Alaska or Canada. And then this comparison became even more uncanny when I began to scan the trees along the shores with my binoculars and started to see the striking, distinctive white heads of adult bald eagles perched on the limbs. I spotted one after another sitting in the trees, regally overlooking their domains. I saw immature eagles, too, which were more difficult to pick out because of their uniformly dark plumages. By the end of that memorable day I had seen 21 bald eagles perched on trees, fighting on the ice over a frozen deer carcass, flying on immense, dark wings overhead, and even screaming and grappling with each other in spectacular aerial courtship displays.

Since 1972, when the pesticide DDT was banned for use in this country, the bald eagle has been staging a gradual comeback from critically low population levels everywhere outside of Alaska (where their numbers have always been high). This comeback has been aided in no small part by the efforts of biologists from universities and state wildlife agencies, both by protecting important eagle habitats from development and disturbance and by artificially augmenting the eagle's numbers through hacking and transplanting programs. Eggs from healthy eagle populations in Canada, for example, have been put into eagles' nests in our country where the lingering effects of DDT spraying in the 1950s and 1960s still cause the older eagles to lay eggs too thin-shelled to withstand the weight of the incubating parents. These eggs are then successfully hatched and their eaglets raised by the foster parents.

At the same time, selected eggs have been taken from the wild, brought into laboratories, and artificially incubated. Then the chicks are transferred to carefully protected wild areas where they are fed natural foods by humans who make sure they are never seen by the young eagles, to prevent their imprinting on people (this process is called "hacking"). Meanwhile, the adult eagles from whose nests these eggs were taken often lay replacement eggs, thus further increasing the number of young eagles. The bald eagle has now become reestablished as a nesting bird in such states as New Jersey, New York, and Pennsylvania, where only one or two breeding pairs had existed by 1980.

Since 1979 the National Wildlife Federation has been taking an annual census of the number of bald eagles spending the winter in the lower forty-eight states. Our country as a whole now has from 11,000 to 13,000 wintering bald eagles outside of Alaska, a large increase over the 1970s. About 70 percent of these eagles probably migrate down from Canada and Alaska. Our region's wintering eagles are also on the increase: In 1983 New Jersey counted fewer than 10 bald eagles spending the winter there; in 1990, 70 were counted. In our northeastern region bald eagles spend the winter along the coasts of Maine and New Hampshire; around the Delaware Bay; on large, unfrozen lakes and reservoirs throughout our area (especially the Quabbin Reservoir in Massachusetts and the Mongaup, Rio, and Rondout reservoirs in New York); and on any of the large, free-flowing rivers that retain open waters for fishing. One of the largest concentrations of wintering eagles in the eastern United States is at the Aberdeen Proving Grounds in Maryland, where 182 were counted in January 1990.

Along the upper section of the Delaware River, near where New York, Pennsylvania, and New Jersey meet, a well-studied population of bald eagles returns every winter. Depending on the severity of the weather and the amount of ice-free, open water in the river for the eagles to fish in, this population may contain as many as 32 bald eagles. Since 1983 a cooperative study of these eagles has

————Observations————

————*Observations*————

been carried out by East Stroudsburg University and the National Park Service, which manages the 72,000-acre Delaware Water Gap National Recreation Area along both the New Jersey and Pennsylvania sides of this stretch of the river. Besides actually taking annual censuses of the eagles, this study has attempted to discover the factors that make this area such a prime wintering region and to formulate a management plan to ensure that the area continues to support these birds.

This study has ascertained that the eagles spending the winter in the area are birds that return from the North every year, starting to arrive in December and then reaching peak numbers in January and February. They disperse back to the North sometime in March. During this period they eat mainly fish, although dead deer and other carrion are occasionally consumed. The three most important factors ensuring the continued success of this region (and probably other areas throughout the Northeast where bald eagles spend the winter) in supporting eagles are open water for fishing; large stands of coniferous and deciduous trees where the eagles can rest during the day and roost at night, and from which they can hunt for fish; and—perhaps most critically—freedom from human disturbance. Eagles are very shy and are quick to flee an area that experiences too much human activity.

For these reasons many of our region's prime bald eagle wintering areas are now being protected from undue disturbances and patrolled by state wildlife or conservation personnel. Signs have been posted directing visitors to remain in their vehicles while observing the eagles in order to keep disturbance to a minimum. The National Park Service has conducted eagle watches on certain winter weekends in the Delaware Water Gap Recreation Area in order to give people the opportunity to view eagles as a group under carefully controlled conditions to minimize frightening the birds. Hundreds of people have participated in these outdoor programs, and they have experienced the incomparable thrill of watching our national symbol, recently rescued from the brink of extinction and now flying free in increasing numbers amidst some of our region's finest scenic beauty.

42

New Year Babies

The birth of black bears

————Observations————

Each January, during the so-called dead of winter, a miracle occurs in the northeastern United States, mainly in our larger, more remote forests but sometimes surprisingly close to major roads and population centers. It is the miracle of birth: the reproduction of the black bear, our area's second-largest animal (after the moose). It usually occurs during the first three weeks of January, when the dormant pregnant female bears are safely hidden in their winter dens away from human eyes. There she gives birth to cubs (generally from two to five) that are so tiny that each weighs less than one two-hundredths of its mother's weight. Yet, after nursing on her milk during the next two and one-half to three months, each cub emerges in spring weighing from four to ten times its birth weight, and by the end of its first summer it may weigh as much as 100 pounds.

The typical winter den of a black bear in the northeastern United States is a far cry from the large, roomy cave so often portrayed in children's books and cartoons. It may be a tunnel excavated by the bear within a large, exposed root system of a tree or a simple shelter created beneath toppled trees or heavy brush piles. Many bear dens are inside small caves or rock cavities or under fallen, leaning slabs of rock. Other bears sleep away the winter months right on the ground, either within the cover of thick growths of rhododendron or mountain laurel or in small, exposed depressions dug out of the forest floor, which differ little from the "day beds" they use during the warmer months. Mother bears with cubs have been found snoozing away the winter in the crawl spaces of summer cabins or inside culverts beside busy highways. Dens are usually provisioned with leaf litter, rotting wood, branches, and other material for bedding, and many have openings with northerly exposures so they get covered with drifting snow. Even if a bear's den seems to be an ideal place in which to spend the winter, its occupant almost always selects a different one the following year.

Since the late 1960s and early 1970s the miracle of the black bear's reproduction has been studied by such pioneering bear biologists as Michael Pelton in Tennessee, Charles Jonkel in Montana, Lynn Rogers in Minnesota,

Gary Alt in Pennsylvania, and Patricia McConnell in New Jersey. Their research has revealed some remarkable facts about this intriguing creature. Bears mate anytime from mid-May to mid-September, the peak season being June and July. However, no matter when a female bear has been impregnated during that four-month period, she gives birth in her den sometime in January.

This paradox is explained by the phenomenon of delayed implantation. After conception the fertilized egg floats freely in the female's uterus and doesn't attach itself to the wall to begin further development until late November or December. Then, after only six weeks of development in the mother's body, cubs only 9 inches long and weighing a mere 10 to 16 ounces each are born to mothers weighing 200 pounds or more. In this way the cubs come into the world in the relative safety of a den, to a mother that is fat and restful. After birth the tiny cubs instinctively crawl through the mother's fur to her nipples, guided by the heat emanating from this hairless region of her body. After two and one-half to three months of nursing on their mother's rich milk, the cubs emerge in April weighing 4 to 10 pounds. The following winter the fast-growing cubs may weigh half as much as their mother, with whom they once again hibernate in a den, emerging their second spring to leave her for independent lives. For this reason a female black bear mates and gives birth only every other year.

Black bears are doing very well throughout most of the country, including the Northeast, although they have disappeared from such states as Rhode Island, Nebraska, and Illinois; have been reduced to only a handful of individuals in Ohio and Indiana; and survive as marginal populations in Alabama, Louisiana, Mississippi, Kentucky, and much of the Southeast. In many states there are now more black bears than there were fifty years ago. Over 25,000 are estimated to roam Maine's vast forests; more than 4,000 live in New York (mostly in the Adirondack Forest Preserve), a state with 20 million people. Pennsylvania has as many as 8,000 black bears—more than double the number estimated to have lived in that heavily wooded state in 1970, and the most in recent history. Even New Jersey, our country's most densely populated and urbanized state,

——Observations——

now has over 250 black bears, most of which have dispersed from the very productive and expanding bear population in the nearby Pocono Mountains of Pennsylvania to colonize thousands of acres of newly acquired state and federal woodlands in New Jersey's northwestern corner.

This is all very good news to those who enjoy hiking the northeastern woods hoping to see one of these magnificent but timid animals. Others can take pleasure just knowing that there's enough room in our crowded, busy world for these huge creatures to continue bearing their cubs in the "dead of winter."

43

Insects on Ice

Snow fleas, stoneflies, and other winter insects

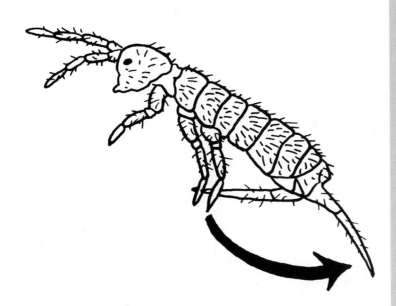

F ew things seem more out of place in the northern woods than insects fluttering about on a January day—except, perhaps, a colony of thousands of them actively crawling on top of the snow. Yet, both are annual occurrences during the so-called January thaw, or whenever temperatures warm up toward the freezing point throughout the winter. To be sure, the great majority of insects in northern latitudes lie dormant and unseen during the winter. A very few species, however, not only become active in the cold weather but even mate and reproduce in the snow and ice.

The counterpart to hibernation in the insect world is called diapause, a complete cessation of development and activity that usually begins long before the onset of cold weather. For example, the eggs of several species of moths, like the tent caterpillar and gypsy moth, enter diapause during the summer and don't hatch into caterpillars until after experiencing the entire winter season. Other species, like the swallowtail butterflies and giant silk moths, enter diapause in the pupal stage, spending the winter months, respectively, as a naked, twiglike chrysalis or a pupa wrapped in a silken cocoon. There are also insects that overwinter as caterpillars (woolly bear, viceroy butterfly) or adults (ladybird beetles, mourning cloak butterfly), each species awakening from its state of suspended animation and completing its development (or reproducing, in the case of adults) in the spring.

These overwintering insects have evolved a variety of strategies for surviving the subfreezing temperatures during their long periods of dormancy. Many avoid freezing by retreating deep beneath the soil or burrowing into the mud at the bottom of lakes and ponds. But others simply become dormant above the ground, fully exposed to winter's most severe weather. These insects, like the amphibians that are exposed to winter's subfreezing weather during their seasonal dormancy (see chapter 31), practice one of two methods to survive the freezing temperatures.

Some form glycerol or other antifreeze compounds in their body fluids, enabling their blood and other internal fluids to drop well below the freezing point of water without turning into ice. The antifreeze compounds perform this apparent miracle by binding with particles of dust, bits of food, bacteria, or other seed nuclei in the body fluids and preventing them from growing into harmful ice crystals. This method of supercooling enables an insect's internal fluids to drop as low as 30 degrees Fahrenheit below zero without turning into ice.

Other insects can actually freeze solid during the winter and thaw out in spring without experiencing any internal damage. This is accomplished (like the frogs mentioned in chapter 31) by restricting the formation of ice to the extracellular fluids in the blood and body cavity so that the cells themselves avoid damage to their walls from intracellular ice formation. In this way some insects live through the winter frozen alive and thaw out in spring to complete their life cycles. In the Arctic a species of woolly bear caterpillar spends ten months of the year frozen solid!

There are a very few exceptions to the general pattern of insects remaining dormant all winter, and these species provide rare and delightful glimpses of "insects on ice," adding a touch of mystery and wonder to an otherwise cold, dreary winter day. One of these species is the snow flea, a tiny, $1/8$-inch insect that is almost impossible to notice individually. But snow fleas live in big colonies, so densely packed together that there appear to be thousands of grains of pepper sprinkled all over the snow, especially near the bases of tree trunks. Upon closer examination these dark, bluish black specks can be seen crawling and jumping on the snow.

Snow fleas have received their common name from their jumping ability. But they aren't even related to fleas; they are members of the most ancient and primitive group of insects, the springtails (order Collembola). The oldest fossil insects ever found (over 300 million years old) are of springtails, and they are virtually indistinguishable in appearance from modern springtails. Unlike other insects, springtails lack compound eyes, they continue to molt their skin even after reaching reproductive maturity, and they experience no metamorphosis—each successive growth stage following a molt resembles the previous one

———Observations———

except in size. For these reasons some insect taxonomists consider springtails not insects at all but, rather, members of a more primitive, ancestral group.

Springtails also lack wings, but this doesn't prevent them from getting around. Their name is derived from an unusual two-pronged, forklike tail (the furcula), which can be flexed and bent forward under the body, where it is held in place in a cocked or tensed position by a pair of short projections that function as a catch. When this catch is released, the furcula snaps down, strikes the ground, and flings the insect as much as 6 inches into the air.

When winter temperatures approach freezing, and the humidity is consequently higher, snow fleas emerge through the snow cover and feed on decaying leaves, bark, algae on the tree trunks and snow surface, and sap—they can become pests by falling into maple syrup buckets by the hundreds. During some winters the numbers of snow fleas in a given area may become unbelievable, and these tiny insects accumulate in depressions on the snow and around the bases of trees literally by the millions. The darkened snow surface appears to be in constant movement from their bodies. Then, when night falls they all disappear by simply scurrying down through the snow toward the leaf litter on the forest floor.

Several species of winter stoneflies are also active in the cold weather. Emerging from icy streams as nymphs in midwinter, they clamber onto the snow to shed their skins and become dark, flattened, winged adults that retain the nymphs' paired tails. After mating the females then return to the streams and rivers and lay their eggs, which hatch into another generation of nymphs that spend a year underwater.

On mild winter days scores or even thousands of small flies known as winter gnats appear in the woods. They swarm together and perform distinctive dancing flights in the air above the snow. There are also winter crane flies and winter scorpion flies, two species of essentially flightless, wingless insects (tiny vestiges of wings are all that remain) that crawl from the earth out onto the snow in winter with six long, spindly, spiderlike legs. The winter crane fly resembles a large wingless mosquito (like the winter gnat, it is actually closely related to the mosquitoes, and its harmless, winged, summer relatives are often mistaken for them), while the winter scorpion fly possesses a long, trunk-like beak and, in the male, a harmless set of claspers at the tip of its abdomen, which it sticks up like a scorpion.

Indeed, insects that are active in winter are rare exceptions to the rule. Most humans never see them, but their presence and activity in the middle of winter proves that there is still life out there in the silent winter woods. Winter is not as frozen and devoid of wild creatures as it appears. Seeing these winter insects carrying out their life cycles makes it a bit easier to believe that the woods will once again be bursting with an infinite variety of plants and animals in spring.

44

First to Nest

The great horned owl breeds in midwinter

Observations

Long before the first sounds of spring signal the end of this cold and difficult winter season, a voice echoes in the darkness of night from the woods to proclaim that another nesting season has indeed begun. It is a deep, booming voice, almost human in quality, and often answered by a similar voice some distance away. Beginning in mid-November and increasing in intensity through December and January, these are the calls of our most powerful predatory bird, the great horned owl. Calling in a series of five to seven deep, muffled, uninflected hoots—hoo, hoo-hoo (pause), hoo, hoo—the male owls stake out their territories in late autumn, and then pairs of owls hoot to each other to attract mates or to cement their already established bonds.

By late January or early February female horned owls are already sitting on their eggs, making them the earliest nesting birds in the northeastern United States. Two or three (rarely as many as five) large, dull white eggs are laid in an old hawk, crow, or heron nest (often in a large beech tree), or simply in a hollow tree, the top of a broken snag, or on a rock ledge upon which the female places some of her feathers to soften the surface. The preferred habitat is deciduous forest mixed with some hemlocks and white pines, although the great horned owl is found in a great variety of habitats throughout the country.

Egg laying follows an elaborate courtship ritual in which the male entices and stimulates his lifelong mate by fluffing out his feathers, bowing his head, spreading his wings, and dancing in a shuffling fashion along tree limbs. Aerial acrobatics are also added to this repertoire as the male performs dives and loops and flies from tree to tree. Both partners may then snap their beaks like castanets (a habit also used to intimidate humans and other larger animals), rub their heads and bills together, and hoot to each other before mating.

The female alone incubates the eggs, and she begins this duty as soon as the first one is laid. The other eggs are produced at intervals of several days so that there is always a difference of a few days between the hatching of the first and last eggs after their thirty-five-day incubation periods. Thus, the nestlings are not all the same age and size, and in times of food shortage the older, more aggressive owlets will snatch the food from the parents, and the younger siblings may perish. The male not only shares in feeding the young, he must also bring food to his mate daily during her incubation period since, without the mother's body warmth, the subfreezing winter temperatures would quickly kill the eggs and new nestlings. Female great horned owls often sit on their nests covered with snow and ice in the middle of winter storms.

The owlets are born in late February or March completely helpless, with soft, white downy feathers and eyes that remain closed for over a week. They don't begin to learn how to fly for nine to twelve weeks after hatching, but by this time they have probably already left the nest and are perched on branches, stumps, or even the ground. Here they continue to be fed by their parents for several more weeks into late spring or early summer—one of the longest periods of dependency of any bird in our region. Biologists believe the reason for this long delay in reaching independence is to synchronize the young owls' initial attempts at hunting on their own with the peak period of the appearance of young mammals and birds. This new generation of inexperienced prey represents comparatively easy pickings for owls that are honing their newly acquired predatory skills.

The great horned owl has been called the "king of the forest" and the "tiger of the air." These birds will fiercely and aggressively defend their nests and young even from humans (several of whom have been attacked and injured by getting too close to the nests), and the animals that horned owls consider prey include everything from large insects to house cats: fish, snakes, frogs, mice, rats, shrews, squirrels, songbirds, muskrats, woodchucks, rabbits, opossums, minks, weasels, ducks, geese, grouse, herons, pheasants, large hawks, foxes, skunks, and even other owls. Of all these items the most commonly selected prey are mice and rabbits, although scientists who study the great horned owl claim that almost every one smells of skunk. Its ability to dispatch such a variety of large creatures stems not only from the great horned owl's size—up to 24 inches in height, 4 pounds in weight, and with wings

—————Observations—————

spreading 5 feet—but also its powerful, hooked beak and tremendous, needle-sharp talons that can easily go through a man's hand.

The horned owl's most remarkable and legendary capacities, however, are its senses. Its eyes are as large as a human's and are over thirty-five times more sensitive, enabling it to easily detect prey moving about at night. Its hearing may be the most acute of any animal's, which explains the horned owl's uncanny ability to accurately capture mice scurrying on the snow or leaf litter on the darkest, most overcast nights when vision is impossible. With these impressive physical attributes and its ability to adapt to a variety of different habitats (including urban parks, cemeteries, and golf courses, provided rodents and other prey are available), the great horned owl appears to be holding its own throughout our region. Over 130 (more than one per square mile) were counted during the 1988 Christmas Bird Count in Cumberland County, New Jersey, alone! The "tiger of the air" is secretive and not often seen, but its unearthly hooting continues to elicit chills from those who listen to the sounds of the winter nights.

45

Winter's Deep Sleep

The woodchuck is sound asleep on Groundhog Day

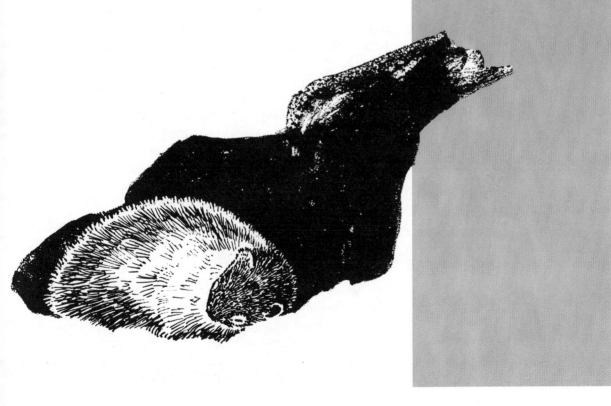

Observations

Every year on February 2, fat, furry, and sleepy animals are coaxed out of their dens and brought before the eyes of television cameramen, newspaper photographers, and reporters. (The most famous place for these annual events is in Punxsutawney, Pennsylvania.) Tongue in cheek, each person carefully observes whether or not these animals see their shadows and then goes on to predict the longevity of the winter. In a tradition dating back to the early German farmers, the woodchuck, or groundhog, has been used as the country's most famous weather prognosticator, but, like the width of a woolly bear caterpillar's colored bands or the thickness of a squirrel's fur, the woodchuck's observation of his own shadow is of absolutely no use in forecasting the severity or length of winter.

The choice of the woodchuck as this region's primary weather forecaster stems from its vague resemblance to the European badger and hedgehog, two other burrowing animals that were traditionally used by the Germans for the same purpose every year on February 2, the Catholic holy day of Candlemas. In actuality almost all woodchucks in the Northeast are unavailable for this task at this early date, for they are deep under the ground in a state of hibernation from which most will not emerge until later this month or early March. The woodchuck is one of the world's few true hibernators among the mammals. After retiring to its den in the autumn, its metabolic functions and body temperature drop to fractions of their normal levels, and no food or water is taken for the next several months. In this country the only mammals besides the woodchuck that truly hibernate are the marmots (western cousins of the woodchuck), ground squirrels (including, to some extent, our eastern chipmunk), jumping mice, and several species of bats.

Mammalian hibernation is undoubtedly one of nature's most amazing adaptations to surviving periods of hardship. Faced with the very difficult or impossible task of finding enough food during the winter months to produce the internal heat necessary to maintain their high body temperatures, mammals such as bats (which eat flying insects) and woodchucks (which eat green plants) become completely inactive and temporarily abandon being warm-blooded. Unlike the black bear and other so-called false hibernators (see chapter 38), these true hibernators spend the winter with body temperatures just a little above freezing, thus saving an enormous amount of fuel and consequently losing very little weight throughout their dormant periods.

As the days decrease in length in late summer and fall, the woodchuck's hypothalamus gland (a portion of the brain) responds by triggering a series of specific actions that ultimately lead to a long winter's sleep. It is thought that the special hormones involved in causing these responses are the same throughout the animal kingdom in any species that experiences winter dormancy. For example, if blood taken from a hibernating woodchuck or dormant black bear is injected into an active and awake mammal, even a species that normally never exhibits dormancy, it enters a state of hibernation. The search for this mysterious "hibernation hormone" has been an active area of scientific research in recent years.

The usual sequence of responses in a hibernating species like the woodchuck begins in autumn with an increased appetite and period of food-gorging. The woodchuck may double its body weight and put on $3/4$ inch of fat by eating as much as $1^1/_2$ pounds of vegetation daily, and a jumping mouse's body may be fully 50 percent fat by the time it enters hibernation. Its periods of sleep also increase in length daily, and finally there comes a time when it does not awaken in its den. This may be late September in New England, mid-October in Pennsylvania, or early November in New Jersey. The woodchuck's den is usually a chamber at the end of an extensive underground tunnel system, perhaps 10 to 45 feet in length, dug in loose soil on a well-drained hillside to avoid flooding. In this snug den it enters its winter sleep curled up in a tight ball, head tucked beneath its tail and fur standing erect. Bats differ from the other true hibernators in selecting caves rather than underground burrows for hibernation, and each species— little brown myotis or little brown bat, social bat, eastern pipistrelle, and big brown bat—generally hangs upside down from a different section of a cave for its winter sleep.

The next step in the sequence is a dramatic lowering of the metabolic processes. A woodchuck's heart rate falls

————Observations————

——Observations——

from one hundred to four or five beats per minute during hibernation, and its breathing drops from sixteen breaths per minute down to only one breath every few minutes while it sleeps in its den. Some ground squirrels exhibit even greater degrees of suspended animation during winter, experiencing decreases in their breathing rates from one hundred breaths per minute when active to only a couple of gasps of air every three minutes while hibernating.

This drop in the hibernating mammal's metabolism results in a decrease in both its consumption of oxygen and its production of internal heat, leading to one of the other hallmarks of true hibernation: a much lower body temperature. That of a hibernating woodchuck, for example, may be as low as 38 degrees Fahrenheit (the same as the temperature of its burrow) as compared to its normal temperature of 99 degrees. Thus, unlike hibernating snakes, frogs, and other cold-blooded animals in which colder winter temperatures bring about passive drops in their body temperatures and then consequent decreases in their metabolic rates, hibernating mammals exercise complete control over their winter sleep, experiencing drops in body temperatures only after decreasing their metabolic rates first.

A hibernating mammal like a woodchuck takes in no food or water for as long as five months all winter. Its body water is conserved by simply not urinating until spring. Our eastern chipmunk occasionally enters periods of true hibernation, especially during severely cold or snowy winters or after autumns when acorns, nuts, and other food are in short supply. But, unlike the woodchuck, jumping mice, and bats, chipmunks store food in their dens and feed on this larder whenever they awaken during the winter, so they don't have to rely on their body fat to get them through this season. Instead of gorging on food in autumn, the chipmunks' response to the shorter days and cooler temperatures is to busily gather food and store it underground in their chambers. In the South, chipmunks may remain active all year long.

Although the woodchuck's hibernation temperature may be lower than 40 degrees Fahrenheit, the dormant animal still exercises some control over it by not allowing its body temperature to drop too close to the lethal freezing

———Observations———

point. Its skin remains sensitive to temperature, and if it gets too close to freezing, the woodchuck's body temperature no longer passively follows the temperature in its den. Instead, at some critically low level the woodchuck begins to shiver its muscles to produce internal heat and avoid freezing. Thus, a hibernating mammal can be said to have lowered its thermostat to a new "set point," around which it continues to regulate its body temperature during its winter sleep. So far, the arctic ground squirrel (which may hibernate for eight months of the year) is the only mammal in the world known to be capable of supercooling, or surviving unfrozen with body temperatures a few degrees below 32 degrees Fahrenheit.

Hibernating woodchucks, jumping mice, and bats remain in their dens all winter long without food, but every week or two they slowly reawaken, temporarily raise their body temperatures up to normal levels, and then go back into their deep sleep. The reason behind these brief, periodic arousals (which are fueled by a special "brown fat" concentrated around the neck and shoulders) is unclear, but some scientists believe the animals need to take a few deep breaths to rid their bodies of gaseous wastes. Other researchers think that the hibernators must periodically regain consciousness to check the temperature of their dens or other environmental signals to keep their internal, biological clocks synchronized with the outside world.

Sometime around the end of February or beginning of March (perhaps a couple of weeks earlier in southern Pennsylvania and New Jersey) the first male woodchucks emerge from their dens to seek mates. Later, the females and yearlings will also awaken after their long winter sleep. During this final reawakening from hibernation it takes two to four hours for the woodchuck to sharply increase its heart rate and respiration and generate enough heat to achieve its normal body temperature (it takes bats only ten to fifteen minutes to warm up and become active from their hibernating state). Food is still in very short supply at this late winter date, but, because of the extremely low energy demands during hibernation, much of the woodchuck's body fat acquired last fall still remains to keep it alive and healthy until spring's green explosion in a few weeks.

46

Mating Mammals

FEBRUARY II

A great variety of wildlife breeds in February

————*Observations*————

Winter's carpet of snow has often been compared to a book upon which are recorded the comings and goings of all the wildlife that is active during this season. Many of these animals are nocturnal and very secretive, and their footprints in the snow are often the only clues they leave about their secret activities and hiding places and, indeed, the very fact that they exist in our region at all. One of the most exciting and educational pursuits for those humans who venture outdoors during the cold days is to study these tracks in the snow, identify their makers, follow them to their dens or burrows, and perhaps learn what they have been eating . . . or what ate them!

At this time of the year there may suddenly be revealed on the surface of the snow a new flurry of activity, as well as the additional footprints of animals that had been mostly dormant during winter's earlier weeks. This season, the "dead of winter," is the mating period for many of the mammals in the northeastern United States. In order to synchronize the birth of their young with spring's milder weather and their subsequent growth to independence during the warm, productive days of summer and fall, these species must mate during the middle of winter. In this way their babies are brought into the world in April or May when freezing weather is gone and the world is experiencing its great annual flush of regreening of the vegetation, return of the birds, reawakening of the insects, reptiles, and amphibians, and rebirth of a new generation of wildlife.

Unfortunately, another visible sign that these animals have increased their activity levels at this time is the presence of their dead bodies along the roads and highways. Every February the sight of road-killed skunks and raccoons suddenly serves as a reminder that these two mammals have emerged from their dens, where they have been hiding from the colder temperatures, and have gone searching for mates. Even though these two animals are not closely related (the skunk is in the mustelid, or weasel, family), each has a gestation period of sixty-three days, so the first young raccoons and skunks usually appear about mid-April.

Another northeastern mammal with a similar gestation period (sixty to sixty-three days) is the eastern coyote, a species that has now become firmly established throughout our region since first migrating here in the 1930s and 1940s from Canada and the western United States. Fully a third larger than its western ancestor (up to 50 pounds in weight), the eastern coyote is thought to have taken advantage of our region's forest regrowth after farms were abandoned as well as the absence of the timber wolf (extirpated by the turn of the century) and an expanding deer population. Coyotes mate in late January or February, bringing forth a litter of five to ten pups in April.

Our two smaller relatives of the coyote—the red fox and the gray fox—each have a gestation period of about fifty-one days, and the females begin to come into heat sometime in late January. Mating occurs in February (March in the more northern or mountainous regions), and young are born in April. Likewise, the bobcat, one of our region's most elusive animals, also mates in mid-February, sometimes to the accompaniment of much squalling and screaming, and after a fifty- to sixty-day gestation period the kittens are born in April.

By late February and early March other mammals begin to find mates in our northeastern states—mink and muskrats in the streams, ponds, and wetlands; cottontail rabbits and woodchucks in the meadows and early successional woodlands; snowshoe hares in the bogs and spruce forests; and chipmunks in the mixed-oak and northern hardwood forests. Each of these species is characterized by a gestation period of approximately one month (perhaps a week or two longer in the mink). In this way they bring forth a new generation of their species during that tremendously prolific month of April when the natural communities of our region experience their annual rites of reproduction.

47

Winter's Silence Ends

FEBRUARY III

Our resident birds begin to sing as days get longer

————Observations————

There is a silence in the outdoors of winter that occurs at no other season. Except for a few beeches and oaks that hang on to their bleached, dried leaves, the deciduous trees no longer rustle or whoosh to the sound of winds pushing against their foliage and bending their green branches. The blanket of snow muffles even the crunching sounds of human footsteps. No frogs or insects are calling or buzzing to attract mates, and on the lakes and ponds only the periodic sound of ice cracking and reverberating disturbs the profound sense of quiet and emptiness.

But the most important element that contributes to winter's lack of sound is the silence of the birds. Most species have departed to the southern states or tropical America for the winter. The few that remain move through the forests like phantoms, quietly searching for insects and seeds without revealing their presence by song or call. Those birders who venture out in winter to find birds, as during the annual Christmas Bird Count, may hear the tinkling calls of tree sparrows, the chips of cardinals, and the taps of woodpeckers, but these slight sounds are heard only close to their source. To the great majority of people in the Northeast, the winter woods are indeed silent.

There comes a time, however, in middle to late February when suddenly this silence is broken. It usually occurs on a sunny, clear day when for the first time in months the sounds of birds singing once again start the day. For many people it is only upon hearing these forgotten, beautiful melodies that they realize that winter, indeed, is losing its firm grip on the landscape. Even the most confirmed snow-worshipper and winter sportsman can't help but feel cheerful and optimistic upon awakening to the songs of birds on a late February morning.

For the birds themselves this newly regained urge to sing is beyond their control. Once again it is the result of photoperiod, or daylength, acting on the birds' hormones via the pituitary gland. As the days increase in length in late winter the birds begin to respond to this increased light by returning to their breeding condition. Reproductive glands break out of their dormancy and males begin to use their voices to attract mates and stake out their territories. Perched in the tops of trees or shrubs in plain view, they sing their characteristic melodies to stimulate prospective mates (or lifelong partners, as in the case of cardinals) and to warn potential usurpers to stay away from their home courts.

In our northeastern states winter's silence is usually broken first by the permanent residents, those few species that don't migrate but remain the entire year. One of the earliest singers is the black-capped chickadee, that familiar, engaging, acrobatic bird that travels in roving bands in winter and commonly visits bird feeders. Male chickadees produce a clear, two-noted whistle that sounds like "fee-bee," with the accent on the first note. Often the first chickadee to sing elicits a reaction from several others, and the woods are filled with the plaintive whistles.

A close relative of the chickadee, the tufted titmouse, is another of our region's permanent residents, and its loud "peter-peter-peter" or "here-here-here" whistles are also heard during the sunny days of February. The titmouse was formerly a southern bird, but it has been expanding its range northward during the past few decades. It is now well established up to southern Ontario although still absent from our region's high mountainous areas and northern New England.

A series of nasal, low, "yank-yank-yank" notes characterizes both our region's nuthatches, the white-breasted (a permanent resident) and the smaller red-breasted, which often leaves in fall for more southern areas. Another easily recognized sound of late winter is the sad cooing of the mourning dove, which, like the tufted titmouse, has been expanding its range northward. Two additional winter birds that have successfully spread to our region from the South are the cardinal and the mockingbird, both of which are nonmigratory and among the first songsters of late winter. The cardinal's loud, piercing whistles are repeated over and over in several distinct variations from the top of an exposed perch where all the world can appreciate its flaming red color. The dull gray mockingbird usually practices its imitations, each repeated three or more times before switching to the next, from the safety of dense thickets or shrubbery around homes.

————*Observations*————

Two of the most cheerful, melodic songsters of our region are finches that closely resemble each other in appearance. One, the purple finch, is a native species that occasionally migrates southward in great numbers but otherwise remains in the Northeast to some extent every winter. The other, the house finch, is a recent import from the western United States, brought over as caged birds by the pet shop industry about 1940 and then becoming successfully established around northeastern residential areas when birds were released to the wild. It is now found up to Ontario, Maine, and the Great Lakes states. Both finches produce lively, warbling songs that can't help but brighten up a February day.

Not all of the February bird sounds can be described as songs. The woodpeckers break the winter silence in a different way. Drumming, or rapidly tapping on a resonant tree trunk or branch, is just as characteristic a sound on a sunny, late February day as the whistle of a chickadee. The small downy woodpecker, its similar but larger relative the hairy woodpecker, and the huge, 19-inch-long pileated woodpecker are all common permanent residents of our region (although the pileated's secretive nature and extensive territory may make it seem rarer than it is). Each one's drumming (becoming louder and more reverberating as the species' size increases) serves the same function as the songs of the other resident birds: to attract a mate and establish the territorial boundaries within which a new family will soon be raised during the approaching season of spring.

The Swamp's Symbol of Spring

Observations

At the end of February, deep in the dark recesses of woodland swamps and along the murky banks of shaded watercourses, a strange-looking plant begins to poke up from the frozen muck and snow. Streaked with purplish brown and greenish yellow, each thick, fleshy plant resembles a pointed monk's hood. Known as a spathe, this unusual, open structure, from 3 to 6 inches high, contains the plant's tiny flower parts on a knoblike club, or spadix, hidden inside the hood. Later in the season huge, cabbagelike leaves emerge and cover the swampy ground. When crushed or broken, both the flowers and leaves produce a disagreeable, strong, skunklike odor, which is responsible for the other half of this plant's name—skunk cabbage—a rather unlikely candidate for the very first flower of spring.

Skunk cabbage is able to literally melt its way up through the ice and snow by producing its own heat. For about two weeks in late winter the plant increases its respiration and rapidly burns starch in its massive underground root system to maintain an amazingly high temperature of 72 degrees Fahrenheit in its insulated hood. This may be as much as sixty degrees higher than the outside air temperature, and skunk cabbage can even vary its metabolic rate according to how cold the air is. On warmer days its respiration slows down, while on colder days it may burn starch to produce internal heat at rates comparable to a shrew or hummingbird. In this way a steady, 72-degree temperature is maintained for about two weeks, no matter how cold it is outside.

Producing its own warmth is unique to skunk cabbage among all the plants of our region. This adaptation not only enables skunk cabbage to get a head start on the spring flowering season, but the heat intensifies the odor given off by its flowers to attract any pollinating flies and bees at this very early date. As they take pollen inside the insulated hoods, these insects are temporarily warmed up from the chilly late winter air and are thus able to continue flying from plant to plant to spread pollen. Skunk cabbage plays the role of "warming hut" to these hardy pollinators, and its pollen is usually the first food of the year for reawakening honeybees.

In our northeastern region close relatives of the skunk cabbage include golden club, wild calla, and the familiar jack-in-the-pulpit, all members of the arum, or aroid, family of plants. These plants all have acrid, pungent juice and thousands of needlelike crystals of calcium oxalate, which produce a burning, painful sensation if eaten. Nevertheless, these plants are among the favorite early spring greens for migrating Canada geese and reawakening black bears. The Native Americans made the skunk cabbage and some of the other arums edible (and nutritious) by cooking them in several different waters to destroy the acrid juices and in some cases pounding the plants to crush the sharp crystals.

Most members of the arum family are tropical, including common house plants like the philodendron and the caladium, and a Sumatran species, *Amorphophallus titanum*, one of the world's largest flowering plants with blossoms up to 6 feet high and 4 feet across! In fact, some scientists believe that skunk cabbage also may have been a tropical plant eons ago and gradually spread northward to exploit new environments. In its northward dispersal, skunk cabbage evolved its heat-producing ability to retain a tropical environment for its flowers, thus enabling it to fill the niche of the earliest wildflower of the year.

As skunk cabbage's pointed spathes emerge from the frozen earth to signal the end of winter, the forest is still cold and bare. But the sap is now rising in the maple trees, and the next evening rains may bring hordes of wood frogs and spotted salamanders out of the leaf litter and soil toward the vernal ponds to lay eggs. The thawing of the damp earth brings a new, fresh fragrance to the air, and the cold blasts of winter are periodically replaced by balmy breezes from the south.

Soon the honks of northwardly migrating Canada geese will be heard overhead, and the "peents" and whistling wings of courting woodcocks will once again lure naturalists away from the comfort of their homes into the wetlands to witness nature's ancient rituals. For those of us who delight in keeping track of all these wonderful annual events, another year is about to begin.

Bibliography

Able, K. 1983. "A migratory bird's Baedeker." *Natural History*, (September): 22–27.

Alt, G. 1984. "Characteristics of bear cubs at birth." *Game News*, (June): 10–13.

———. 1980. "Rate of growth and size of Pennsylvania black bears." *Game News*, (December): 7–16.

Altman, L. 1977. "Scientists brave bears and winter in hunt for a sleep hormone." *New York Times*, November 21: 39.

Aschenbach, J. 1989. "Researchers looking into tricks of some web-weaving spiders." *The Pocono Record*, May 20: D-1.

Baker, M., K. Spitler-Nabors, and D. Bradley. 1981. "Early experience determines song dialect responsiveness of female sparrows." *Science*, (November 13): 819–20.

Barron, G. 1992. "Jekyll-Hyde mushrooms." *Natural History*, (March): 46–53.

Beck, R. 1971. "A study of wood thrush song." *Cornell Laboratory of Ornithology Newsletter*, (Fall): 6.

Behler, J., and F. King. 1979. *The Audubon Society Field Guide to North American Reptiles and Amphibians*. New York: Alfred A. Knopf.

Bellrose, F. 1979. "The drama of bird migration." *The Nature Conservancy News*, (September-October): 14–18.

Bergman, C. 1985. "Invaders from the far north." *National Wildlife*, (October-November): 34–38.

Betts, W. 1979. "Hard times strike the timber rattler." *Defenders*, (February): 14–19.

Biderman, J. 1983. "Food for flight." *Audubon*, (May): 113–19.

Bishop, S. 1941. *The Salamanders of New York*. Albany: University of the State of New York.

Bock, C. 1979. "Christmas bird count." *Natural History*, (December): 7–12.

Bohlen, J. 1984. "New threat of a silent spring." *Defenders*, (November-December): 20–29.

Boraiko, A. 1980. "The pesticide dilemma." *National Geographic*, (February): 145–83.

Borror, D., and D. DeLong. 1971. *An Introduction to the Study of Insects*. New York: Holt, Rinehart and Winston.

Borror, D., and R. White. 1970. *A Field Guide to the Insects*. Boston: Houghton Mifflin.

Boyle, R. 1987. "Autumn's hidden harvest." *National Wildlife*, (October-November): 4–8.

———. 1969. *The Hudson River*. New York: W. W. Norton.

Breckenridge, W., and J. Tester. 1961. "Growth, local movement, and hibernation of the Manitoba toad." *Ecology*, (Fall): 637–46.

Brett, J. 1987. "Birder's guide to Hawk Mountain." *Wild Bird*, (October): 37–43.

Brett, J. (curator). Various years. *Hawk Mountain News*. Hawk Mountain Sanctuary Association, Kempton, PA.

Brett, J., and C. Nagy. 1973. *Feathers in the Wind*. Hawk Mountain Sanctuary Association, Kempton, PA.

Brewer, J. 1982. "A visit with 200 million monarchs." *Defenders*, (April): 13–20.

Briggs, S., and J. Criswell. 1979. "Gradual silencing of spring in Washington." *Atlantic Naturalist*, 32: 19–26.

Brown, W. 1981. "Conserving the timber rattlesnake." *The Conservationist*, (July-August): 27–29.

Bull, J. 1974. *Birds of New York State*. New York: Doubleday.

Burns, A. 1960. "The insect orchestra." *Audubon Nature Bulletin*, 14 (10).

Burt, W. 1964. *A Field Guide to the Mammals*. Boston: Houghton Mifflin.

Cade, T. 1963. "Observations on torpidity in captive chipmunks." *Ecology*, (Spring): 255–61.

Cade, W. 1978. "Of cricket song and sex." *Natural History*, (January): 64–72.

Campbell, R. 1981. "Forest succession and the gypsy moth." *The Conservationist*, (July-August): 37–39.

Carey, C., and R. Marsh. 1981. "Shivering finches." *Natural History*, (October): 58–63.

Carpenter, C. 1953. A study of hibernacula and hibernating associations of snakes and amphibians in Michigan." *Ecology*, (January): 74–80.

Clauson, A. 1976. "The American woodcock." *The Conservationist*, (July-August): 34–35.

Conant, R. 1957. *Reptiles and Amphibians of the Northeastern States.* Zoological Society of Philadelphia.

Conover, A. 1983. "Getting to know black bears." *Smithsonian*, (April): 87–96.

Cowen, R. 1991. "Liquid crystal bridges silk-spinning gap." *Science News*, (February 23): 119.

————. 1990. "Vanishing amphibians: why they're croaking." *Science News*, (February 24): 116.

Davis, D. 1967. "The role of environmental factors in the hibernation of woodchucks." *Ecology*, (Summer): 683–89.

Dawkins, M., and D. Hull. 1965. "The production of heat by fat." *Scientific American*, (August): 62–67.

Ditmars, R. 1952. *A Field Book of North American Snakes*. New York: Doubleday.

Dodge, J. (ed.). Various years. *Hawk Migration Studies*. Hawk Migration Association of North America, Braddock Bay Raptor Research Center, Hilton, NY.

Douglas, M. 1979. "Hot butterflies." *Natural History*, (November): 56–65.

Dunne, P., and W. Clark. 1976. "Fall hawk movement at Cape May Point." *New Jersey Audubon*, (July-August): 113–24.

Edwards, J. 1987. "Sounding taps for the sugar maple." *National Wildlife*, (October-November): 20.

Elzinga, R. 1981. *Fundamentals of Entomology*. Englewood Cliffs, NJ: Prentice-Hall.

Environment Canada. 1981. *Downwind: The Acid Rain Story*. Minister of Supply and Services, Ottawa.

Essman, J. 1991. "Waging war with caterpillars." *The Conservationist,* (March-April): 55.

Evans, H. 1968. "In defense of magic: the story of fireflies." *Natural History,* (November): 40–42, 68–71.

Faber, H. 1977. "Deadly rain imperils two Adirondack species." *New York Times,* March 28: 31.

Fellman, B. 1991. "When the going gets cold." *National Wildlife,* (December-January): 7–12.

———. 1990. "A case of spotted fervor." *National Wildlife,* (April-May): 13–16.

Fergus, C. "Woodcock." *Wildlife Notes* 175–21. Pennsylvania Game Commission, Harrisburg.

Finch, R. 1986. "September song." *Orion,* (Summer): 63–65.

Fischer, R. 1991. "Exploring the world of goldenrods." *The Conservationist,* (July-August): 34–37.

Gansner, D., and O. Herrick. 1985. *Host Preferences of Gypsy Moth on a New Frontier of Infestation.* Forest Service Research Note 330. Northeastern Forest Experiment Station, Broomall, PA.

———. 1979. *Forest Stand Losses to Gypsy Moth in the Poconos.* Forest Service Research Note 273. Northeastern Forest Experiment Station, Broomall, PA.

Geller, A. 1980. "The groundhog is a lousy weatherman." *National Wildlife,* (February-March): 25–28.

George, J. 1978. "My search for secret agent 25238." *National Wildlife,* (April-May): 16–19.

Gibbons, E. 1962. *Stalking the Wild Asparagus.* New York: David McKay.

Gibo, D. 1972. "Hibernation sites and temperature tolerance of two species of Vespula and one species of Polistes." *N.Y. Entomological Society News,* (June): 105–8.

Graham, F. 1984. "Shorebirds: images and projections." *Audubon,* (March): 81–92.

Grenoble, S. 1984. "A barn full of bears." *American Forests,* (December): 24–28, 61–62.

Grossman, J. 1990. "Learning to live with bears." *National Wildlife,* (April-May): 4–10.

Gwynne, D. 1983. "Coy conquistadors of the sagebrush." *Natural History,* (October): 70–74.

Halfpenny, J. 1991. "The cold facts of winter." *Natural History,* (December): 50–60.

Harlow, W. 1957. *Trees of Eastern and Central U.S. and Canada.* New York: Dover Publications.

Harrison, G. 1991. "Little dynamo." *National Wildlife,* (February-March): 41–44.

———. 1981. "Taking off the velvet." *National Wildlife,* (October-November): 46–47.

Harrison, K., and G. Harrison. 1990. *The Birds of Winter.* New York: Random House.

Hawkins, J. 1979. "Aroids." *Horticulture,* (February): 35–38.

Heinrich, B. 1991. "Nutcracker sweets." *Natural History,* (February): 4–8.

Heller, H., and G. Colliver. 1974. "CNS regulation of body temperature during hibernation." *American Journal of Physiology,* (September): 583–89.

Hendry, G. 1990. "Making, breaking, and remaking chlorophyll." *Natural History,* (May): 37–40.

Hornblower, M. 1983. "How dangerous is acid rain?" *National Wildlife,* (June-July): 4–11.

Horton, T. 1991. "Deer on your doorstep." *New York Times Magazine,* April 28: 29–31, 38–42, 74.

Howard, R. 1979. "Big bullfrogs in a little pond." *Natural History,* (April): 31–36.

Hubley, J. (ed.). 1991. "Woodcock need helping hand." *Pennsylvania Wildlife,* (January-February): 6.

Huth, P., and D. Smiley. 1980. *Blueberries and Huckleberries of the Shawangunk Mountains.* The Mohonk Trust Research Report, Lake Mohonk, New Paltz, NY.

Jackson, J. 1982. "Golden islands of life." *National Wildlife,* (August-September): 20–24.

Jacobs, L. 1989. "Cache economy of the gray squirrel." *Natural History,* (October): 41–46.

Katzmire, J., L. Rymon, and A. Ambler. 1991. "The development of a wintering population of bald eagles in the Delaware Water Gap National Recreation Area." *Proceedings of 1991 Delaware Water Gap 25th Anniversary Symposium:* 82–87.

Kealy, P. (ed.). 1990. "The gypsy moths are here." *Spanning the Gap*

(Delaware Water Gap), (Spring): 2.

Keiper, R., and L. Solomon. 1972. "Ecology and yearly cycle of the fire-fly *Photuris pennsylvanica.*" *N.Y. Entomological Society News*, (March): 43–47.

Kelsey, P. 1979. "White-tailed deer." *The Conservationist*, (September-October): 3–7.

———. 1978. "The seven sleepers." *The Conservationist*, (January-February): 28–32.

Kerr, R. 1972. "Sugaring off." *The Conservationist*, (February-March): 48.

Kirk, R. 1977. *Snow*. New York: William Morrow.

Kiviat, E. 1980. "Low tides and turtle trails." *Hudson Valley*, (September-October): 27–29.

Knight, J. 1944. *Woodcock*. New York: Alfred A. Knopf.

Knutson, R. 1981. "Flowers that make heat while the sun shines." *Natural History*, (October): 75–80.

———. 1979. "Plants in heat." *Natural History*, (March): 42–47.

Kricher, J. 1976. "Nature's cold light." *The Conservationist*, (July-August): 14–17.

Kroodsma, D. 1989. "What, when, where, and why warblers warble." *Natural History*, (May): 50–59.

Lawren, B. 1989. "Something to sing about." *National Wildlife*, (December-January): 20–26.

Lawrence, G. 1984. *A Field Guide to the Familiar*. Englewood Cliffs, NJ: Prentice-Hall.

Laycock, G. 1982. "The urban goose." *Audubon*, (January): 44–47.

Leberman, R. 1984. "Studying the spring warbler migration." *Bird Watcher's Digest*, (March-April): 81–85.

Lipske, M. 1979. "Insects in danger." *Defenders*, (June): 130–35.

Lloyd, J. 1969. "Flashes and behavior of some American fireflies." *The Conservationist*, (June-July): 8–12.

———. 1966. *Studies on the Flash Communication System in Photinus Fireflies*. Ann Arbor: University of Michigan.

Loucks, B., and K. Kogut. 1985. "The peregrine returns." *The Conservationist*, (March-April): 12–17.

Luoma, J. 1987. "Black duck decline." *Audubon*, (May): 19–24.

Lyman, C., and P. Chatfield. 1955. "Physiology of hibernation in mammals." *Physiological Reviews*, 35: 403–25.

Lyman, C., and R. O'Brien. 1974. "A comparison of temperature regulation in hibernating rodents." *American Journal of Physiology*, (July): 218–23.

Lynch, W. 1983. "Great balls of snakes." *Natural History*, (April): 65–68.

Lyons, C. 1985. "The migration of the monarchs." *The Conservationist*, (September-October): 38–41.

MacKay, B. 1982. "City honkers." *Defenders*, (April): 8–12.

Marchand, P. 1987. *Life in the Cold*. Hanover: University Press of New England.

———. 1987. *North Woods*. Appalachian Mountain Club, Boston.

Marshall, E. 1981. "The summer of the gypsy moth." *Science*, (August): 991–93.

McCarty, S., and D. Decker. 1983. "Woodchuck—New York's industrious digger." *The Conservationist*, (March-April): 6–11.

McConnell, P. 1991. "The black bear in Delaware Water Gap National Recreation Area." *Proceedings of 1991 Delaware Water Gap 25th Anniversary Symposium:* 97–101.

———. 1987. "Bears—in New Jersey?" *New Jersey Outdoors*, (November-December): 3–5.

McCormick, J. 1966. *The Life of the Forest*. New York: McGraw-Hill.

McKee, R. 1987. "Peregrinations and permutations of a contrary eight-toed beast." *Audubon*, (May): 52–80.

McNeil, R. 1974. *Deer in New York State*. Extension Bulletin 1189, Ithaca, NY: N.Y. State College of Agriculture and Life Sciences, Cornell University.

Menzel, P. 1983. "Butterfly armies are now under guard in annual bivouac." *Smithsonian*, (November): 175–82.

Mertz, C. 1990. "Swan song for our songbirds?" *Pennsylvania Wildlife*, (November-December): 29–30.

Miller, J. 1991. "The American shad recreational fishery of the Delaware River." *Proceedings of 1991 Delaware Water Gap 25th Anniversary Symposium:* 88–96.

Miller, O. 1979. *Mushrooms of North America*. New York: E. P. Dutton.

Mitchell, J. 1980. *The Curious Naturalist*. Englewood Cliffs, NJ: Prentice-Hall.

Mohr, C., and T. Poulson. 1966. *The Life of the Cave*. New York: McGraw-Hill.

Monastersky, R. 1990. "The fall of the forest." *Science News*, (July 21): 40–41.

Moon, L., and N. Moon. 1985. "Braddock Bay spring hawk migrations." *The Kingbird*, (Winter): 7–31.

Morris, G. 1972. "Phonotaxis of male meadow grasshoppers." *N.Y. Entomological Society News*, (March): 5–6.

Morris, J. 1991. "Of shad, time, and the river." *New Jersey Outdoors*, (Spring): 21–23.

Moser, J. 1985. "Canada geese—the call from on high." *The Conservationist*, (November-December): 32–35.

Mrosovsky, N. 1968. "The adjustable brain of hibernators." *Scientific American*, (March): 110–18.

Myers, J. 1989. "Delaware Bay: a spectacle of spring passage." *Nature Conservancy Magazine*, (March-April): 14–19.

———. 1986. "Sex and gluttony on Delaware Bay." *Natural History*, (May): 68–76.

Nardi, J. 1990. "Mycorrhizae: an underground alliance of fungi and green plants." *Nature Study*, 43 (3&4): 4–5.

Necker, C. 1969. "Dwellers of the forest floor." *National Wildlife,* (April-May): 51–54.

Nelson, R., et al. 1973. "Metabolism of bears before, during and after winter sleep." *American Journal of Physiology*, (February): 491–96.

Nero, R. 1985. "Great gray ghost of the north." *Animal Kingdom*, (February-March): 25–33.

Newcomb, L. 1977. *Newcomb's Wildflower Guide*. Boston: Little, Brown.

Niles, L. 1991. "The return of the bald eagle." *New Jersey Outdoors*, (Spring): 64.

Noble, G. 1954. *The Biology of the Amphibia*. New York: Dover Publications.

Nye, P. 1990. "A second chance for our national symbol." *The Conservationist*, (July-August): 16–23.

O'Pezio, J. 1984. "Unraveling the mysteries of bear denning." *The Conservationist*, (January-February): 23–25.

Ozoga, J. 1986. "The social role of buck rubs and scrapes." *Pennsylvania Outdoors*, (September-October): 23–27, 74–78.

Paladino, L. 1983. "The horseshoe crab." *The Conservationist*, (May-June): 23–27.

Palmer, E. 1957. "Insect life in winter." *Nature Magazine*, (January): 25–32.

Pennisi, E. 1991. "Out for the count." *National Wildlife*, (December-January): 38–40.

Peterson, R. 1980. *A Field Guide to the Birds East of the Rockies*. Boston: Houghton Mifflin.

Peterson R., and M. McKenny. 1968. *A Field Guide to Wildflowers*. Boston: Houghton Mifflin.

Pettingill, O., and S. Spofford. 1971. *Enjoying Birds in Upstate New York*. Ithaca, NY: Cornell Laboratory of Ornithology.

Pielou, E. 1988. *The World of Northern Evergreens*. Ithaca, NY: Comstock Publishing Associates.

Platt, R. 1952. *American Trees*. New York: Dodd, Mead.

Pope, C. 1946. *Snakes Alive and How They Live*. New York: Viking Press.

Pyle, R. 1983. "Migratory monarchs: an endangered phenomenon." *The Nature Conservancy News*, (September-October): 21–24.

Quinn, V. 1983. "Clean-up crew." *National Wildlife*, (April-May): 12–14.

Revkin, A. 1989. "Sleeping beauties." *Discover*, (April): 62–65.

Rhoads, L. 1987. "The gypsy moth parasite release program in Pennsylvania." *Pennsylvania Forests*, (Summer): 7–11.

Robbins, C. 1980. "Effects of forest fragmentation on breeding bird populations in the Piedmont of the mid-Atlantic region." *Atlantic Naturalist*, 33: 31–36.

Robinson, L. 1984. "A sky with 10,000 broadwings." *Bird Watcher's Digest*, (January-February): 40–41.

Rogers, L. 1981. "A bear in its lair." *Natural History*, (October): 64–70.

Russell, H. 1971. *Winter Search Party*. New York: Thomas Nelson.

Ryden, H. 1984. "The white-tailed deer." *Country Journal*, (November): 18–23.

Sayre, R. 1980. "An invasion to remember." *Audubon*, (January): 52–55.

Schmid, W. 1982. "Survival of frogs in low temperature." *Science*, (February 5): 697–98.

Schmidt, K. 1980. "Jackwax and hogwallers." *The Conservationist*, (January-February): 19–20.

Schultz, J. 1991. "The multimillion-dollar gypsy moth question." *Natural History*, (June): 40–44.

Scriber, J. 1987. "Puddling by female Florida tiger swallowtail butterflies." *The Great Lakes Entomologist*, 20 (1): 21–23.

Seideman, D. 1984. "Homing in on the hunter." *National Wildlife*, (April-May): 51–54.

Serrao, J. 1991. "Bear facts." *Pocono World*, (Summer): 102–8.

———. 1986. *The Wild Palisades of the Hudson*. Woodcliff Lake, NJ: Lind Publications.

———. 1985. "Decline of forest songbirds." *Records of New Jersey Birds*, (N.J. Audubon Society), 11 (1): 5–9.

———. 1979. "Autumn hawk migration." *Biology Digest*, (September): 13–38.

———. 1978. "Winter's long sleep—the biology of hibernation." *Biology Digest*, (February): 11–29.

Sexton, O.J., C. Phillips, and J. Bramble. 1990. "The effect of temperature and precipitation on the breeding migration of the spotted salamander." *Copeia*, (September 19): 781–87.

Shoop, C. 1968. "Migratory orientation of *Ambystoma maculatum*." *Biological Bulletin*, (August): 230–38.

Skeen, S. 1982. "Lord of the Adirondack night." *Adirondack Life*, (November-December): 28–32, 43–45.

Smiley, D. 1980. *Gypsy Moths and Man*. The Mohonk Trust Research Report #5. Lake Mohonk, New Paltz, NY.

Smith, C. 1986. "What's killing the sugar maples?" *Country Journal*, (March): 46–49.

Smith, H. 1986. "Pimentel vs. pests." *Cornell Alumni News*, (October): 36–37.

Smith, R. 1966. *Ecology and Field Biology*. New York: Harper and Row.

Spier, D. 1980. "Derby Hill." *The Conservationist*, (May-June): 33–37.

Stegeman, L. 1963. "A glimpse of the animal life of the topsoil." *The Conservationist*, (December-January): 12–16.

Steinhart, P. 1989. "Portrait of a deepening crisis." *National Wildlife*, (October-November): 5–12.

———. 1989. "Standing room only." *National Wildlife*, (April-May): 46–51.

———. 1984. "Trouble in the tropics." *National Wildlife*, (December-January): 16–20.

Stephens, G. 1984. "Long-range effects of defoliation." *Connecticut Woodlands*, (Spring): 19–21.

Stewart, M., and C. Ricci. 1988. "Dearth of the blues." *Natural History*, (May): 64–70.

Stiles, E. 1984. "Fruit for all seasons." *Natural History*, (August): 43–52.

Stokes, D. 1983. "Weathering the world of snow." *National Wildlife*, (December-January): 4–10.

Storey, J., and K. Storey. 1992. "Out cold." *Natural History*, (January): 23–25.

Storey, K., and J. Storey. 1990. "Frozen and alive." *Scientific American*, (December): 92–97.

Sullivan, W. 1982. "Hibernation chemical identified." *New York Times*, March 9: C1–C2.

———. 1979. "Variety of sensors tell plants it's spring." *New York Times*, March 20: C1, C3.

Swan, H., and C. Schatte. 1977. "Antimetabolic extract from the brain of the hibernating ground squirrel." *Science*, (January): 84–85.

Symonds, G. 1963. *The Shrub Identification Book*. New York: William Morrow.

Terres, J. 1987. "Hitchhikers in the sky." *National Wildlife*, (October-November): 38–40.

———. 1980. *Audubon Society Encyclopedia of North American Birds*. New York: Alfred A. Knopf.

Tiffany, L., G. Knaphus, and R. Nyvall. 1981. *Mushrooms and Other Related Fungi*. Cooperative Extension Service, Iowa State University.

Tyning, T. 1981. "Night of the salamanders." *Defenders*, (April): 33–37.

Urquhart, F. 1976. "Found at last: the monarch's winter home." *National Geographic*, (August): 160–73.

Vernberg, F. 1953. "Hibernation studies of two species of salamanders." *Ecology*, (January): 55–62.

Verts, B. 1967. *The Biology of the Striped Skunk*. Champaign, IL: University of Illinois Press.

Vogelmann, H. 1982. "Catastrophe on Camel's Hump." *Natural History*, (November): 8–14.

Vogt, B. 1988. "The squirrel we love and loathe." *National Wildlife*, (August-September): 30–34.

———. 1980. "Nurtured on nuts." *National Wildlife*, (October-November): 51–54.

Walcott, C. 1989. "Show me the way you go home." *Natural History*, (November): 40–46.

———. 1984. "Mysteries of migration." *The Conservationist*, (March-April): 24–31.

Wallace, J. 1986. "Where have all the songbirds gone?" *Sierra*, (March-April): 44–47.

Webster, D. 1969. "Temperatures and related factors in lakes." *The Conservationist*, (December): 12–16.

Weiss, R. 1990. "Relying on more than wings and prayers." *Science News*, (March 3): 140.

———. 1989. "Blazing blossoms." *Science News*, (June 24): 392–94.

Welty, J. 1969. *The World of Birds*. Philadelphia: W. B. Saunders.

Wexler, M. 1989. "A case of urban renewal." *National Wildlife*, (June-July): 11–13.

Wickelgren, I. 1989. "Spider webs: luring light may be a trap." *Science News*, (May 27): 330.

Wigglesworth, V. 1964. *The Life of Insects*. New York: The New American Library.

Wilcove, D. 1990. "Empty skies." *The Nature Conservancy Magazine*, (January-February): 4–13.

Wilcove, D., and R. Whitcomb. 1983. "Gone with the trees." *Natural History*, (September): 82–91.

Wille, C. 1990. "Mystery of the missing migrants." *Audubon*, (May): 82–85.

Williams, T. 1982. "Ah, gypsy moth." *Audubon*, (March): 14–23.

Williams, T., and J. Williams. 1978. "An oceanic mass migration of land birds." *Scientific American*, (October): 166–76.

Wishner, L. 1982. "Chipmunks: lively lords and ladies of our woodlands." *Smithsonian*, (October): 76–84.

Zim, H. 1955. *Fishes*. New York: Golden Press.

Index